Aggression, Time, and Understanding

Frank-M. Staemmler

Aggression, Time, and Understanding

••••••••••••

Contributions to the Evolution of Gestalt Therapy

A GestaltPress Book

published and distributed by
Routledge, Taylor & Francis Group
New York

All rights reserved. No part of this publication may be reproduced, stored in a retrieval system, or transmitted, in any form or by any means, electronic, mechanical, photocopying, recording, or otherwise without the prior written permission of the publisher:

Copyright 2009 by: The GestaltPress
　　　　　　　　　　　127 Abby Court
　　　　　　　　　　　Santa Cruz, CA 95062

　　　　　　　and　　　165 Route 6A
　　　　　　　　　　　Orleans, MA 02653

Email: gestaltpress@aol.com, gestaltpress@comcast.net

Distributed by: Routledge, Taylor & Francis Group
　　　　　　　　　　270 Madison Avenue
　　　　　　　　　　New York, NY 10016

Library of Congress Cataloging-in-Publishing Data
　1. Gestalt therapy, 2. psychology, 3. aggession,
　4. anger, 5. regression, 6. Frank-M. Staemmler, 7. Perls

ISBN: 978-0-415-87098-6

This book is dedicated
to
my international friends and students.

Contents

Preface xii
The Author xviii

Section 1 — Aggression

1. Ego, Anger, and Attachment –
   A Critique of Perls's Aggression Theory and Method
   Frank-M. Staemmler & Barbara Staemmler 3
   Chapter Reference Points 6

   Part One 9
      1. 1. *Frederick S. Perls's Theory of Aggression* 9
      1. 2. *Problems* 21

   Part Two 36
      2. 1. *Motivational Systems* 36
      2. 2. *The Everyday Side Effects of Aggression:*
         Repercussions on the Aggressor 45
      2. 3. *Catharsis* 62
      2. 4. *Inhibition and Control* 75
      2. 5. *Between Scylla and Charybdis* 82
      2. 6. *Can Anger and Aggression Ever Be*
         Recommended? 85

   Part Three 92
      3. 1. *Appraisal* 92
      3. 2. *Anger Appraisal* 100
      3. 3. *Case Example 1* 105
      3. 4. *Importance* 113
      3. 5. *Needs* 134
      3. 6. *Responsibility* 148
      3. 7. *Power* 160

   Final Remarks 164
   References 168

Section 2 — Time

2. The Here and Now is not What it Used to Be –
The Tail of the Comet, the Face of Janus, and
The Infinity of Possibilities
   Frank-M. Staemmler 187

Misunderstandings *190*
   The "Out of Sight – Out of Mind"
      Misunderstanding 190
   The "Nothing Exists Apart from the
      Here and Now" Misunderstanding 192
   The Hedonistic Misunderstanding 201
Subjectivity *202*
Continuity *205*
Memory *212*
Process Activation *220*
Kairos *224*
References *226*

3. Towards a Theory of Regressive Processes in
Gestalt Therapy – On Time Perspective,
Developmental Model and the Wish to Be
Understood
   Frank-M. Staemmler 235

*The Psychoanalytic Term of "Regression" –
   A Brief Explanation and Some Critical Comments* *237*
Approaching a Gestalt Therapy View of "Regression" *247*
*Proposal for a Gestalt Understanding of
   Regressive Processes* *254*
*Balint's Theory of Regression and Its Yield for a
   Gestalt Understanding of Regressive Processes* *264*

3. Continued

Final Considerations 281
References 297

Section 3 — Understanding

4. Dialogue and Interpretation in Gestalt Therapy – Making Sense Together
   Frank-M. Staemmler 305

   Part 1 – In which I try to reconstruct how interpretation acquired a bad reputation in Gestalt therapy and a grand delusion was born 306

   Part 2 – In which old friends meet surprisingly, start to communicate, and a lot of interpretation unavoidably takes place 309

   Part 3 – In which I compile a few quotations, for instance from phenomenological and hermeneutic writings, and make a distinction between the micro- and macrolevels of interpretation ... 313

   Part 4 – In which two people (one of them called the "client," the other one called the "therapist") engage in an interpretative dialogue (called "therapy") trying to make some more sense of the client's experience 316

   Part 5 – In which his majesty, the German Jewish theologian and philosopher Martin Buber, is invited to share his throne with the Russian linguist and literary theorist Mikhail Mikhailovich Bakhtin, and in which the meaning of "dialogue" is enlarged 323

   Part 6 – In which the contents of the previous sections are integrated and brought to a conclusion 329

   References 331

5. **Cultivated Uncertainty –**
   An Additude of Gestalt Therapists
   Frank-M. Staemmler 335
   "I Only Came to Use the Phone." 336
   The Need for Certainty 338
   Diagnoses and Certainty 339
   The Significance of Meanings 340
   The Power of Interpretation and Its Distribution 341
   Pseudo-certainty 342
   Rosenhan's Research 346
   Context and Meaning 347
   One-Sided Power of Interpretation and Necessary
      Uncertainty 348
   Cultivated Uncertainty 349
   I-Thou-Relationship 350
   Phenomenology 351
   Constructivism 352
   Field Theory 354
   Process 355
   References 356

Preface

●●●●●●●●●●●●●●●●●

At many occasions — conferences, seminars, workshops etc. — I have been asked by English speaking people for translations of the papers that I originally wrote in German. So far I have had to point them to different issues of different journals in which some of my articles have been published in the past. Obviously, it has not always been easy for them to find access to these publications.

The book at hand will solve this problem at least with respect to a part of my writings. It includes four of those former papers that I have been asked for most frequently — as well as a very recent one on aggression which has not been published in English before. I am glad that from now on my English speaking colleagues and students will have easy access to this collection thanks to the efforts of the GestaltPress.

The GestaltPress as represented especially by Robert Lee, Deborah Ullman, and Gordon Wheeler deserves of my high appreciation for the courage that it appears to take to publish an English Gestalt therapy book written by a German author. My German publishers have many times before tried to offer my written and edited books to English and US-American pub-lishing companies; they were never accepted because of the presumed small number of readers (i. e. buyers).

However, the GestaltPress does not only do a personal favor to me as a writer, I think it also renders a valuable service to the international Gestalt therapy community, the published communication among which has only too long been a one-way street: most of the books that were written in

English have been translated into German and other languages, but almost never *vice versa*. In sum, for all these reasons I am more than happy to see this book in print now.

The Contents of This Book

It is subdivided into three sections and five chapters. These sections deal with aggression, time, and understanding, respectively — hence the title of the book. *Section 1* consists of only one chapter which is also the lengthiest and most recently written paper among the five in this collection; my wife, Barbara Staemmler, has contributed to it with her knowledge of Buddhist texts. It addresses one of my most important concerns, i. e. the question of how as citizens we can educate ourselves for peace (to allude to one of Laura Perls's essays) and of how as therapists we can support our clients to discover peaceful ways of coping with the challenges that life confronts them with.

Moreover, my heart beats for changes and developments in Gestalt therapy's theory of aggression that are more adequate than our original theory to reach the aforementioned aims. As you will see, my own point of view deviates essentially from that of the Perls' and is much closer to that of their teacher Kurt Goldstein, who at the end of his life wrote the following remarkable sentences that might be read as his legacy:

> The help we give patients in therapy is not an external, merely practical, activity but something that originates in the most characteristic property of man, the tendency to help and the desire to be helped. This is the expression of the original unity of men ... Man can be an individual only in this unity with the other.... Only in a unity with the "other" is the self-realization of the individual guaranteed.... This living in communion guarantees, on the one hand, the uniqueness of the individual; on the

other hand, it makes possible the feeling of responsibility for the other's actions in the attempt to realize oneself. This may appear to justify even the encroachment upon the "other" in the interest of his self-realization. The distinction between this behavior and aggression cannot be taken too seriously. Aggression never has a positive value, neither for the aggressor nor for those aggressed against. It is essentially a reaction to those situations in which the individual cannot come to terms with the demands of self-realization. (1959, 185ff.)

Section 2 deals with the significance of time in Gestalt therapy. Time has always been a fascinating topic for me. From the beginning of my career as a Gestalt therapist the catchword of the "here and now" has been both captivating and puzzling and has motivated me to think about it again and again. The two chapters in this section display some results of these efforts. The first paper picks up the classical catchword and tries to endow it with more differentiation and complexity by drawing on various philosophical as well as psychological sources.

The second paper deals with the theoretical and practical problems that regressive processes present to our understanding of time and to our clinical work with clients who tend to regress to — and this is the question: — to what? The answer to this question depends essentially on the developmental model that one adopts. I explore the traditional psychoanalytic notion of development and compare it to more recent ideas as have been put forward by modern infant research. Here I think we can find a more adequate frame of reference for what might meaningfully be called "regressive processes" in the context of Gestalt therapy and its concept of the here and now.

Section 3 broaches the issue of understanding that has also been one of the major concerns in my theoretical work for the past twenty years. In fact, one of the most compelling

Preface ... xv

motivations that led to my choosing the therapeutic profession had to do with my strong curiosity and interest in the hermeneutic dimension of human relationships. However, I did not find this dimension to be satisfyingly treated by traditional Gestalt therapy theory (see, for example, Staemmler, 1999; 2005; 2006). So I began to read the hermeneutic philosophers (Heidegger, 1962, and Gadamer, 1989, for instance) and occupied myself quite a bit investigating the significant dimensions of empathy in psychotherapy (see Staemmler 2007; in print).

Among my various writings on this issue the two papers that are included in this book in *Section 3* are the ones that elicited the strongest resonance in my readers. The first one, about dialogue and interpretation, tries to overcome the paralyzing presumption that in Gestalt therapy we do not interpret. I demonstrate that interpretation cannot be avoided; it takes place on many different levels and is a substantial aspect not only of any human dialogue but, more radically, of any human way of being in the world. In this paper I give some hints to how this aspect of the human condition can be meaningfully integrated into the practice of Gestalt therapy.

The last paper in this book proposes "an attitude for Gestalt therapists" that I have named "cultivated uncertainty" and that I find absolutely important for a proper handling of the interpretive dimension in the therapeutic encounter including diagnosis. I am happy about the fact that this paper has been published and republished in German and in other languages many times and that the term "cultivated uncertainty" has become fairly well known in the Gestalt community. I hope that its reprint in this volume will even more support the spreading of an attitude in Gestalt therapists which represents a both honest and professionally competent use of the fact that very often as therapists we are facing the unknown — in our clients' experience as well as in our own.

Acknowledgements

Not being a native English speaker I had to rely very much on the help of my English and American friends to make the translations of my papers a comfortable reading for those who were raised in the English language. Lynne Jacobs spent reams of hours to edit the papers on aggression and on dialogue and interpretation; moreover, she provided me with helpful comments on some aspects of these papers and, thereby, contributed to their quality. When Malcolm Parlett was the editor of the *British Gestalt Journal* he, among other things, committed himself to publishing papers of non-British authors, including my papers on cultivated uncertainty and on the here and now. He took great care in facilitating the translations (the paper on the here and now was translated by Valerie Curen), and was instrumental as a thorough and supportive editor. Joe Wysong, the then-editor of *The Gestalt Journal* edited my paper on regressive processes. Last but not least, Robert Lee was so kind as to take on the busy task of editing this book as a whole and of looking after all the tiny bits and pieces that needed to be taken care of before it went to the printer. — To all of these people I give my heartfelt and grateful thanks.

I hope that you, the readers, will find the following pages useful and inspiring.

June 2008, Frank-M. Staemmler

References

Gadamer, H.-G. (1989). *Truth and Method*. New York: Crossroad.
Goldstein, K. (1959). Health as value. In A. H. Maslow (Ed.), *New knowledge in human values* (pp. 178-188). New York & Evanston: Harper & Row.
Heidegger, M. (1962). *Being and time*. San Francisco: Harper.
Staemmler, F.-M. (1999). Hermeneutische Ansätze in der klassischen Gestalttherapie [Hermeneutic approaches in classical Gestalt therapy]. *Gestalt 36*, 43-60.
Staemmler, F.-M. (2005). Cultural field conditions: A hermeneutic study of consistency. *British Gestalt Journal 14/1*, 34-43.
Staemmler, F.-M. (2006). The willingness to be uncertain: Preliminary thoughts about interpretation and understanding in Gestalt therapy. *International Gestalt Journal 29/2*, 11-42.
Staemmler, F.-M. (2007). On Macaque monkeys, players, and clairvoyants: Some new ideas for a Gestalt therapeutic concept of empathy. *Studies in Gestalt Therapy: Dialogical Bridges 1/2*, 43-63.
Staemmler, F.-M. (in print). Das Geheimnis des Anderen – Empathie in der Psychotherapie aus neuer Perspektive [The secret of the other: Empathy in psychotherapy from a new perspective]. Stuttgart, Germany: Klett-Cotta.

Original English Publications of the Papers in This Book

Cultivated uncertainty: An attitude for Gestalt therapists. *British Gestalt Journal* (1997) 6/1, 40-48.
Towards a theory of regressive processes in Gestalt therapy – On time perspective, developmental model and the wish to be understood. *The Gestalt Journal* (1997) 20/1, 49-120.
The here and now: A critical analysis. *British Gestalt Journal* (2002) 11/1, 21-32.
Dialogue and interpretation in Gestalt therapy: Making sense together. *International Gestalt Journal* (2004) 27/2, 3

The Author

••••••••••••

Frank-M. Staemmler, Ph.D., born in 1951, is a psychologist and Gestalt therapist. He has been working as a Gestalt therapist in private practice since 1976, and as a supervisor and trainer in Gestalt therapy since 1981. He is the co-founder and co-director of the *Zentrum für Gestalttherapie* in Würzburg, one of Germany's most distinguished training institutes.

Frank has contributed greatly to the Gestalt therapy literature: he has written over seventy articles and book chapters as well as five books, and he has (co-)edited six other books. He teaches internationally and is a frequent presenter at conferences in Germany and other countries. He was editor of the *International Gestalt Journal* from 2001 to 2006, and is now co-editor of the *Studies in Gestalt Therapy: Dialogical Bridges*. He also served as an organizer of several conferences in Germany by which he promoted the exchange between different orientations in Gestalt therapy and between representatives of different therapeutic modalities.

Frank and his wife, who integrates Gestalt therapy, musical therapy, and meditative approaches, enjoy working as a couple with couples. They have two adult children and live in a small winegrowers village in central Germany. Frank's non-professional interests include classical music, Himalayan cultures and — *l'art de vivre*.

Section 1
Aggression

1

Ego, Anger, and Attachment –

A Critique of Perls's Aggression Theory and Method

Frank-M. Staemmler & Barbara Staemmler

> Man is born for mutual help; anger for mutual destruction. The one desires union, the other disunion; the one to help, the other to harm; one would succour even strangers, the other attack its best beloved; the one is ready even to expend himself for the good of others, the other to plunge into peril only if it can drag others along.
>
> (Seneca, *De Ira*, book 2, chap. 5)

In the course of our preparations for an interdisciplinary conference titled "Aggression, Self-Assertion, and Civil

Courage"[1] (see Staemmler & Merten 2006) we have occupied ourselves again intensely with the "classical" theory of aggression in Gestalt therapy as it was first formulated by Perls (1942; 1947) in *Ego, Hunger, and Aggression* and later reiterated with little variation in *Gestalt Therapy* (Perls et al. 1951).

Basically we agree with Richard Kitzler — a member of the first group of Gestalt therapists who gathered with Laura and Frederick Perls and with Paul Goodman at the end of the 1940s and early '50s in New York — who maintains:

> ... indeed except for Paul Goodman's amazing restatement of the body of Perls's work and Goodman's section on "Verbalizing and Poetry" in the theory section of the book, ... there is nothing in Perls, Hefferline, and Goodman that is not in *Ego, Hunger and Aggression*. (Kitzler 2006, 46)

Indeed, the differences in content between the two books, as far as the theory of aggression is concerned, are so minimal that we will not deal with them in what follows.

In Perls's later books (Perls 1969b; 1973; Perls & Baumgardner 1975), in essence the earlier positions are also only repeated; however, this is not done systematically but in the form of sporadic remarks — which is in accordance with the general character of these books, the major parts of which are transcripts of sound recordings and films that were taken during workshop sessions. Therefore, we think it is justified to refer to these texts only in a sporadic manner too.

---

[1] Since this term does not appear to be used in English as frequently as in German, we quote its definition from Wikipedia:

> Civil courage (sometimes also referred to as 'social courage') is defined by many different standards, but the term is usually referred to when civilians stand up against something that is deemed unjust and evil, knowing that the consequences of their action might lead to their death, injury, or any other negative effect.

We will be concerned with the *essential* features of this theory that in our present-day view appears even more doubtable than before. Our increasingly critical opinion has received additional support from our reading of a number of research reports from the field of academic psychology as well as from our simultaneous studies of various practical and theoretical aspects of Buddhist psychology and spirituality.

In what follows we will outline the positions that we have worked out with respect to Perls's theory of aggression and to the therapeutic treatment of human aggression. We understand this paper as a preliminary proposal that we want to make available to our colleagues in the hope of stimulating a discussion that will contribute to a critical reflection on the traditional understanding of aggression in Gestalt therapy and that will possibly lead to a revision of that theory.

More than sixty years have gone by since it was first formulated, and during this span of time research has not stood still. New ideas might be useful and maybe even necessary. When Perls et al. wrote *Gestalt Therapy*, they emphasized "... that by assimilating whatever valuable substance the psychological sciences of our time have to offer we are now in the position to put forward the basis for a consistent and practical psychotherapy" (1951, p. viii). We are convinced that Gestalt therapy, if it is to remain a consistent and practical psychotherapy, has to keep on integrating the valuable substances of the psychological (and other) sciences that have emerged since 1951 and that will emerge in the future.

The following text is subdivided into three parts: in Part One, we deal with the intrinsic logic of Perls's theory of aggression: we summarize it, discuss it critically, and point out its weaknesses and internal contradictions. In Part Two we will transcend the frame of reference of this theory and take a closer look at some of its elements from the perspective of other theories and that of recent research results. And finally, in Part Three, we will propose a Gestalt therapy approach to the work with aggression as we find it reasonable and effective today.

Because of the complexity of the topic we will again and again make references to thoughts we have expressed in earlier or later parts of our paper. In order to make it easier for you, our readers, to find the respective text passages, we have marked them as "points of reference" by adding parentheses in which the sign "↪" along with a certain number can be found. If at another place in our text we refer to such a point of reference, you will find in parentheses the remark "see reference point(s) ...," with the respective number(s) instead of the three periods. In addition, for your convenience we have included below a listing of the chapter reference points, locating them within the chapter outline as well as giving their page numbers:

Chapter Reference Points

PART ONE

1. 1. Frederick S. Perls's Theory of Aggression

    1. 1. 1. *Biting, Chewing, and Digesting: The Biological Level*
    1. 1. 2. *"Mental Metabolism": The Psychological Level*
    1. 1. 3. *Intermezzo*
    1. 1. 4. *Aggression as Expression and Action: The Interpersonal Dimension* (↪1, *p. 17;* ↪2, *p. 18*)
    1. 1. 5. *History of Effect* (↪3, *p. 19*)

1. 2. Problems

    1. 2. 1. *Confusion of Terms* (↪4, *p. 21;* ↪5, *p. 22;* ↪6, *p. 22*)
    1. 2. 2. *Category Mistake* (↪7, *p. 23*)

1. 2. 3. Out-Dated Psychology of Development, Emotion, and Cognition
1. 2. 4. Individualistic Picture of Mankind (➲ 8, p. 27; ➲ 9, p. 28; ➲ 10, p. 29)
1. 2. 5. Problematic Notion of Growth (➲ 11, p. 34)

PART TWO

2. 1. Motivational Systems (➲ 12, p. 36)

2. 2. The Everyday Side Effects of Aggression: Repercussions on the Aggressor (➲ 13, p. 45)

2. 2. 1. Repulsive Expression
2. 2. 2. Reduced Cognitive Performance (➲ 14, p. 52)
2. 2. 3. Culture-Blind "Authenticity" (➲ 15, p. 55)
2. 2. 4. "Anger Kills" (➲ 16, p. 57)
2. 2. 5. Summary

2. 3. Catharsis (➲ 17, p. 62)

2. 3. 1. An Old-Fashioned Concept
2. 3. 2. The Investigation by Bushman, Baumeister and Stack (1999)
2. 3. 3. Summary

2. 4. Inhibition and Control (➲ 18, p. 75)

2. 5. Between Scylla and Charybdis

2. 6. Can Anger and Aggression Ever Be Recommended?

PART THREE

3. 1. Appraisal

3. 1. 1. Personal Meanings in Social Context
3. 1. 2. Cognition and Feeling (➲ 19, p. 95)
3. 1. 3. Cultural and Social Influences

8 ... AGGRESSION, TIME, & UNDERSTANDING

3. 2. Anger-Appraisal

3. 3. Case Example 1 (➲ 20, p. 105)

    3. 3. 1. Vignette
    3. 3. 2. Interpretation

3. 4. Importance (➲ 21, p. 113)

    3. 4. 1. Important Occasions
    3. 4. 2. Self-Esteem and Slight (➲ 22, p. 116; ➲ 23, p. 123)
    3. 4. 3. Case Example 2
    3. 4. 4. Reduction of Importance (➲ 24, p. 129)
    3. 4. 5. Selflessness (➲ 25, p. 130)

3. 5. Needs (➲ 26, p. 134)

    3. 5. 1. The Function of Needs in Gestalt Therapy (➲ 27, p. 136)
    3. 5. 2. The Plasticity of Needs
    3. 5. 3. Basic Needs (➲ 28, p. 140)
    3. 5. 4. Alteration of Referential Need
    3. 5. 5. Selfish Entitlement (➲ 29, p. 145)

3. 6. Responsibility (➲ 30, p. 148)

    3. 6. 1. Agency and Control
    3. 6. 2. Freedom, Limitations and Interdependence (➲ 31, p. 156)

3. 7. Power (➲ 32, p. 160)

Final Remarks

References

PART ONE

1. 1. Frederick S. Perls's Theory of Aggression

To make the context of our considerations identifiable we first need to recapitulate the central notions of the tradition to which we refer.

At the end of the 1950's Frederick S. Perls recalled the point of departure of his theory of aggression:

> Nearly twenty years ago, when I was still an orthodox analyst, I took into account the fact that we have two kinds of teeth with two different functions, the cutters and the grinders. The task of the grinders appeared to me to be the destroying of the structure, the de-structuring of food in preparation for its assimilation. This ... changed the role of aggression from an outward-turned death instinct to a life supporting assignment ... (1997, p. 49)

In these few sentences almost all of the terms are included that make up Perls's theory of aggression: "destroying" in the sense of "de-structuring" (to break into parts), "assimilation" and "life supporting" or, as Perls wrote in other places, "growth." This assembly of terms is also illustrative of the historical context, in which Perls developed his theory: the attempt to overcome Freud's negative view of aggression as an outcome of the "death instinct" and to link it instead with the positive force of life.

1. 1. 1. Biting, Chewing, and Digesting: The Biological Level

For Perls aggression is a "biological force" (1969a, p. 5) in the service of life that is closely related to what he calls "assimilation" (see *ibid.*):

> In order to live, an organism must grow, physically and mentally. To grow, we must incorporate external substance, and in order to make it assimilable, we have to

de-structure it. Let us consider just the elementary tool of aggressive de-structuring, the teeth. To build up the highly differentiated proteins of human flesh, we have to de-structure the molecules in our food. (1975, p. 33)

By biting, chewing, and digesting the original structure of food is "destroyed" and transformed so that it becomes similar to the organism (Latin: *ad-similatio*) and usable for survival and growth. If seen in this way, destruction serves life, and aggression can be positively evaluated: "Aggression has one aim in common with most emotions: not senseless discharge, but rather application" (1947, p. 116). It is meaningful mostly because it enables the organism to satisfy its hunger: "The destructive function, although in itself not an instinct ... [is] a very powerful instrument of the hunger instinct ..." (*ibid.*, p. 110).

Being the "orthodox analyst" he was at that time according to his own evaluation, of course Perls regarded this biological function not only as such, but he was also interested in its developmental significance. So it was proximate for him to think in terms of Freud's theory of developmental phases and to define "different stages in the development of the hunger instinct" (*ibid.*, p. 109) — sub-phases of the oral phase, as it were. He started at the "*pre-natal* (before birth)" (*ibid.*) stage, during which the unborn baby "... gets all the food it requires *via* the placenta and umbilical cord — the liquefied and chemically prepared meal as well as the necessary amount of oxygen" (*ibid.*, p. 108). Then,

> with birth, the umbilical cord ceases to function, ... and, in order to keep alive, the newly-born child is faced with tasks ... It has to provide its own oxygen, that is, to start breathing, and it has to incorporate food. ... the molecules of the proteins, etc., of the milk have to be chemically reduced and broken up into simpler substances. (*ibid.*)

This is the *"pre-dental* (suckling)" (*ibid.*, p. 109) stage at which the processes of destruction take place on the biochemical level. With the eruption of the front teeth, the baby enters the "*incisor* (biting)" (*ibid.*) stage. „The task of the teeth is to destroy the food's gross structure..." (*ibid.*, p. 108); they enable the infant to prepare the metabolic destructuring of food in an additional, however imperfect, manner. The so-called "dental aggression" takes shape.

With the occurrence of the next phase that Perls calls the "*molar* (biting and chewing" stage and that presupposes the eruption of grinders, the child achieves the additional capability of further mincing bitten-off pieces.

> The task of the molars is to destroy the lumps of food; mastication is the last stage in the *mechanical* preparation for the forthcoming attack[2] by *chemicals*, by body juices. The best preparation for proper digestion is to grind the food into an almost fluid pulp... (*ibid.*, p. 109)

1. 1. 2. "Mental Metabolism": The Psychological Level

Similar to Freud who did not restrict himself to looking at the biological level of development, Perls also concerned himself with the question of which psychological processes are associated with the biological ones in terms of time and taxonomy. Basically he took as his point of departure a concept he adopted from J. C. Smuts (1926/1973) whose book *Holism and Evolution* had impressed him deeply. Perls introduced the second part of *Ego, Hunger and Aggression*, the title of which was "Mental Metabolism," by a long quote from Smuts. The passage from this quote that would stamp Perls's subsequent theorizing reads as follows:

---

[2] Note Perls's choice of words!

> The Personality [sic!], like the organism, is dependent for its continuance on a supply of Material, intellectual, social and such-like, from the environment. . . . Just as organic assimilation is essential to animal growth, so intellectual, moral and social assimilation on the part of the Personality [sic!] becomes the central fact in its development and self-realisation. (Smuts, 1926/1973, p. 301; see Perls, 1947, p. 105)

As the headline "Mental Metabolism" already announces, the central thought now is the establishment of a correlation between the level of biological metabolism and the mental or psychological level — the fourth chapter of this part of his book is called "Mental Food." Perls claims to ". . . look upon psychological material in the same way as upon physical food" (*ibid.*, p. 132). He does not clarify, however, if for him this claim follows from an alleged analogy, an isomorphism, or a causality. In any case, he attributes to each developmental stage a certain style of a human being's "intake of the world" (*ibid.*, p. 130).

To be sure, here he does not speak about material food, but about "the world," i. e. about other people or "psychological material" such as the content of thoughts or imaginations. To the pre-dental stage he assigns "total introjection" (*ibid.*); the person behaves ". . . 'as though he had no teeth' — the introjected person or material remains intact. . . . The image is incorporated more or less *in toto*" (*ibid.*); mental content is uncritically absorbed lock, stock, and barrel.

The incisor stage is associated with "partial introjection" (*ibid.*, p. 131). "Here only parts of a personality are introjected" (*ibid.*); cognitive material and other people's opinions are only in part subjected to scrutiny. Finally, the molar stage parallels assimilation, which in Perls's view is the most mature way of dealing with mental content;

assimilation involves the complete destructuring of the material. Therefore Perls maintains that "... aggression is required to assimilate the world. If we don't assimilate what is available, we can't make it our own part of ourselves. It remains a foreign body in our system — something which Freud recognized as introjection" (1973, p. 186).

In sum one can say: from the biological stages in the development of food intake Perls derives respective stages of psychological development as well as psychological styles in the way people deal with other people, opinions, imaginations, and other content. Also on the psychological level for him aggression is a necessary means for people's quarrel with the (mental) world, without which people would not be able to destroy (destructure) mental content they are confronted with and to come up with their own responses to the world. He concludes: "Thus aggression is essential for survival and growth" (Perls, 1975, p. 33).

1. 1. 3. Intermezzo

If you look at Perls's understanding of aggression we have described so far, you will find that he only refers to the "*intra*psychic" realm. Although the world, other people, and their opinions do exist, the process through which the aggressive destructuring takes place so far only appears as the *internal* psychological work of the person who "takes the world in." In other words, at first aggression is not an act by which a person intervenes in the world, not even an emotion expressed or a feeling experienced, but exclusively an "intrapsychic" *function*.

This comprehension of aggression follows logically from its derivation from the biological processes of food intake and digestion. What is experienced in this context may be hunger, but certainly not any irritation, annoyance, or anger: usually you do not go to a restaurant because you harbor hostile feelings against the offered meals and, therefore, wish to annihilate them. The destruction of the food that takes place is *functionally* necessary; it has nothing to do with what we mean in everyday parlance when we talk about aggression and destruction. The same applies to the critical investigation of cognitive material: it is not necessarily accompanied by aggressive experience; fortunately one can carefully and thoroughly think about most matters without having a temper tantrum.

So we have to state: wherever in Perls's theory the terms "aggression" or "destruction" occur *in the context of biological or psychological "metabolism" subserving assimilation, survival, and growth* they acquire a meaning that does *not* conform to their colloquial use. In contradistinction, both in everyday speech and in scientific psychology "aggression" usually denotes an offensive attack intending the infliction of harm — frequently associated with emotions of anger or rage — either on an interpersonal or an international level (see reference point 6).

Of course, with this unusual application of the term "aggression" the danger of misunderstandings is given; in Gestalt therapy literature some authors try to avoid it by speaking of "positive aggression." Such misunderstandings would have to be traced back to a sloppy reception of *Ego, Hunger and Aggression*, if Perls had used the term in his book *only* in the sense he used it in context with metabolism and assimilation. However, that is not the case! In many places he also uses the term "aggression" with exactly the meaning that it has in colloquial and scientific language. Let us take a close look now.

1.1.4. Aggression as Expression and Action:
The Interpersonal Dimension

Perls applies the term "aggression" as well when he speaks about a certain emotion (see, for instance, 1947, p. 116) or about acts of warfare, for instance in context with the German attack against Czechoslovakia (1975, p. 33). And especially in the context of feelings such as anger, rage, and hate he holds views that do not only refer to "*intra*psychic" processing, but also to behavior that directly relates to other people.

In a way similar to the assumption that internal aggressive activity is necessary for healthy metabolism, Perls finds that, in case a person experiences hostile feelings, external aggressive activity towards other people is necessary for the maintenance of psychological health. For example he writes: "If you are afraid to express 'I hate you,' you will soon imagine yourself being hated by the world . . ." (1947, p. 242) — unexpressed anger causes paranoia.

In order to counter such a development he appears to envision a kind of escalating procedure that starts with a fantasy experiment of the kind he would later practice frequently in his work with the "empty chair":

> . . . visualize a person against whom you feel a grudge. Tell him exactly what you think of him. Let yourself go; be as emotional as you can; break his bloody neck; swear at him as you have never sworn before. Do not be afraid that this will become your character. On the contrary, this imaginary work will discharge much hostility, especially in cases of latent hostility, as, for instance, in a strained or estranged marriage. It often works wonders! Instead of forcing yourself to be nice and to hide your irritability behind a mask of politeness, you clear the air. Often,

16 ... Aggression, Time, & Understanding

however, this imaginary action will be insufficient...
(*ibid.*, p. 245)

If that is the case, the next step of escalation is required, i. e. the *direct* expression of aggressive feelings towards the person they are related to. However, as the following examples demonstrate, for Perls the alleged necessity of aggressive expression is only one next step, after which in certain cases — as *ultima ratio*, as it were — their transformation into aggressive *actions* is desirable — of course always in the assumed interest of the well-being and growth of the person who experiences those feelings (and not in the interest of the addressee).

One example deals with a stammering person:

> The chronic stammerer is characterized by his impatience, undeveloped sense of time and by his inhibited aggression. . . . The picture changes completely, however, when he flies into a violent temper. As soon as he is ready to give vent to his aggression, he suddenly finds he has the means at his disposal, and he shouts and swears fluently without a trace of stammering. (*ibid.*, p. 262)[3]

In another example Perls mentions a patient who felt disrespected by his secretary (see reference point 22).

> Unable or unwilling to express the annoyance she aroused in him, he felt awkward, ill at ease and self-conscious in her presence. . . . he felt immediate relief after I had urged him to address her in phantasy as he would like to in actuality, to let himself go. Having a good command over his imagination, he gave full vent to his vituperation, expressing freely all his accumulated anger and annoyance . . . Not that in this case phantasy action

---

[3] In a transcript that was published many years later you can see Perls work exactly according to this theory under the title "The Treatment of Stuttering" (Perls & Baumgardner 1975, pp. 168ff.)

alone was sufficient; he told me later that he had changed his typist. The phantasy explosion had given him sufficient confidence to enable him not only to dress down but dismiss the supercilious employee. (*ibid.*, p. 254)

"Flying into a violent temper," "giving vent to his aggression," "letting himself go" or "giving full vent to his vituperation" are the key words in these examples. Obviously they are the key words of a cathartic concept following the analogy of a steam boiler (➲ 1). Presumably, it is based on the early psychoanalytic idea that held that drive energy should be discharged before it accumulates and, after having reached a certain amount of pressure, explodes and causes damage. If one believes John O. Stevens, for Perls this was not only a therapeutic strategy but also a style he would practice personally: "He kept himself clean — he didn't hold on to shit when he got incensed, he took care of himself, he let it out" (in Gaines 1979, p. 306).

For Perls, aggression would take one of three forms or directions; the first one, which he called "straightforward aggression" (1947, p. 130), was clearly his favorite. The second form comes into being, if straightforward aggression "... is retroflected (e.g. self-destruction)" (*ibid.*), and the third one, if "aggression is projected" (*ibid.*) and experienced as anxiety. Perls thought of the second and third forms as pathological — both if they are practiced in singular cases and especially if they have become habitual and turned into character traits.

The possible overcoming of such pathologies he saw in a return to dental aggression: "The more we allow ourselves to expend cruelty and lust for destruction in the biologically correct place — that is, the teeth — the less danger will there be of aggression finding its outlet as a character feature" (*ibid.*, p. 196). And about forms of sublimination he said:

> All these are excellent outlets for aggression, but they will never equal dental aggression, the application of which will serve several purposes: one rids oneself of irritability and does not punish oneself by sulking and starving — one develops intelligence, and has a good conscience, because one has done something "good for one's health." (*ibid.*, p. 117)

We will discuss the possible repercussions on one's intelligence and health in the second part of this paper (see reference points 13, 14, 16); at this point we would only like to hint at the following: the above quotes and others clearly demonstrate Perls's intent to develop a theory of aggression as well as respective therapeutic methods that can contribute to a *peaceful* living together of people (➲ 2).[4] However, one needs to ask if this concept and his ambiguous use of the term of aggression did not sometimes guide him to statements that make it hard to discern the peaceful intent. Here is an example:

> Aggression has a two-fold purpose: first, to de-structure any threatening enemy to the point where he becomes impotent; and, second, in an expanding aggression, to de-structure the substance that is needed for growth and to render it assimilable. Even Hitler, when setting out to destroy Czechoslovakia, was careful not to destroy the armament factories that he wanted to incorporate into his greater Germany. Thus aggression is essential for survival and growth. (1975, p. 33)

To say it carefully, we find it weird if Hitler's invasion into Czechoslovakia is associated with "survival and growth" instead of dominion and subjugation. Moreover, in

---

[4] His wife, Laura Perls, promoted the same theory in a lecture of 1938 explicitly under the title "How to Educate Children for Peace" (L. Perls, 1992, pp. 37ff.).

the face of the historical events we find it impossible to acknowledge the protection of armament factories by the German military for the purpose of using them for their own ends as a differentiated process of assimilation. Actually, the term of "growth" acquires a very problematic meaning here that we will address in more detail later (see ref. point 11).

1. 1. 5. History of Effect

Perls's notion of aggression and the cathartic practice he derived from it have left visible traces in subsequent generations of Gestalt therapists. The famous and infamous hitting on pillows and yelling at empty chairs, which Yontef once branded as "boom-boom-boom therapy" (1991, p. 7), has become less fashionable in recent years, even though it has not yet died out (see, for instance, Knights 2002; for a critical review see Staemmler 2002c). In the 1970s and '80s many Gestalt therapists worked in a way that Stella Resnick characterized like this: "Gestalt therapy counters societal sanctions against expression by encouraging people to go after and get rid of their stockpiles of unexpressed feeling. People learn ... that expressing themselves is good and right ..." (1975, p. 231).

One can still find similar ideas in more recent publications, for instance in Dreitzel (➲ 3; see reference points 1, 17), who writes:

> As soon as a situation contains obstacles that are hard to remove or even threatening..., aggressive feelings come up, and the organism motivates and energizes itself first by light and then by heavy anger, in extreme cases by destructive rage or by annihilating hate. All of these are normal contact functions. (1995, p. 504)

What looks like the description of a "natural" process here ("the organism energizes itself") of course has nothing to do with 'nature,' but with a questionable notion that our culture in general and its psychoanalytical subculture in particular has created: to assert that "in extreme cases destructive rage or annihilating hate" should represent "*normal* contact functions," in our view points to an equivocal notion of normality.

Behind such assertions one can surmise Perls's cathartic concept that in the *Dictionary of Psychology* is characterized by the idea, ". . . that small aggressions render the big ones unnecessary or impossible (. . . similar to the drive theories)" (Asanger & Wenniger 2000, p. 53). Dreitzel argues exactly in this manner: ". . . he who does not sense his small anger, easily bursts out in rage; he who hardly can say 'no,' will collect resentments; and who finds swearing too violent, will easily dream of weapons of destruction" (1995, p. 505).

As far as we know, a critical discussion of the cathartic notion has hardly taken place among Gestalt therapists until today; we will return to this topic (see reference point 17). And as far as the history of effect of Perls's theory of aggression is concerned we have to state with regret that Gestalt therapists have published very few papers or books that do more than just repeat Perls's theory more or less uncritically — whatever the reason may be. The "dental-aggressive" examination of Perls's theory of aggression among Gestalt therapists has largely been missing; valuable papers such as the ones by Frech (2000) or Wheeler (2006) are rare exceptions and look more at contextual conditions than at the very content of the theory. The most salient critique has been put forward by integrative therapist Hilarion Petzold (see, for instance, 2006).

This is surprising, since the Perlsian theory of aggression — in spite of its positive intentions — is rich with inconsistencies and contradictions that do not stand the test of thorough scrutiny; we will say more about this in the following section. Moreover, Perls's theory is in gross contrast with a long tradition of human experience in general and with a large number of research results in particular that today make its value look more than dubious (see Part Two and Part Three of this paper).

1. 2. Problems

1. 2. 1. Confusion of Terms

In our view, from the very beginning Perls's approach to aggression is based on a confusing use of terms. Above we have quoted his statement saying that the task of teeth is to destroy structures, to de-structure food and to prepare it for assimilation. According to Perls, this process transforms the meaning of aggression and turns it into a "life supporting assignment" (Perls 1997, p. 49).

Here the *decomposition* of food into its raw and chemical components for the purpose of nutrition is equated with "destruction" (◐ 4) — as if a good piece of bread is not eaten but thrown into the garbage pail. That is pretty much like saying that a car mechanic, who *disassembles* an engine with a positive intention (such as wanting to extract spare parts for the repair of other engines), *destroys* the engine. By so saying the *constructive* act is named in a decontextualized and hence misleading way, which makes it seem *destructive* and associates it linguistically with a negative intention. However, even for Perls himself this looked so inadequate that in a next step he needed to reinterpret "destruction" in a positive sense: through this maneuver a "positive" notion of aggression was formed.

This erroneous and pretty laborious construction would have been superfluous if Perls had started his considerations with the useful terminological distinction between "decomposition" on the one hand and "destruction" on the other hand. Admittedly, it can be assumed that his "theory" of aggression would probably never have risen above the status of a very short-lived idea.

An additional argument for a "positive" term of aggression that can frequently be found in the Gestalt therapy literature invokes its etymology: "Aggression," it is maintained, is derived from *ad-gredi* (➲ 5) that originally in Latin only meant to "approach" something "Aggression is the 'step toward' the object of appetite or hostility," Perls et al. (1951, p. 342) write. Hence "aggression" would indicate something like "initiative" or, even more general,

> ... a beneficial, self-expressive, and creative human power to make something or to make something happen, to be willing to give oneself back to the world as well as to receive from the world. This is anything but the hostile warlike exercise of power over others that we generally think of as aggression nowadays. (Miller 1994, p. 77)

At first sight this etymological reasoning appears to be supported by historical truth, but at a closer look it proves to be entirely unhistorical. It rips the term out of its historical (Roman) context and tries to 'transplant' it across millennia into today's language by simply disregarding the change in meaning that has taken place since antiquity: even if it was correct that *aggredi* at *that* time meant to approach something in a more or less neutral fashion, *today* "aggression" denotes something different as Miller in the citation above admits too. In contemporary psychology, "Aggression is any form of behavior directed toward the goal of harming or injuring another living being who is motivated to avoid such treatment" (Baron & Richardson 1994, p. 7). "Harming or injuring" refers to "... damaging, breaching, destroying and annihilating; it also includes '*iniuriam facere*' [Latin: to do injustice] ... i. e. to inflict pain or dysfunction, to evoke irritation and to act in insulting ways ..." (Selg 1968, p. 22 — ➲ 6).

In an attempt to justify Perls's term of aggression one might argue that in certain limited contexts — for instance, in scientific systems of concepts — it is absolutely customary and even necessary to define terms in ways that *deviate* from ordinary language as well as from their uses in other theories. For this reason in physics a second is not defined as a short moment but as the duration of light waves emitted by Cs-133. With the same eligibility, so this argument might continue, Gestalt therapy has the right to define aggression in its own way.

As plausible as this argument may seem at first, it does not take into account one essential aspect: in scientific systems certain terms are defined in *more* specific ways, because their is a need for more precision than in everyday parlance. Perls, however, does not define "aggression" more specifically, but to the contrary, *less* precisely. This does not lead to a gain in conciseness, but to adulteration and confusion. The derangement is carried even further by the fact that, as we have demonstrated above, the unspecific use of the term "aggression" is not applied consistently, but again and again is intermingled with the more specific ordinary use. The result is a hotpot of initiative, critical investigation, creativity, vitality, intake of food, destructivity, hostility and aggressive use of power. If you serve yourself from this hotpot you are likely to also find a few baby teeth in it . . .

1. 2. 2. Category Mistake (➲ ▼)

By making this deliberately polemical statement in which hostility and baby teeth are mentioned in the same breath, we intended to initiate the following point.

"She came home in a flood of tears and a sedan-chair" (Ryle 1949, p. 22) — this sentence provides an example for what Ryle calls a "category-mistake": two things (here: flood of tears and a sedan-chair) are handled in parallel although they belong to different terminological categories. In sentences such as Ryle's this has a funny effect only, but within the framework of serious theories it can lead to grave problems. You can see this, for instance, in the title of a well-respected German book by a well-respected author; the title is *Soul Murder* (Wirtz 1989). Two terms of different categories (here: soul and murder) are linked and thereby suggest — against the intent of the author, to be sure — that the incest survivors, whom the book is about, are psychically dead and do not have a soul anymore.

You can recognize the category error by the fact that the first term (soul) does not specify the meaning of the second term (murder), but *changes* it. "Malicious" murder remains murder, i. e. the malevolent annihilation of a human life, but "soul" murder is not murder in the actual sense of the word; it is a metaphor with all its sometimes useful or, as is the case in the title of this book, detrimental side effects.

The idea of a "mental metabolism" displays the same pattern and yields the same category error. Of course, to take a critical look at something is impossible without metabolic processes, but that does not turn them into mental processes; they remain as biochemical as they have always been. "Mental metabolism" is a metaphor, which brings about a side effect that Perls apparently welcomed but which in our view is problematic:

Since Perls has used the term "metabolism" in the context of digestion of food before, the metaphor suggests that mental processes or emotionally energized encounters between human beings are characterized by the same patterns as digestive processes. However, no human being "digests mental food" with the help of her or his teeth, gastric acid, and enzymes; a "mental stomach" or "gut" is nonsense. What Staemmler has written about Perls's use of the term "field" also applies in this case: "Just the theory that was meant to be holistic turns in part into the exact opposite, i. e. reductionist. The biological, organismic level is predominant; the phenomenal, personal level becomes secondary" (2006, p. 74).

1. 2. 3. Out-Dated Psychology of Development, Emotion, and Cognition

The category error that is implicit in the metaphor of "mental metabolism" has negative consequences for the theory that is based on it. This is not the place to refer in detail to the vast evidence that recent psychologies of development, emotion, and cognition or neurosciences have provided; they make Perls's metaphor look old from today's perspective. Moreover, it would not be fair toward Perls, who for obvious historical reasons had no access to this research. Nevertheless, Kepner is right when he states:

> The original developmental theory in the Gestalt approach, the oral stage of development and oral aggression, was at best a metaphor for dilemmas in adult contact. Not only was it not based on actual observation of children (neither Freud nor Perls appeared ever to actually feed an infant), but it stemmed from a theory that is now vastly superceded by advances in affect theory, cognitive development, and so on. (Kepner 2000, pp. 264f.)

And one must add that even at the time, when Perls wrote his first book, a lot of knowledge was available that was opposed to his considerations. At least he knew something of the Gestalt psychology of the 1930s and '40s, the central term of which he borrowed to name his approach to psychotherapy. Last but not least he dedicated his book *Ego, Hunger and Aggression* "to the memory of Max Wertheimer." By 1945 Wertheimer had published his cognitive psychology under the title *Productive Thinking*, which made Perls's digestive psychology and pathology about "mental food" (1947, pp. 122ff.) or "mental indiges-tion" (*ibid.*, p. 103), respectively, already look out-dated when it was first released.[5]

One needs neither extraordinary introspective capabilities nor much sanity and reason to discern some basic differences between digestive and mental processes: whereas physical digestion predominantly takes place involuntarily and unawares, the processing of mental content, especially the focused critical reflection on data and problems, always *also* is connected with a voluntary direction of attention and with conscious thought.[6] More-over, mental reflections are characterized by something which cannot seriously attributed to digestive organs and to which Wertheimer's book title clearly points: creativity.[7] In addition, mental processes usually take place with reference to certain or to "generalized others" (Mead 1934/1963). Their structure is dialogical (see Bakhtin 1986) — also something one cannot seriously say about digestion. ". . . the mind is no sort of substance at all — metaphysically, minds are not a *bit* like rocks and cats and kidneys" (McGinn, 1989, p. 22 — italics in original).

To another difference Socrates has long ago alerted his conversational partner, Protagoras:

---

[5] To be sure, when Perls wrote his book, which was first published in 1942, he could not know what Wertheimer was going to write in a book that was to be published in 1945. However, this appears irrelevant to us in so far as Wetheimer had published many of the ideas that went into his book in various articles before. And even after 1945 Perls did not change any of his essential statements in the later editions of his book.

[6] This is true in spite of the fact that the majority of cognitive processes does not take place consciously (see our remarks on the cognitive unconscious: reference point 30).

[7] We neglect the old psychoanalytic interpretation that infants experience their faces as creative productions.

When you buy victuals and liquors you can carry them off from the dealer or merchant in separate vessels, and before you take them into your body by drinking or eating you can lay them by in your house and take the advice of an expert whom you can call in, as to what is fit to eat or drink and what is not, and how much you should take and when; so that in this purchase the risk is not serious. But you cannot carry away doctrines in a separate vessel: you are compelled . . . to take the doctrine in your very soul by learning it, and so to depart either an injured or a benefited man. (Platon 1924, p. 109)

Socrates's considerations are especially interesting in the context of Perls's thoughts about "dental aggression" since they are in opposition to Perls and demonstrate that so called "mental food" (in contradistinction to physical food) at first always needs to be taken in ("introjected") — even if at a later point in time it is criticized or rejected. You first have to understand something before you can question it in a meaningful way. The text at hand is an example.

Alas, the category error has even more negative consequences.

1. 2. 4. Individualistic Picture of Mankind
(⊃ 8, see reference points 15, 24, 31)

Above we have underlined the one-sidedness with which Perls both in his theory and in his practice took the aggressor's part. This was a consistent position for him to take: if aggression has a positive valence, because it is seen as being in the service of life and growth, then of course one has to stand up for it to be lived out.

This one-sidedness is closely linked with the metaphor of the "mental metabolism" that is meant to illustrate the adjustment processes that take place between a person and her environment. However, if this metaphor becomes the dominant measure (as it does in *Ego, Hunger and Aggression*), then adjustment takes place in only *one* direction, i. e. the person adjusts the environment *to herself* (she "assimilates" it) and not also herself to the environment (➲ 9; see ref. point 27).[8] In *Gestalt Therapy* one can find the same one-sidedness (and the same equation of the physical with the mental):

> Every organism in a field grows by incorporating, digesting, and assimilating new matter, and this requires destroying the existing form to its assimilable elements, whether it be food, a lecture, a father's influence, the difference between a mate's domestic habits and one's own. (Perls et al. 1951, p. 341)

In the writings of Piaget, who used a similar metaphor to Perls's,[9] besides the term "assimilation" the term "accommodation" can be found; for Piaget only the balance of the two makes up the whole: "We can ... define adaptation as an equilibrium between assimilation and accommodation..." (Piaget 1971, p. 8).

In Perls's writings there is no such balance. Regrettably, this has had an enduring impact on later theoretical developments in Gestalt therapy. They show, for example, in all variants of the "process of contact" (Perls et al. 1951, pp. 403f.

---

[8] There are a few places where Perls uses the terms "alloplastic" and "autoplastic." However, this cannot remedy his "tendency toward exuberant assimilation" (Walter 1999, 59), since he does not attribute any systematic place to them in his theory.

[9] Piaget, however, was much more wary of possible category errors than Perls:

> ... physiologically, the organism absorbs substances and changes them into something compatible with its own substance. Now, psychologically, the same is true, except that the modifications with which it is then concerned are no longer of a physico-chemical order, but entirely functional, and are determined by movement, perception or the interplay of real or potential actions (conceptual operations, etc.). (Piaget 1971, p. 8)

— ⊃ 10).[10] In all these models the environment — including other human beings! — takes the shape of a lifeless constant: following the metabolism metaphor (which in most cases is exemplified by food, sometimes also by some other *object* that does not show any autonomous original activity),[11] that object is thought to be at the (hungry) individual's disposal without constraints — if it only pursues its *own* needs and the resulting impulses without standing in its *own* way by activating any so called "neurotic" mechanisms. This is "... the individualistic ideal of destructuring the environment as if *in vacuo*" (Saner 1989, p. 64).

We have never embarked on this model. To our surprise, besides Saner it seems that Gordon Wheeler is one of the few who have realized its simplicity.

> As customarily drawn ..., the Cycle gives us a schematic of the life history of an impulse in isolation, as if existing separately from its "inner" context of competing or overlapping desires and background of beliefs, expectations, and values — and separately as well from the "outer" context (which is also a living part of our "inner" life) of *other people*, who make up our relevant landscape and our contextual world.... *Alas, examples of such normative, reductionistic teaching and applications of the Cycle model abound, amounting at times to a trivialization*

---

[10] Variants are, for example, the "cycle of experience" (Zinker 1977) or, more recently, the *"Gestaltwelle"* ("gestalt wave," Doubrawa & Blankertz 2000, pp. 63ff.; Blankertz & Doubrawa 2005, pp. 122ff.) bzw. "Kontaktprozess-Welle" ("contact process wave," Dreitzel 2004). — In *Ego, Hunger and Aggression* one can already find the idea of an "organismic circle" or "instinct cycle" (Perls 1947, pp. 55, 70).

[11] A recent example is given by Votsmeier-Röhr (2004, pp. 77ff.). — In the rare cases, in which a human being is taken as an example for the "object" of assimilation (see, for instance, Petzold, 1973, p. 28), this person indeed only functions as an *object* (in this case not as the object of hunger, but as that of sexual desire). For fairness's sake it needs to be added that Petzold has put forward different opinions in later publications.

of the Gestalt perspective itself... (Wheeler, 2003, p. 165 – italics in original; see also Wheeler 2000)

Maybe such a reductionist model can be applied to a gatherer under the presumption that he is the only man in the world. But already the challenges that are posed to the hunter of the Stone Age are not sufficiently described by this model, not to mention the everyday interactions between humans in today's life situations. By no means can it be reconciled with Buber's notion of "I-Thou" (see Frech 2000, p. 5) – not to mention power-critical hermeneutics, which in the attempt at understanding another person necessarily must accept the persistence of differentness, i. e.

> ... the not assimilable comprehension of a different meaning and, on these grounds, the possibility of a substantially new description of one's own familiar understanding of one's self and being. The autonomy of this *other momentum* has to be presupposed in order for the hermeneutic dialogue not to collapse into a monologue of the interpreter with himself. (Kögler 1992, p. 295)

If you apply the idea of a "healthy" aggressor to human relationships, you create the picture of a psychopath who treats other people not as human beings but as *objects*.[12] We do not need to specify the negative consequences for other people that result from a mentality like this, but we would like to mention only in passing the consequences that this mentality – "... replenish the earth, and *subdue* it: and have *dominion* ..." – has already had in respect to our ecology (see Fisher 2002).

The individualist point of view may appear unproblematic as long as we are thinking of aggression in its merely *functional* sense; above we have described the

---

[12] We have already quoted: "Aggression is the 'step toward' the *object* of appetite or hostility," write Perls et al. (1951, p. 342 – italics added).

"*intra*psychic" meaning that Perls first attributed to aggression as a means of "mental metabolism." Even if in the long run the results of this kind of "metabolism" have an impact on other people, this "digestive process" itself does not. Possible "flatulences" or "constipations" primarily hurt the respective person herself.

But as soon as aggression is also understood as a feeling, an emotional expression, or even as a hostile action, it arrives at an interpersonal or political level and yields social consequences. In this context the one-sided partisanship for the aggressor becomes problematic, and both psychological and ethical questions arise that Perls apparently did not consider — not even in his text on "Morality, Ego Boundary and Aggression" (Perls 1975), the title of which might evoke the expectation that these questions are being discussed.

The fact that he did not discuss them can probably be traced back to his "*hyper-individualistic, hyper-autonomous . . . oral-aggression*" (Wheeler 1996, p. 130 — italics in original) picture of mankind, according to which he placed one's *own* growth and well-being first — including the psychic health of the client with whom he happened to work at a given moment. The harmful impact that "giving vent to one's aggression" and "letting oneself go" can have on other people and on one's relationships with them (and on the aggressor himself) apparently were not of major interest for him. However, they are absolutely remarkable, as we will demonstrate below (see reference points 1, 9, 11).

The fulfillment of the needs of the individual (seen in isolation) was Perls's first priority. To him, society and human community appeared more like forces that were *opposed* or, at least potentially, harmful to individual development (this view can also be found in Resnick's quote above). Therefore the person needed to free herself from them or even had to fight against them. A dialectical entanglement of individual and society was beyond his scope of thinking. In contrast to many "field theoretical" reinterpretations by later authors, Perls's theorizing in *Ego, Hunger and Aggression* remained closely tied to a one-person psychology.[13]

He fell prey to a typical individualistic misconception. It consists in the assumption

> ... that the individual would have to prove himself as an individual by developing his individuality in full isolation and independently of the influence from other individuals, and would only subsequently — as an essentially completed individual — enter relationships with other individuals from which then joint action would emerge in the course of time. (Pieper 2003, p. 61/7)

To say it pointedly, individuality (which in some older varieties of psychoanalysis is called "infantile autism" or in Piaget's terminology "egocentrism") is seen as the *primary* entity that is 'domesticated,' if successful social influence is exerted by the community. The social, then, is seen as *secondary* — both chronologically and systemically. Potentially, it even is a threat to individuality, since socialization and individuation are also regarded as *antagonistic* forces: whereas society is interested in socializing the individuals who are part of it — that is to say: to deprive them more or less of their individuality and to accustom them to the social norms —, the individual strives to maintain and develop his individuality against society's pressure.

If, as in Perls's early writings, the striving for individuation and the maintenance of individuality is also seen as a "biological force," the consequence is yet another split, i. e.

---

[13] That also applies to the term of the "field" in this book which deviates from the term "field" as it has been used later in Gestalt Therapy (Perls et al., 1951; see Staemmler 2006). In *Ego, Hunger and Aggression* the "field" is the "aura" of a monade.

... the split between the biological and the social. In this view, the biological is the original, which is contained within the child itself and which forms its psychological substance. The social exercises coercion; it is an external force alien to the child, which squeezes out the modes of thinking that match the internal essence of the child, and replaces them with schemes of thought that are strange to that essence.... Coercion is seen as the mechanism that the social milieu uses in order to steer the development of the child's thinking.... The child is not seen as part of the social whole, not as subject of societal relations which from the first day of its life participates in the social life, of which it is a part. The social is viewed as a strange force situated outside of the child that puts pressure on the child and imposes its own modes of thinking on it. (Vygotski 1972, pp. 53f.)[14]

Not only recent developmental psychology of which Perls was not able to take notice, but already leading thinkers of his time — e. g. Vygotski, whom we have just cited, or, in a different manner, G. H. Mead (1934/1963) — have convincingly explained that, in contrast to the individualistic assumptions described above, the social is primary and that any individuality secondarily emerges from it. And the social does not stand in opposition to biology; without exaggeration one can say: in human beings the social is deeply rooted in their biological condition (see Als 1979). To use Buber's words, "man becomes an I through a You" (1970, p. 80).

---

[14] Vygotski's critique aims at Piaget, but it can be applied to Perls just as well. — The quote is not contained in the English edition, *Thought and Language*, which in comparison to the German edition is shortened very much.

1. 2. 5. Problematic Notion of Growth (⊃ 11)

For Perls, aggression serves assimilation and growth. But what kind of growth? Already on the physical level, growth cannot be a value *per se*, if you understand it primarily and exclusively in *quantitative* ways. Under healthy conditions, the physical growth of a person ends in the second decade of life. And if you think of the growing (!) part of the population in wealthy countries, whose embonpoint is growing faster than is good for their spines, blood parameters, and hearts, it becomes difficult to find this kind of growth desirable. Cancer grows too, and usually it does not do so in the service of survival. The same can be observed in the context of economical development: in contrast to the ritualistic adorations of most politicians, quantitative growth is not conducive to the survival of our planet; this has been clearly said by the "Club of Rome" in the early 1970's (see Meadows 1972; see also Meadows et al. 1993; Kennedy & Merten 2006).

To the "orthodox analyst" Perls, a purely quantitative notion of growth — "the bigger, the better" — should have been suspect of representing a primitive phallic phantasy. But a *qualitative* definition of growth cannot be found is his writings; maybe it is simply impossible to define a term in qualitative ways that is so much quantitatively prearranged in ordinary language.[15] Fuhr and Gremmler-Fuhr hold that a quantitative notion of growth is unfeasible in the psychological field and propose "... to eliminate the term 'growth' from the catalogue of Gestalt therapy's key words ..." (2001, p. 91).

If you read how Perls (1975, p. 33) put the term "growth" in the context of the German occupation of Czechoslovakia,

---

[15] Merten (2003) has proposed to dissolve this dilemma this way: "Growth needs limits."

you will be reminded of the Nazis' propaganda of the "people without space." We do not mean to suggest that anybody, who frivolously uses the term "growth," intends to justify individual or state-run aggressive expansion or other activities disrespecting national or international law; this also applies to Perls, who as a socialist and Jew had personally suffered from Nazi politics. However, we want to underline that these kinds of attitudes and actions become *possible*, if growth *per se* is positively evaluated and, in addition, connected to a confused idea of aggression.

PART TWO

> We can be sure that we will hold on to the deathbed as part of the last balance sheet — and this part will taste bitter as cyanide — that we have wasted too much, much too much strength and time on getting angry and getting even with others in a helpless shadow theater, which only we, who suffered impotently, knew anything about.
>
> (Mercier 2008, p. 378)

In the second part of our investigation of Gestalt therapy's classical theory of aggression we will again pick up some aspects that we have already addressed in the first part. Whereas our critical considerations in the first part predominantly dealt with the internal inconsistency and terminological ambiguity of Perls's theory, which would have been possible in principle in Perls's lifetime, we will now assume another perspective. In what follows we will draw on knowledge of later origin, which we think needs to be integrated into today's reflections on clinical theory and therapeutic practice in Gestalt therapy with respect to aggression.

2. 1. Motivational Systems (➔12)

In the section "Confusion of Terms" we have argued against the laborious and confusing train of thought that is based on an — from our perspective useless — equalization of the meanings of "destroying" and "taking apart," which, in consequence, makes it necessary to reestablish the lost differentiation by establishing a difference between "destroying" and something like "positive destroying" (see reference point 4). In this section we will introduce some *psychological* information with respect to this distinction.

In her lecture on "How to Educate Children for Peace," that we mentioned above, Laura Perls (1992, pp. 37ff. — see reference point 2) has outlined the traditional theory of aggression in a concise fashion. She deplores the educational style of parents who suppress certain behaviors of their child, "... not only ... his so-called 'naughtiness,' his crying and shouting, biting, kicking and scratching, tearing and breaking things, but also ... his curiosity and his inquisitiveness" (*ibid.*, p. 39). And she also shows empathy for the adults: "Of course, the child's inquisitiveness and his physical aggressiveness are very trying for the grown ups. Their satisfaction demands so much time and patience..." (*ibid.* — italics in original).

A few pages later, using the widely defined term of aggression of her own theory, she writes:

> Aggression is not only a destructive energy, but the force which is behind all our activities, without which we could not do anything. Aggression not only makes us attack, it also makes us tackle things; it does not only destroy, it also builds up; it not only makes us steal and rob, it also lies behind our endeavors to take hold and to master what we have a right to. (*ibid.*, pp. 42f.)

If you analyze these three quotes, you will find that — in spite of the confusing fact that Laura Perls always speaks of "aggression" — she continuously mentions *two* categories of behaviors and motivations, respectively. We have compiled them in the table on the following page.

The terms she uses in the second quote appear to be the most useful for labeling the categories to which we have attributed them: on the one hand, category A refers to *aggression* (in the specific sense, as it is used in colloquial language as well as in psychological science, for instance by Baron & Richardson 1994 — see reference point 6). On the other hand, category B deals with "*inquisitiveness*," which in the terminology of motivational psychology is called "investigation" or "exploration" (see Graumann 1969). Ford also distinguishes between the motivation of *"annoyance-anger-rage"* on the one hand, and *"curiosity-interest-excitement"* on the other hand (1992, pp. 148f.).

	Category A	*Category B*
first quote	biting, kicking, scratching, tearing, breaking	curiosity and inquisitiveness
second quote	physical aggressiveness	inquisitiveness
third quote	attacking, stealing, robbing	tackling, building up, taking hold, mastering

We find it remarkable that Laura Perls in the words she uses, as soon as she *describes* certain *experiences* of parents with their children (maybe her own experiences), reintroduces exactly the same differentiation again that she — as well as her husband — has given up on a theoretical level. As a result, she writes sentences such as the following, in which one can find both: "Aggression ... does not only destroy, it also builds up." If Laura and Frederick Perls in their formulation of their theory had lent more weight to their actual experience, they might have ended up where Graumann, Ford and other motivational researchers also have arrived, who do not attribute both categories to the same motivational system. To the contrary, the two categories are investigated as instances of two basically different motivational systems, lately for example by the psychoanalyst and infant researcher Joseph Lichtenberg.

According to his investigations, five human motivational systems must be distinguished:

(1) the need for psychic regulation of physiological requirements, (2) the need for attachment and later affiliation, (3) the need for exploration and assertion, (4) the need to react aversively through antagonism or withdrawal (or both),[16] and (5) the need for sensual enjoyment and sexual excitement. (Lichtenberg et al. 1992, p. 1; see also Lichtenberg 1989)

Here, under the numbers 3 ("exploration and assertion") and 4 ("aversion through antagonism" = aggression), you find exactly those motivations to which the Perls refer also (see categories B and A in our table above), although they throw them into the same hotpot called "aggression" — with the consequence that they need to differentiate them laboriously again later by introducing their idea of "positive aggression" (= the exploratory-assertive motivational system in Lichtenberg's terms).

The above mentioned motivational and developmental psychologists have a number of good reasons (not only terminological ones) why it makes sense to them to assume *two different* categories of motivations. They

> ... distinguish *assertiveness* from aggression. Aggression, either in subtle or direct ways, aims to demean or harm another, whereas assertiveness aims to put one's own needs or wishes forward and not to harm another. The aim for assertiveness is to attain one's own goal or safeguard one's own rights without harming or belittling another person. (Dreikurs Ferguson 2000, p. 277 — italics in original)

This insight of the psychologists is clearly supported by the neuroscientists. We would like to cite one of them, Jaak

---

[16] The two sides of this aversive motivation might be better known as *"fight or flight."*

Panksepp, who has done extensive research on emotions and has categorized them on the basis of neurophysiologic data:

> 1. The SEEKING[17] system . . . .: This emotional system is a coherently operating neuronal network that promotes a certain class of survival abilities. This system makes animals intensely interested in exploring their world and leads them to become excited when they are about to get what they desire. It eventually allows animals to find and eagerly anticipate the things they need for survival, including, of course, food, water, warmth, and their ultimate evolutionary survival need, sex. . . . In humans, this may be one of the main brain systems that generate and sustain curiosity, even for intellectual pursuits. This system is obviously quite efficient at facilitating learning, especially mastering information about where material resources are situated and the best way to obtain them. (Panksepp 2005, pp. 52f.)[18]
>
> 2. The RAGE system . . .: Working in opposition to SEEKING is a system that mediates anger. RAGE . . . energizes behavior when an animal is irritated or restrained. Human anger may get much of its psychic "energy" from this brain system. (*ibid.*, p. 54)

In our context it is most important that Panksepp characterizes the "RAGE system" as "*working in opposition* to SEEKING"; and he adds: ". . . the RAGE and SEEKING circuits may normally have mutually inhibitory interactions" (*ibid.*, p. 191). They also differ in that the SEEKING system is *proactively* activated, whereas the RAGE system is *reactively* activated: exploratory behavior starts *before* its target is

---

[17] The author capitalizes words that in his theory have *systematic* meaning and that he uses not only in the colloquial sense.

[18] These formulations strongly remind us of the phenomena that in the traditional literature of gestalt therapy are subsumed under the "positive" meaning of "ad-gredi" (see reference point 5).

perceived, whereas anger refers to something already *given* (see also Nell 2006, p. 215).

In passing we would like to mention that with respect to Perls's theory of aggression and the meaning he attributes to *hunger* it is interesting that for Panksepp, seeking for food and for other resources relevant to survival is clearly part of the SEEKING system — and not of the antagonistic RAGE system as one would have to expect, if one would follow Perls's understanding of aggression.

The difference in subjective feel of these two systems is easily illustrated. For example, remember a situation in which you wanted to find out something, wished to investigate a certain matter, intended to pursue a certain interest or decided to achieve something. You collected more and more information, acquired certain capabilities, made some well-planned steps, and at some point in time you experienced with relish a powerful feeling, when you found out or achieved what you were aiming at. In the end you had the pleasant experience of your own efficacy, and on the way to that end you felt the excitement and the stimulation that were the concomitants of your engagement with new situations and facts. The subject matter of your activity as well as your activity itself were *attractive*.[19]

And now, in contradistinction, imagine an occasion at which you were annoyed and angry and maybe had the fantasy of hurting or even killing the person who has triggered your wrath. What did you experience physically and mentally in that situation? Probably you were tense in an unpleasant way, you may have been occupied with an

---

[19] An impressive example for the joyful character of a strongly activated explorative-assertive motivational system can be found in the highly engaged, both extremely emphatic and humorous disputations that are practiced in Tibetan-Buddhist monasteries (see Bräutigam & Ribowski 2003, DVD, tracks 05/06ff.).

indignation that may have felt somewhat tantalizing to you, your thinking may have been narrowed and tied to the cause of your anger and, in the event that you vented it, you may have experienced some brief relief, but certainly no enrichment (as in the previous example). The subject matter of your activity as well as most of the activity itself was *aversive*.

The fact that we are confronting two different motivational systems, which in general are also experienced differently, does indeed not entirely exclude the possibility that in certain situations both systems are activated in parallel.[20] However, because of their "mutually inhibitory interaction" described by Panksepp (i. e. the relative incompatibility of attraction and aversion), it must be assumed that in these cases the weighting will be distributed very much on *one* of these systems and that one will have to expect a rather sudden transition from the predominant activation of the one system to that of the other.[21] For instance, increasingly intense feelings of anger may reach a climax and may then capsize into a pleasurable feeling of strength — or *vice versa*, as one can observe when the playful mutual trial of strength by squabbling children suddenly turns into bitter seriousness.

In spite of all critique we agree with the Perls in one respect: frequently the style of education Laura Perls

---

[20] "Parallel activation" may also mean that for a certain span of time one motivational systems works in the service of another. Grawe, who uses a different taxonomy of motivations than Lichtenberg, provides an example: "In situations in which helplessness is experienced, destroying something can acquire . . . a liberating positive meaning with respect to the frustrated need for control" (1998, p. 392).

[21] For the combination of other motivational systems, which are not mutually inhibitory, one must expect that they can be activated in parallel in a more balanced fashion. An obvious example is the parallel activation of Lichtenberg's motivational systems 2 (attachment-affiliation) and 5 (sensuality-sexuality). However, that does not mitigate their basic differentness.

describes in the first quote induces a confusion between the two kinds of motivation in children; this confusion may continue into adulthood and can therefore be found in some therapy clients too. This personal, *psychic* confusion must be taken seriously; nevertheless, this does in no way justify the *terminological* and *theoretical-psychological* confusion introduced by the Perls:

> ... fear, shame, and guilt are the affects parents most commonly evoke to erect prohibitions against exploratory-assertive activities they regard as dangerous or damaging: climbing on tiltable chairs, running after a ball into a street, grabbing a toy away from another child, pulling on mother's earring or glasses to inspect them. A subtle but important interplay exists in the parent's perception of the child's motive. Parents who recognize their child's activity as exploratory, self-assertive, and playful in nature, after effectively prohibiting a dangerous pursuit, will help the child to switch to another exploratory-assertive goal, including exploring the danger when appropriate. *Parents who regard their child's exploratory-assertive activity as aversive, that is, as antagonistic and rebellious* because they do not like it, after prohibiting the dangerous pursuit, shame the child as foolish, malicious, and bad. Consequently, the child will confuse assertion with antagonism and the persistent carrying out of a self-conceived agenda as shameful and evil. The subsequent permutations of this confusion of assertion and aversion will be pathogenic beliefs (Weiss and Sampson, 1986) that others are hostile suppressors to whom one must be compliant, that the self is faulty and bad and that self-exploratory motives are not to be trusted. (Lichtenberg et al. 1992, p. 55 — italics added)

By highlighting a part of Lichtenberg's et al. observations we intended to draw special attention to a certain aspect: a potentially pathogenic factor in those parenting styles consists exactly of a *lack of differentiation* between the child's two different motivations, i. e. of a parental behavior that treats the explorative-assertive activity of the child as if it had its source in the aggressive side of the aversive motivational system. However, "perhaps the best way to foster cruelty-dissolving empathy is to better deploy one of our most under-utilized social resources, childhood rough-and-tumble play . . ." (Panksepp 2006, p. 234). Without such experience, children will have a hard time learning to discern self-assertion and exploration from aggression and will tend to activate both motivational systems undifferentiatedly.

Then, to assert themselves will not be possible; they will have to attack the one towards whom they actually only want to assert and try out themselves; the intended self-assertion easily becomes an aggressive activity. The lacking ability to differentiate fosters unnecessary (and actually unintended) aggression, since it either confuses aggression with self-assertion or puts aggression in the service of self-assertion. Reversely, the lack of differentiation may also contribute to a lack of self-assertion, for instance when self-assertion gets under the impact of aggression inhibition that, given a clear differentiation, would not have to affect it.

If the confounding of different motivations by parents can yield detrimental effects in their children, one has to ask the question whether the same confounding, which exists in the theoretical assumptions of Perls's theory of aggression, is useful or noxious. After all, it is a theory that is made and — as experience demonstrates — apt to influence the behavior of therapists. Presumably, for their clients it is as little helpful as for children, if their explorative-assertive motivations on the one hand and their aversive-aggressive motivations on the other hand are not seen in their respective own rights and are not responded to in the respective appropriate ways. If they are thrown into one and the same hotpot, this lacking differentiation might foster the emergence of aggression in clients in the same manner that it does in children.

As we have said before, for Laura and Frederick Perls the idea of "positive aggression" appeared instrumental in therapy or in "education for peace." However — to use the appropriate martial metaphor, — their shot was off target. The explorative-assertive motivational system has to be clearly distinguished from the aversive — both theoretically and in education and psychotherapy. Thereby a multitude of aggressive expressions and behaviors might not emerge in the first place — which many people display assuming they have to be ("positively") aggressive, when all they want is to follow their needs, interests, and opinions. Moreover, experienced and expressed hostility might decrease in frequency, if people would know better and make more use of the really positive alternative to aggression, i. e. their explorative-assertive capacities. To them, much too often aggressiveness seems to be the only viable option if it comes to standing up for themselves.

Whereas in most cases it is desirable to support clients in developing explorative-assertive attitudes and behaviors, this cannot at all be said of aversive-aggressive coping strategies. Therefore, in what follows we will deal with exploration and self-assertion only marginally, but will turn our attention primarily to the aggressive part of the aversive motivational system.

2. 2. *The Everyday Side Effects of Aggression: Repercussions on the Aggressor* (➔ 13)

We take it as a widely known and well-established matter of fact that human aggressiveness can have a large variety of negative consequences for those who are exposed to it. The high print run of psychological literature on the aftermath of traumatic experience that has been published in recent years speaks for itself. We would only like to quote one source, one which refers to the correlation between the earlier victimization by the aggression of others and the later development of aggressiveness that sometimes turns victims into perpetrators:

> Many studies show that the experience of violence in childhood increases the likelihood of later delinquency because of violent actions by the factor two to four, but does not necessarily lead to violence... There are also other possibilities to process childhood experience of violence: you can become a drug addict, get depressive or develop panic attacks, become unable to form reliable relationships, suffer from psychosomatic or posttraumatic disorders, develop a chronic pain condition or begin to injure yourself — all of these diseases as well as some others yield a significant correlation with childhood abuse... One thing, however, is rare: that one remains healthy... (Dornes 2006, p. 336)

However, human aggression does not only catch children in its wake. To an extraordinary degree, women (especially in its sexualized form), are prey to agression from others. And violence against male adults can take on the shape of extreme physical damage, in some cases even with deadly consequences for the victims, as the cruelties that sometimes occur in prisons illustrate. More often than not it is the dismay about the fate of these victims that motivates the public to question the possibility of a more peaceful living together.

Frequently and rightly it is complained how soon after such events the public furor and outrage abates again and how easily the extraordinary events can distract from the ordinary, less figural, and by the mass media less attended aggressiveness that takes place in families, work places, and schools every day. Yet, in our observations of the public discussion and the media we have recognized an additional and regrettable phenomenon: lack of interest in the actions of the "normal" perpetrators that take place within the realm of what society readily accepts.

Of course, there is the sensationalist interest in the person of an "Ipswich Strangler" as well as an increasing number of serious and valuable approaches to the work with adolescent, right wing and other violent persons (see, for instance, Lempert 2006). But the entirely "normal" situation of the average citizen — eking out his living oriented at success, competitively, impatiently, drinking coffee or smoking cigarettes, always ready to take somebody on — usually gets as little attention as that of a chronically overloaded single mother of three children, who slaps a kid that does not want to do its homework, or as that of the couple — who over a period of twenty or more years do not miss a chance to cynically deprecate one another, icily remain silent, or irascibly jangle at each other.

Those are examples of the inconspicuously ordinary perpetrators, whose actions sometimes may yield more harmful effects for themselves than for those who, from the observer's point of view, seem to be the ones suffering the most.[22] In many cases chronic aggressiveness leads not only to psychic and social, but also to physical problems for the ones who are easily irritable *themselves*: their anger can kill them. (See reference point 16., later in the chapter.)

---

[22] This is not to down play the suffering of children who are exposed to parental aggression, if only indirectly:

> Children of all ages find adults' anger stressful and emotionally arousing; exposure to interadult anger may sensitize children toward anger and make them more likely to be aggressive. (Lemerise & Dodge 2000, p. 599)

2. 2. 1. Repulsive Expression
Intermittent Explosive Disorder
Affects up to 16 Million Americans[23]

> A little-known mental disorder marked by episodes of unwarranted anger is more common than previously thought, a study funded by the National Institutes of Health's (NIH) National Institute of Mental Health (NIMH) has found. Depending upon how broadly it's defined, intermittent explosive disorder (IED) affects as many as 7.3 percent of adults — 11.5-16 million Americans — in their lifetimes. The study is based on data from the National Comorbidity Survey Replication, a nationally representative, face-to-face household survey of 9,282 U.S. adults, conducted in 2001-2003.
>
> People with IED may attack others and their possessions, causing bodily injury and property damage. Typically beginning in the early teens, the disorder often precedes — and may predispose for — later depression, anxiety and substance abuse disorders. Nearly 82 percent of those with IED also had one of these other disorders, yet only 28.8 percent ever received treatment for their anger, report Ronald Kessler, Ph.D., Harvard Medical School, and colleagues. In the June, 2006 Archives of General Psychiatry, they suggest that treating anger early might prevent some of these co-occurring disorders from developing.
>
> To be diagnosed with IED, an individual must have had three episodes of impulsive aggressiveness "grossly out of proportion to any precipitating psychosocial stressor," at any time in their life, according to the standard psychiatric diagnostic manual. The person must have "all of a sudden lost control and broke or smashed something worth more than a few dollars . . . hit or tried to hurt someone . . . or threatened to hit or hurt someone."
>
> People who had three such episodes within the space of one year — a more narrowly defined subgroup — were found to have a much more persistent and severe disorder, particularly if they attacked both people and property. The latter group caused 3.5 times more property damage

---

[23] http://www.nih.gov/news/pr/jun2006/nimh-05.htm — Posted April 8, 2007

> than other violent IED sub-groups. Affecting nearly 4 percent of adults within any given year — 5.9-8.5 million Americans — the disorder leads to a mean of 43 attacks over the course of a lifetime and is associated with substantial functional impairment.

On a German internet-website[24] the translation of the announcement on IED was illustrated with the following photograph:

The picture demonstrates one of the side effects of aggressiveness that at first sight may look rather innocuous: from an esthetic perspective, anger does not have a favorable face, as the Dalai Lama once observed with his inimitable smile: "Hatred ... brings about a very ugly, unpleasant physical transformation of the individual" (1997, p. 10 — italics added). The concurring description of the Stoic philosopher Seneca[25] sounds more grim:

---

[24] http://www.handicap-network.de/handicap/Handicaps/psyche/psychea. htm#psy60 — January 6, 2007
[25] An useful overview on Seneca's attitude on anger and aggression is given by Toch (1983).

For as the marks of a madman are unmistakable — a bold and threatening mien, a gloomy brow, a fierce expression, a hurried step, restless hands, an altered color, a quick and more violent breathing — so likewise are the marks of the angry man; his eyes blaze and sparkle, his whole face is crimson with the blood that surges from the lowest depths of the heart, his lips quiver, his teeth are clenched, his hair bristles and stands on end, his breathing is forced and harsh, his joints crack from writhing, he groans and bellows, bursts out into speech with scarcely intelligible words, strikes his hands together continually, and stamps the ground with his feet; his whole body is excited and "performs great angry threats;" it is an ugly and horrible picture of distorted and swollen frenzy... (Seneca, 1614, *De Ira*, book 1, chap. 1)

Although in the tradition of Gestalt therapy esthetic criteria are valued (see Bloom 2005; Perls et al. 1951; L. Perls 1992) among others, one may find these manifestations negligible, if one looks at them *only* from an esthetic point of view. However, those manifestations do not only mean that an angry person is abhorrent to look at; her appearance also has an *expressive* character, i. e. she frequently also has a threatening or repulsive effect on others. To be confronted with aggressive expressions often triggers distress and aversive reactions such as withdrawal or counter-aggression. "It takes a near-saintly character not to respond angrily to another person's anger, especially when that person's anger seems unjustified and self-righteous. So another person's anger can be considered another cause of anger" (Ekman 2003b, p. 111)[26].

---

[26] In the reverse case, it is very difficult for an angry person to maintain this feeling, if she is confronted with someone, who obliviously remains friendly, as Ekman has demonstrated in an interesting experiment. In the debriefing the angry person said: "I couldn't be confrontational. I was always met with reason and smiles; it's

If one's anger elicits another one's anger, relational disturbances can hardly be avoided; in these cases social and physical side effects are closely interconnected:

> ... hostile persons both experience more interpersonal difficulties and respond to them with greater physiological reactivity. They also experience less social support and display less favorable physiological responses to it when available. Hence, hostility is characterized by both greater exposure and reactivity to unhealthy psychosocial contexts ... the greater exposure occurs because hostile persons create more conflict and undermine sources of social support through a variety of cognitive and behavioral processes ... (Smith et al. 2004, p. 1247)

Importantly, faces that display anger have the — evolutionary meaningful — feature of becoming figural in the perception of the observer and of attracting special attention: "... angry faces in happy crowds were found more efficiently than happy faces in angry crowds. Likewise, angry faces in neutral crowds were found more efficiently than neutral faces in angry crowds" (Hansen & Hansen 1988, p. 922; see also Buck 1994). So we are not only concerned with the phenomenon that anything which differs from the background is more easily perceived; an angry face obviously has an *extraordinary* "demand character."

In interpersonal conflicts this *"pop-up"*-effect often contributes to a negative spiral, since human beings not only perceive the other's anger preferentially[27], they also tend to evaluate the *other's* aggressive expression as more *inappropriate* than their own. "... an initiator of an aggressive interaction even evaluates her/his own behaviour as more

---

overwhelming. I felt something — like a shadow or an aura — and I couldn't be aggressive" (Goleman 2003, p. 18).

[27] This is true to a particularly large degree for the perception of a *male* angry face by a *male* (see Williams & Mattingley 2006).

appropriate than the subsequent reaction directed against herself/himself which (s)he apparently provoked" (Mummendey et al. 1984, p. 308). This makes an escalation of the conflict likely, because both participants have the impression of an inappropriate reaction of the respective other, whereas their respective own behavior appears to be commensurate to them.

> This dissent may produce something like a slope of respective perceptions of inappropriate actions, which gives speed or energy for the development of an escalating progress of an aggressive interaction: the recipient, being oriented to norms and expectations concerning suitable behaviour in a certain situation, perceives and evaluates this action as violating a norm and inappropriate; (s)he feels provoked and justified to pay back to get even with the opponent. Now the new victim feels attacked and mistreated ... and so on. (*ibid.*, p. 309)

If one desires a *de*-escalation one has to conclude from this investigation the following: only if I express my response to an experienced attack in a noticeably *slighter* manner as compared to the intensity of my experience, I can expect that the other person will experience my response as appropriate!

To keep this in mind during conflict is certainly not always easy, especially since in such situations humans tend not to perform at the peak of their mental capacities ...

2. 2. 2. Reduced Cognitive Performance (⊃ 14)

Escalations in aggressive conflicts are frequently boosted and enforced by a reduced differentiation of cognitive performance: "... when such intense anger and hatred arise, it makes the best part of our brain, which is the ability to judge between right and wrong and assess long-term and short-term consequences, become totally inoperable" (Dalai Lama

1997, p. 10). Typically, when people are angry, they insist in an entirely self-uncritical way on their opinion as being right, even though their view of the situation tends to be colored by their anger one-sidedly and might be in need of correction or at least refinement more than in other situa-tions. Nevertheless, they only perceive what can give rise to new irritation. They hold in their hearts an unquestionable conviction, which later may appear to them as an imprudent statement made out of anger; sometimes they even harshly demand an apology from the other when they might as well have reasons to apologize themselves.

However, even if the other makes a clear effort at deescalation and, say, apologizes, angry people usually do not find it easy to respond positively quickly and to accept the apology. Anger, once activated, cannot be easily deactivated; it has its own dynamics that for a certain period of time makes it at least partly resistant to a situation that has already changed for the better. "For a while we are in a *refractory* state, during which time our thinking cannot incorporate information that does not fit, maintain, or justify the emotion we are feeling" (Ekman 2003b, p. 39 — italics in original).

In addition, not only the intake of new information is restricted, but also the retrieval of information which is ordinarily available in memory. The working of our memory to a considerable degree is dependent on our overall condition as well as on the relational situation we are in: our memory is "*state dependent*" (Bower 1981). If we are angry with somebody, we recall instances that have similarly triggered our anger much easier and in much more detail than we remember situations in which we have felt in accordance with the other person or have even been happy.

This may help to explain, for instance, why struggling partners often find it difficult to focus their argument on the current situation and not to extend the subject matter boundlessly by referring to all kinds of events in the more or less distant past. Moreover, those past events are typically only seen in ways that seem to *confirm* a partner's experience of the current situation and that provide her or him with justifications for the given view of things.

Refractory state *and* state dependent memory have one effect in common: both information that is perceptible in the here and now as well as information that is available in memory is *ignored if it contradicts the current angry feeling and is apt to modify it*. Anger leads to self-righteous cantankerousness and to a lack of self-critical thinking. In his article on "narcissistic rage," Kohut correctly states that in such a situation "... the reasoning capacity [is] ... totally under the domination and in the service of the overriding emotion..." (1972, p. 382). The reasoning of an anger-driven person may be astute, but it is so only within a very narrow frame; there are no traces of long-sightedness or even wisdom; "... rage enslaves the ego and allows it to function only as its tool and rationalizer" (*ibid.*, p. 387).[28]

Of course, the willingness and capacity to engage in a dialogue with the other person are also restricted. Even people who otherwise are smart, may be made to believe by their anger-corrupted intellect "... that our expressions of rage will change the other person's view of themselves and even lead to an apology. Most of the time, however, our rage only locks the other person into the very stance that led to the affront in the first place" (Lazarus 2001, p. 61). So the wish to resolve the interpersonal conflict that has triggered the anger will not be fulfilled — on the contrary: the gap that has opened up between the opponents is likely to deepen along with the feelings of isolation and of not being understood in which the angry person is imprisoned.

---

[28] These behaviors may be interpreted and treated as *regressive processes* (see Staemmler, 1997 and this book).

2. 2. 3. *Culture-Blind "Authenticity"*

These observations are widely known, although they still do not always lead to adequate consequences both in everyday life and in therapeutic traditions like that of Gestalt therapy. Within the tradition of Gestalt therapy this may be related to the fact that here the "authentic" expression of feelings has almost acquired the status of a "hypergood" (see Taylor 1992, 62ff.[29]); and it seems that — as is the case with hypergoods in general — this hypergood is almost unquestionable, the more so as in this case it can also rely on a tacit alliance with the culturally anchored ideology of catharsis (see ref. points 1, 3, 17). The "spontaneous" and "authentic" expression of feelings, then, is taken to be "healthy," and not much space is left for a critical analysis of the developmental conditions of what is seen as "authentic" within culture and socialization (➲ **15**; see reference points 8, 24, 31):

> In general, the emotion of anger is regarded as a universal emotion that is related to the individual achievement of goals. It signals that the person is barred from reaching her goal or is treated in an unjust way; it leads to the action tendency to remove the obstacle.... At exact analysis, however, one finds that frequency, occasion, expression and regulation of potentially anger-triggering situations are subjects to cultural peculiarities that are associated with the predominant views of the self in that culture.

In so-called collectivistic cultures such as Japan or China, in which people mostly adhere to an interdependent notion

---

[29] "Let me call higher order-goods... 'hypergoods,' i. e., goods which not only are incomparably more important than others but provide the standpoint from which these must be weighed, judged, decided about..." (Taylor 1992, p. 63).

of self, feeling and showing of anger is not desirable, since this confrontive emotion endangers the harmony of the social reference group. People in these cultures tend to avoid situations that might trigger anger and do not focus on the other person who may have precipitated the hindrance. Rather, they withdraw and try to minimize their angry reaction by distracting themselves; or they do not ascribe any intention to the opponent in the first place and, therefore, do not respond with anger, but with equanimity...

> In contrast, in so-called individualistic cultures such as in the United States of America, in which people primarily subscribe to an independent view of the self, anger is seen as adequate and functional, since it fosters the person's development of uniqueness, autonomy, and self-expression. Anger is tolerated in the interest ... of individual rights and latitudes... Hence, in these Western cultures people tend to engage in anger-triggering situations and stay angry as long as it appears to be useful for the achievement of their own goals... (Holodynski 2006, p. 34)

The citation underlines: the "authentic" feeling in our individualistic culture in infiltrated by social norms that favor the achievement of people's *"own* goals," even if they are sometimes understood in a very narrow-minded way — as if detrimental effects on the relationships with other people would have no impact on one's "own" interests.

The cultural narrow-mindedness also shows in the way in which the above-mentioned cognitive restriction is evaluated. Although it is bemoaned occasionally, most of the time it is appreciated as a focusing of attention and fighting strength that helps the enforcement of one's own interests *against* those of others. Moreover, a large number of research results are more or less ignored that hints at the negative *long-term* effects of chronic aggressiveness.

These research results include studies which prove the adverse long-term impact of a low aggression threshold on the development of intelligence. As a partial outcome of a longitudinal study that investigated children, adolescent and young adults from their ninth year of life on over a period of twenty-two years, Huesmann et al. found "... that early aggression is the precursor of diminished intellectual functioning [in adults]" (1987, p. 236); high aggressiveness scores at the age of eight predicted poor intellectual functioning of the adult subjects in later years (whereas, surprisingly, early cognitive functioning that was associated with high aggression scores at the age of eight years, did *not* provide a reliable prognosis of aggressiveness in the adult subjects). Here Geen sees the following connection:

> Once an aggressive strategy has been encoded, it tends to persist and to exert a reciprocal effect on intellectual processes. By hindering good relationships between the child and both teachers and peers, aggressive behaviour interferes with the child's chances at intellectual opportunities and advancement. The aggressive child is not popular and is not afforded many chances for growth through positive social interactions. (2001, p. 55)

2. 2. 4. "Anger kills" (➲16)

The negative side effects of anger and aggression concern not only the psychic dimension, but also the physical. Since the sensation-causing publication of the *Western Collaborative Group Study* (WCGS — Rosenman et al. 1975) more and more evidence has been gathered for the observation that subjects who can be sorted as the so-called "Type A" personality, suffer more frequently and to a higher degree from increased blood pressure, constricted blood vessels, *angina pectoris* and — in some cases — heart attack (Houston & Snyder 1988; Müller 1993).

Hence, *Anger Kills* is the striking title of a book in which Williams & Williams (1993) have compiled their own research results as well as those of other investigators to mark this widespread and yet too little noticed problem. One of the most prominent insights from these studies is: although in general Type-A individuals do not look after themselves very carefully (exercise less, pay less attention to their hygiene, sleep less, drink more alcohol, stick to a more unhealthful diet, smoke more — all of which may be additional contributions to coronary heart disease), it has been demonstrated that Type-A personality also forms a self-contained pathogenic factor that functions *independently* from the other behaviors mentioned, but is, of course, particularly noxious in combination with them.[30]

"Type A" is the name of a syndrome of ways of experience and behavior that consists of the following elements: strong purposefulness, ambitiousness, and striving for success; impatience and hastiness (including rapid speech); irritability and increased readiness for anger and aggressive behavior — the latter element is often called "hostility." This is useful to know, because since the 1960s and '70s research on the Type A syndrome was especially concerned with the question of which element of the syndrome is particularly pathogenic.

In the course of these investigations, the factor called "hostility" (abbreviated: "ho") was checked out with the aid of psychometric instruments especially designed for this purpose. Contrada et al. summarize the results: "Evidence that has accumulated since the WCGS supports the hypothesis that hostility may represent the 'toxic' element of

---

[30] Perls himself presumably practiced some Type A behaviors; we have already quoted Stevens: "... he didn't hold on to shit when he got incensed, ... he let it out" (in Gaines 1979, p. 306). Maybe Perls's grave heart disease was not only a result of his smoking habits.

Type A behavior" (1990, p. 647). Other researchers demonstrated this in longitudinal studies with children (e. g. Fackelmann, 1989), mid-age adults (e. g. Shekelle et al., 1983), and elderly people (e. g. Kawachi et al., 1996); there was always a significant correlation between hostility and abnormal alterations, particularly with respect to coronary blood vessels.[31]

In the light of these studies the following statement by the Buddhist physician and yogi Gambopa (1079-1153), which at first sight may appear merely metaphorical, acquires a very real meaning: "Anger is like a poisonous arrow that spears your heart" (quoted in Ladner 2005, p. 14). This is so not only because of the physical harm that their anger does to hostile people, it is also because of the social isolation into which they maneuver themselves; this isolation is an additional risk factor. In an investigation including 1,300 cardiology patients it was established:

> Among unmarried patients who told us that they had no one to whom they could confide major concerns, 50 percent were dead within five years. In marked contrast, only 17 percent were dead among patients who were married, reported they had a confidant, or both. This profound impact of social isolation on survival in our heart patients could not be explained by their underlying heart condition. Clearly, the lack of social ties increased the risk of dying for all patients, no matter how severe their disease. (Williams & Williams 1993, p. 66)

---

[31]. In recent years, an increasing number of investigations have been published that also demontrate the negative impact of hostility on other organs such as the lung (see, for instance, Kubzansky et al. 2006).

2. 2. 5. Summary

Anger and aggression, in particular if they become habitual, yield a number of detrimental concomitant phenomena with respect to a person's expressive behavior, intellectual achievement, social competency and physical health. The more frequently, intensely, and continuously a person experiences anger and behaves aggressively, the more he will not only cause distress in other people, but will also burden his social relations and harm his own physical health. The frequent "free" expression of anger is not healthy, as is still maintained sometimes, but — to say it pointedly — makes you ugly, dumb, lonesome, and sick. Perls's idea that one could "rid oneself of irritability" and "develop intelligence" (1947, p. 117) by uninhibited expression, is an illusion.

Thus, there are many reasons to call anger a "poison of the mind," as the Buddhists do, or to see it as a "mental sin," as Seneca does (1614, *De Ira*, book 1, chap. 16).[32] Whether or not one wants to do so within the frame of our culture is probably a tactical question, since such denotations are likely to be understood as supporting the widespread attitude that condemns aggression in moralizing ways and thereby contributes to its equally problematic repression (see reference point 12).

One thing, however, is clear: anger and aggression cannot be lived out in a way that is healthy for the person who is angry (for women, however, the risks appear to be smaller than for men[33]). The evidence leaves no doubt that the

---

[32] An excellent overview on the considerations on anger and aggression by antique authors is provided by Harris (2004).

[33] In our culture, women tend to express their anger differently than men, especially in the form of what is called "relational aggression," i. e. by attempts to damage the social relationships of the ones at whom they are angry, through malicious gossip or other intrigues (Crick & Grotpeter 1995). "... relational aggression [is] defined as behavior that does harm to

expression of angry feelings and the acting out of aggressions is in effect always also *retroflective*; there is no aggression that is *only* outgoing and not detrimental to the aggressor himself. The idea, which still exists among Gestalt therapists, that in the "ideal" case one could direct one's aggressions directly outward and only against the person who triggered it, *without* retroflecting it, does not merely reveal odd ethics. Moreover, it is simply a chimera, since anger always strikes back against the person who is angry.

In a meta-analysis of numerous studies about the connection between hostility and physical health Miller et al. come to the following conclusion:

> This meta-analytic review supports the age-old hypothesis that chronic anger and hostility is an independent risk factor for the development of CHD and premature mortality. Evidence from both cross-sectional and prospective studies suggests that hostility is a robust risk factor. (1996, p. 344)

However, an occasional outburst of anger will not immediately be deadly. Of course, the dose of the "poison of the mind" plays its part, i. e. frequency, duration, and intensity of experienced anger will determine the probability with which the above mentioned harmful effects will occur: hence the therapeutic aim will not be the complete absence of aggressive experience, but rather the development of *resilience*. Davidson defines resilience ". . . as the maintenance of high levels of positive affect and well-being in the face of adversity. It is not that resilient individuals never experience negative affect, but rather that the negative affect does not persist" (2000, p. 1198).

---

the relationships of a person with her peers or damages her feelings of belonging and being accepted . . ." (Werner et al. 1999, p. 154).

For people who lack this resilience, the research results proving the harmful effects of anger are of utmost relevance. Therefore we strongly recommend taking them into account in the discussion about the treatment of aggression in Gestalt psychotherapy (and other modalities).

For risks and adverse effects, please also see the following section.

2. 3. Catharsis (⮕ 1▼)

"I want to punch the pillow," I said.

"Hmm!" he said. "Good." And he handed the pillow to me.

I sat with it for a moment, then began jabbing my fist into it. "I'm angry, Dad," I said three or four times.

"That doesn't sound too angry," Dan said. "More like annoyance."

"I'm angry, Dad!" I said louder.

"Good — let's hear it, and see you beat the pillow."

I kept repeating that I was angry and beating the pillow and getting more and more caught up in my emotion until I was screaming and sobbing with rage and burying my fists in the pillow as hard as I could. (Lee & Stott, 1993, pp. xxf.)

Those who know the history of Gestalt therapy will probably be reminded by this report of some of their own experiences. As we have shown in the first part of this paper, Perls's concept of aggression did not only amount to the general recommendation, "expression of resentment is one of the most important ways to help you to make your life a little bit more easy" (Perls 1969b, p. 48); it also led to practical procedures that can best be characterized by the term "catharsis": "Express your resentment — kind of present it right into his or her face", Perls (*ibid.*) suggested, because, as he held, "any anger that is not coming out, flowing freely, will turn into sadism, power drive, and other means of torturing" (*ibid.*, p. 76). Similarly Rosenblatt: "I permitted fights, arm wrestling, some body wrestling and other physical forms of aggression..." (1998, p. 12).

2. 3. 1. An Old-Fashioned Concept

The psychological concept of catharsis, which is based on a kind of steam boiler model and implies the idea of "emotional hydraulics" (Seligman 2002, pp. 68ff.), can be traced back to a time and to a theoretical context in which there was more thinking and writing on "drives" and "instincts" than on "motivations" and "relations." Its dynamic, it was assumed, was similar to a pretty simple hydraulic mechanism; a kind of a reservoir was continuously or at certain occasions filled up and, therefore, needed emptying (or "discharge") at times in order not to overflow or even to "explode." In the logic of this model, to control aggression in the long run was "... as judicious as trying to counteract the increasing pressure in a continuously heated boiler by screwing down the safety valve more tightly" (Lorenz 1967, p. 239). Aggression had to be discharged every now and then, preferably by directing it toward an object that could not easily be harmed or destroyed:

> A simple and effective way of discharging aggression in an innocuous manner is to redirect it at a substitute object.... Redirection as a means of controlling the functions of aggression and other undischarged drives has been known to humanity for a long time. The ancient Greeks were familiar with the conception of catharsis, of purifying discharge... (Lorenz 1967, pp. 240f.)

Hence, the expression of aggression at those, who are seen to be its cause, or at "substitute objects" "... is called catharsis, and the reduction of aggressive action tendencies that is assumed to be its outcome is called the cathartic effect" (Zumkley 1978, p. 19).

With certain variations, this model can be found, for instance, in the ethology of Konrad Lorenz (1967), in some older versions of psychoanalysis or, again in a different form, within frustration-aggression-theory (Dollard et al. 1939[34]). At least with respect to its application to human beings, it has frequently been criticized as mechanistic or hydraulic (see the following sketch); it has also been refuted on empirical bases (see Geen & Quanty 1977; Tavris 1988; Warren & Kurlychek 1981). Moreover, it represents a blatant manifestation of individualist anthropology: if seen in its light, people seemingly only have the problem of regulating their *own* internal pressure (see reference points 6, 9, 15).

However, in our view emotions are *personal responses*; they are aspects of the *relations* of a person to other people and to the wider environment, on which they may have a forming influence. They are not objects (including steam), but *social processes* in *social situations* (see Averill 1990; Nichols & Efran 1985, pp. 51f.).[35]

---

[34] We have the impression that frustration-aggression-theory is still rather popular, although it has been disproved — at least in its strong variant — long ago; in this variant, aggression always springs from frustration, and every frustration leads to aggression. However, frustrations can also result in resignation or in productive efforts at overcoming their causes, for instance.

[35] Of course, this applies to anger too. In a large investigation Averill (1982) found that only in 6 % of the cases in which subjects became angry, the anger was directed at a non-human target. And even in those 6 % many anthropomorphisms were included, as is, for instance, the case, if a person, who has hurt herself at a table, calls it with invectives such as "you son-of-a-bitch."

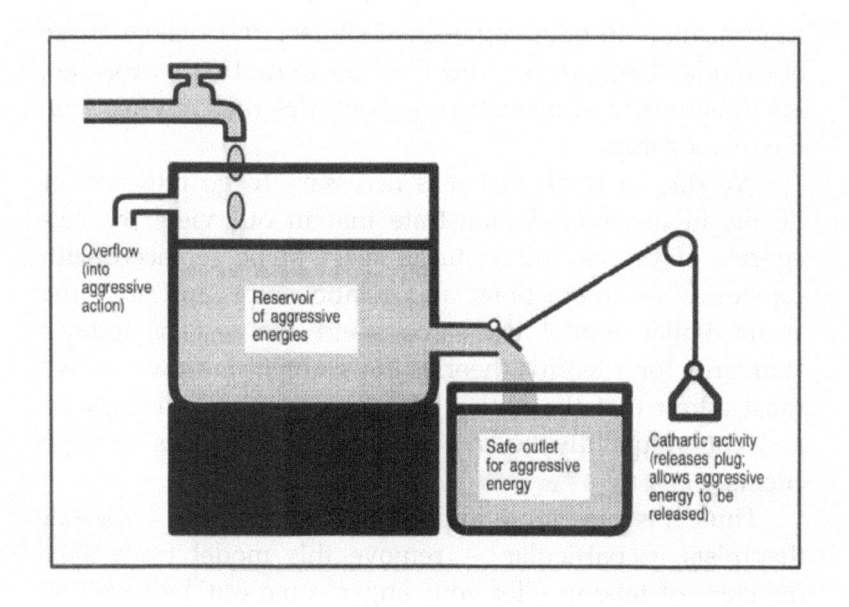

[Figure: Hydraulic model of aggression showing a reservoir of aggressive energies with overflow into aggressive action, safe outlet for aggressive energy, and cathartic activity that releases plug allowing aggressive energy to be released.]

(from Eysenck 1996, p. 99)

It is not adequate to reify emotions and to talk of them as of material things that can be piled up, stored, and discharged later. In contrast to many of his other statements, even Perls once claimed: "Actually nature is not so wasteful as to create such a powerful energy as aggression just to be 'got rid of' or 'abreacted'" (1975, p. 33). Here he drew on a more modern concept of emotion that can be found in some places in *Gestalt Therapy* besides the cathartic concept: "An emotion is the integrative awareness of a relation between the organism and the environment" (Perls et al. 1951, p. 407).

As everyday experience shows, in general it is more or less harmful to human relations when someone follows the catharsis model and, in order to achieve the hoped-for release, gives vent to his anger without situational attunement to the other person. If expression is more an end in itself than an offer of personal contact and dialogue (see Staemmler 1993), it may quickly lead to mutual reproaches, invalidations, and alienation — with destructive effects on the relationship.

We do not think that it is necessary to go into further details in order to demonstrate that in our view the categories of drives and instincts need to be replaced with categories of interactions and relationships and that the steam boiler model does not stand the test of today's standards for scientific theories in psychology. However, we must admit that the notion of catharsis is still widespread and can frequently be met in layperson such as therapy clients.

Thus, it is even more important that therapists — Gestalt therapists in particular — remove this model from their manners of talking ("let your anger come out") as well as from their theoretical repertoire. As a regrettable example for an adherence to the steam boiler model we have already mentioned Dreitzel (1995 — see reference point 3); but he does not stand alone. Whatever the reason(s) may be[36] — especially in the context of psychotherapy, in which much

---

[36] Why Dreitzel uses Scheff's (1979) book as his only source on the dynamics of catharsis is hard to understand. Scheff is a sociologist, whose sociological competence we cannot evaluate, whose psychological and psychotherapeutic knowledge, however, appears limited. In addition, the author, whose thinking tellingly oscillates "... between emotion as distress, and emotion as discharge" (ibid., p. 50 — italics added), downplays the significance of research that he has read, but that provides evidence against catharsis theory. For instance, he writes: "In a typical study, he [Berkowitz] has shown that active retaliation against an aggressor not only does not lower the level of hostility of the person who is retaliating but may actually raise it. Although this seems to be an important finding, its relevance to the theory of catharsis is limited" (ibid., p. 23). Why so? The author does not give an explanation. And Dreitzel follows him uncritically.

more differentiated models are urgently called for (see, for instance, Holodynski 2006), the steam boiler model persists in particularly obstinate ways.

Thus, if you as a therapist offer it to your clients, you are very likely to find open ears and to be considered as the enunciator of enjoyable news — especially by people who tend to act out their aggressions anyway (Bushman et al. 2001, p. 23)! Anger is an extremely *unpleasant* feeling; people want "to get rid of it" as soon as possible. The enunciation that catharsis may serve this purpose has a seductive effect, since it is the announcement of a seemingly successful affect regulation, which in many cases has already been established before. Using an ingenious experimental design, Bushman et al. have been able to demonstrate that

> ... participants behaved aggressively toward someone who had criticized and insulted them, but they were much less aggressive if they believed that they had taken a pill that would prevent their mood from changing. This pattern suggests that people aggressed *because they believed it would be a good way of getting rid of their anger*. When the prospect of mood repair was eliminated, aggression lost its appeal. (2001, p. 21 — italics added)

Folk psychology promises the efficacy of catharsis; and it has all the power of contingency on its side, since the *immediate* experience seems to prove the believers in catharsis right: at first cathartic activity feels pretty good (see below), and its consequences are impressive: "If you tire yourself by wood-chopping, you will not have much strength left for a big punch-up ..." (Selg 2000, p. 53). Nevertheless, we have to accept the fact that "most of the evidence fails to support the catharsis hypothesis. Indeed, the findings of many studies are exactly the opposite of what would be expected on that hypothesis" (Eysenck 1996, p. 106).

2. 3. 2. The Investigation by Bushman, Baumeister and Stack (1999)

How strongly and easily people can be influenced as to whether or not they seek refuge in cathartic emotional expression, is illustrated by an interesting investigation. The researchers subdivided a sample of 360 individuals of both sexes into three subgroups. The first group was given a "newspaper article" (especially designed for the purpose of this investigation), in which the positive effect of cathartic behavior was highlighted; the second group was presented with a largely identical, but in its message contrary article (for both versions see the text box on the adjoining page); the third group served as a control group and was given an article whose content had nothing to do with catharsis.

A while after the subjects had read the respective article they were exposed to a situation that was likely to trigger irritation: an essay they had written in the meantime was evaluated in an extremely negative and derogatory way. Subsequently, those who reported to have been angered by this evaluation, were given a list of ten coping strategies with respect to their anger, one of which was "hitting a punching bag" (others were, for instance, "playing solitaire" or "watching a comedy"). The subjects were requested to rank these strategies "... in the order of his or her preference for doing them later in the experiment" (*ibid.*, p. 369). The results were striking:

> ... the content of the article had a significant effect on angered participants... Angered participants who read the procatharsis article wanted to hit the punching bag more than did angered participants who read either the anticatharsis article or the article unrelated to catharsis... (*ibid.*)

> ### Research Shows That Hitting Inanimate Objects Is an Effective [Ineffective] Way to Vent Anger
>
> Cambridge, Mass. (AP) Do you believe that you can vent anger by hitting a punching bag? According to the results of a study published this week in *Science*, you could not be more right [wrong].
>
> The study confirms a long history of research on the effectiveness [ineffectiveness] of displacing anger to inanimate objects. The study was conducted by Dr. Elias Boran, a psychological researcher at Harvard University. Boran says that his results provide direct confirmation of the idea that anger can[not] be vented harmlessly when people can displace their anger to an inanimate object.
>
> The findings are the results of a 2-year study involving 1,000 university students living in the university's residence halls. Participants in the study were randomly divided into one of two groups. One group hit a punching bag (a portable floor model provided by the experimenter) when they were angry. The other group tried to relax when they were angry. Boran found that students who hit a punching bag when angry were 4 times less [more] likely to have complaints filed against them by other students in the residence hall and were 2 times less [more] likely to have been reported to campus police for aggressive incidents than were students who tried to relax.
>
> Boran says that his study is consistent with the results of scores of studies showing that people can[not] effectively vent anger to inanimate objects. According to Boran, "When you are angry, the best [worst] thing that you can do is to find something inanimate to hit or kick to vent your anger."

Bushman et al. 1999, p. 376

It can be assumed that the persuasive potency of therapists relating to their clients will be even greater than that of psychological researchers handing a fake newspaper article to a sample of research participants. In other words, if therapist think that cathartic procedures will be helpful for their clients to become less aggressive and, therefore, make respective therapeutic suggestions, it is likely that they will be successful to an even higher degree of significance than were the researchers who used the article. Briefly, if a therapists wants to have a client hit a pillow, she or he is *relatively* likely to be successful.[37]

Even if cathartic procedures should not have *specific* therapeutic effects, it could be surmised that the expression of anger by means of aggressive actions might yield therapeutic effects through *non-specific* factors such as placebo effects or self-fulfilling prophecies (see Frank 1961). In this case one could think, "Things could be worse." Things would in fact be worse, if it could be shown that cathartic procedures lead to the contrary of what they promise, i. e. that subjects would tend to more aggressive behavior than they did before the catharsis. And things would be extremely bad, if the undesirable effects would reach a degree that is *not* counterbalanced by the non-specific positive factors.

And a number of serious indicators point to exactly that. The research by Bushman et al. (1999), for instance, included a second part that was design to answer the question if people "... who were led to believe in the catharsis effect would actually feel a reduction in anger after hitting the punching bag and therefore show diminished aggression toward the other person ..." (*ibid.*, p. 370).

---

[37] As we are told by our supervisees, this relative success is contrasted by a considereable number of situations in which clients refuse to accept this kind of therapeutic suggestions. Those therapists who still believe in cathartic strategies are in danger of interpreting their clients' refusals as avoidances. For reasons we will explain soon, we think that this interpretation is misguided; we interpret those refusals as healthy resistances of the clients against inadequate suggestions.

The reverse was the case! "... hitting a punching bag does not produce a cathartic effect: it *increases* rather than decreases subsequent aggression" (*ibid.*, p. 373 — italics added). The degree of aggressive tendencies in subjects who read the procatharsis article (in comparison to the anticatharsis article readers and the control group) already increased as a result of the reading only. Moreover, this effect was still verifiable *after* they had had the opportunity to "*abreact*" — which after these research results clearly has to be called a misnomer — their anger by hitting the punching bag. For, although the hitting itself was frequently experienceed in a positive manner, it did *not* have a minimizing effect on aggressive behavior after this situation. Particularly remarkable was the fact that the increase of aggressiveness after the hitting was not only directed at those persons who through their negative evaluation had provided the subjects with a "reason," but was equally directed at *uninvolved* persons.

The study authors hypothesize that the positive experience of the hitting might be the basis of the unsubstantiated good reputation of catharsis. Presumably this experience can be traced back to a pleasant physical perception that may function as a reinforcement since "in fact, the people who enjoyed hitting the punching bag the most were also the most aggressive ... later" (Bushman et al. 2001, p. 18). In addition, Geen reports research observations in which transitionally something like a "... 'physiological catharsis' did occur; aggression was accompanied by a return of blood pressure to normal levels. However, 'behavioral catharsis,' defined as a reduction in aggression following aggression, did not occur — in fact, the opposite was found" (Geen 2001, p. 134). Maybe, besides the immediate reinforcing effect, the following explanation is also possible: "The person may interpret his relaxed condition as being due to the aggression he has just committed and may therefore experience a weakening of socialized restraints against further violence" (Geen et al. 1975, p. 725).

This means that we are confronted with a twofold phenomenon: (1) already the message or, respectively, the belief it induced, namely that the aggression that was vicariously directed at an object would bring about a cathartic effect, *intensified* subjects' aggressiveness. And (2) the activity that is expected to have a "cleansing" (= cathartic) effect does not lead to the desired result — to the contrary: it boosts the person's aggressiveness in spite of her opposite expectation, i. e. *against* the placebo-effect, which suggest a high effect size.

If the research by Bushman et al. (1999) has any representative value (after all, the sample size included 360 subjects), one does not only have to draw the conclusion that we ought to give up cathartic practices for the purpose of aggression reduction, one must also stop propagating them, if one does not want to reinforce human aggressiveness inside and outside of therapeutic settings. And that does not only apply to any kind of aggressive action in the strict sense of the word, it also applies to verbal expression of anger[38] (Mallick & McCandless 1966).

To end of this section we would like to refer briefly to another investigation Bushman (2002) conducted a few years after the study mentioned above, in which he tried both to re-check and to specify his earlier results. Basically, he was able to replicate his results, this time with an even larger sample of 602 subjects. The additional specifications are of special interest in that they display a great proximity to certain psychotherapeutic techniques:

In this study, half of the subjects were asked to think very precisely of the person, against whom their anger was

---

[38] For instance, swearing or yelling at somebody.

directed, *while* they were hitting the punching bag. In contrast, the other half of the subjects were exposed to a "distraction condition," i. e. they were requested to think of training their muscular power while they were hitting the bag. The increase of subsequent aggressiveness was significantly higher under the experimental condition than under the distraction condition.

As we can conclude from these research results it cannot be justified to support clients in venting their anger or to invite them to indulge in violent fantasies; this also applies if the person towards whom they experience their anger is absent and only imagined. Such procedures not only increase clients' aggressive tendencies and do harm to the relationships with the people with whom they have to cope in their lives. They also do harm to the clients themselves since, as we have shown in the previous section, an increase in the frequency of anger and aggression is correlated with an increasing risk for coronary heart disease and other health problems.

In conclusion, the "therapeutic" strategies mentioned above have to be classified as malpractice that are not in keeping with the state of the art. This is the case in general, but of course to an extraordinary degree for clients who — such as the "average citizen" described above (see reference point 13) — already suffer from a heightened aggressive potential. Such strategies become entirely counterproductive if applied to clients who tend to temper tantrums anyway, such as those who have been (or could be) diagnosed with *Intermittent Explosive Disorder* (IED) according to DSM-IV (see textbox i previous section), "... since with each expression of anger the neuronal aggressive pattern is strengthened; it is not controlled better. This is neuroscientifically 'logical' (Grawe 2004) and has been confirmed by psychological research in aggression again and again" (Petzold 2006, p. 52).

2. 3. 3. Summary

In sum, we must agree with Darwin who observed that "he who gives way to violent gestures will increase his rage..." (Darwin 1898, p. 365). The hoped-for cathartic effect cannot be proved; the contrary is the case: "Aggression, whether against an antagonist or some other target, is generally followed by *more*, not less subsequent aggression" (Geen 2001, p. 134 — italics in original; see also Krahé 2001, p. 213). Not only do so-called "cathartic" activities themselves increase people's aggressiveness, but even the (erroneous) belief that cathartic activities will be helpful increases aggression as well. And the more precisely these activities are tailored to the actual target person, as is, for instance, the case in some variants of the therapeutic techniques that use an "empty chair" ("Picture your father..."), the stronger the aggression-enhancing effect.[39]

If these techniques are applied in a *group* setting, an additional impact has to be taken into account that has to do with the effect that group members observe each other's aggressive actions. You only need to think of group situations in which members witness another member's aggressive action with benevolence, thereby supporting and reinforcing his aggressiveness.[40]

---

[39] Frequently these techniques are applied in context with the idea of "finishing unfinished business" — an idea that has its conceptual problems. In any case, research on catharsis demonstrates that one can not finish one's unfinished business with one's own aggressiveness by the use of these technical variants.

[40] Frequently (as well as typically, as we will explain later) anger is activated out of the mindset of the victim; and in our culture sympathy almost automatically is on the side of those who are considered to be the victims (see Hafke 1996). Therefore, almost anybody who behaves

In addition, while they are witnessing this, they are probably not aware of the model learning that takes place simultaneously and that enhances their own aggressive potential. Investigations in "mirror neurons" and their functions show "... that the observation of other people's actions does not only activate an internal program of identification and simulation in the observer, but also that this resonance of mirror neurons blazes a trail for action tendencies" (Bauer 2005, p. 39).[41] In children, the after effects of aggressive demonstrations, particularly those given by male adults to boys, can be detected for many months (see Hicks 1965).[42] And Selg had to state: "Rapes that are pleasurably depicted change the attitude of the observer toward women and toward the deed: women are seen more negatively, the deed more positively" (2000, p. 49; see also Selg 1986).

2. 4. Inhibition and Control (⊃ 18)

We have placed the two previous sections in front of the following one to give them a certain position effect since we assume that information on harmful side effects of the *expression and acting-out* of anger and hostility (sometimes briefly called "anger-out") is much less known than are the

---

aggressively tries to define himself as the victim of aggression that has been primarily excerted by others.

[41] Recently, Philippson (2006, p. 62) has referred to neuroscientific findings on mirror neurons as an argument for the advantages of group therapy. His argument is correct, but it ignores the dangers.

[42] It may not be because of the effects of imitation only, but also because of other processes such as the identification with the aggressor, "... that the hard core of the 5 % of severely criminal and repeatedly violent adolescent perpetrators who are responsible for 50 % of all criminal violence come from violent family backgrounds. In their childhood, these adolescents have themselves been victims of the violence that they act out later" (Dornes 2006, p. 18).

detrimental consequences of the inhibition of expression and the holding-back of anger (called "anger-in"). Today, it is almost commonplace to assert that it does not do you good to "swallow" (or "retroflect") your anger. After all, it is this commonplace that provides the point of departure for the reverse assertion that one has to externalize one's anger in order not to get ill from it.

As we have seen, this reverse assertion is wrong, but that does not mean that the observation on which it is based is wrong too: the observation that the "retroflection" of aggressiveness has harmful consequences as they are described so impressively in Mercier's fascinating novel:

> When others make us angry at them — at their shamelessness, injustice, inconsideration — then they exercise power over us, they proliferate and gnaw at our soul, then anger is like a white-hot poison that corrodes all mild, noble and balanced feelings and robs us of sleep. Sleepless, we turn on the light and are angry at the anger that has lodged like a succubus who sucks us dry and debilitates us. We are not only furious at the damage, but also that it develops in us all by itself, for while we sit on the edge of the bed with aching temples, the distant catalyst remains untouched by the corrosive force of the anger that eats at us. On the empty internal stage bathed in the harsh light of mute rage, we perform all by ourselves a drama with shadow figures and shadow words we hurl against enemies in helpless rage we feel as icy blazing fire in our bowels. (Mercier 2008, pp. 377f.)

The harmful psychic and physical consequences of chronically held-back anger and/or of anger directed against one's own self that manifest, for instance, in the form of depression, high blood pressure (see Manuck et al. 1985) and impairments of the immune system (see Esterling et al. 1990), have been documented abundantly and can hardly be disputed (Siegman & Smith 1994), although they are not as univocal and pronounced as those of expressed anger (see also Huber & Gramer 1993; Siegman 1993). In addition, more recent studies such as the ones by Dormann et al. (2002) confirm the previous evidence: the psychologists from Frankfurt (Germany) examined the employees of call-centers who are instructed to be persistently friendly toward their customers, even if this is in contrast to what they actually feel. It was found that these demands resulted in symptoms such as burnout, heightened irritability, psychosomatic diseases and impaired sense of self-esteem.

Hence, self-control can — to the degree that it works — provide a certain amount of protection of others from the aggressions of hostile people, if they do control themselves; from this point of view it has to be welcomed. However, there are also serious disadvantages to this strategy, because the (continuous) antagonism between aggressive tendencies on the one hand and their deliberate control on the other hand yields the afore-mentioned physical and psychic problems. Moreover, as experience shows the balance between hostility and control is difficult to maintain. It easily collapses and then does not guarantee any reliable protection of others.

> ... attempts to control behavior arbitrarily — one's own or that of other people — accomplish nothing in the long run but to produce conflict and consequent pathology. What do I mean by arbitrary control? I mean attempts to make behavior conform to one set of goals without regard to other goals (and control systems) that may already be controlling that behavior — that must already exist, since behavior exists. (Powers 1973, p. 259)

Since this is so, Gestalt therapists frequently appeal to Beisser's "paradoxical theory of change," in which he says:

Change does not take place through a coercive attempt by the individual or by another person to change him.... The Gestalt therapist rejects the role of "changer".... He believes change does not take place by "trying," coercion, or persuasion, or by insight, interpretation, or any other such means. (1970, p. 77)

And Staemmler & Bock (1998), in their theory of the process of change, emphatically underscore that when polarization has been reached — i. e. the phase in which two contradictive forces are opposed to each other keeping each other in check —, the therapeutic process in no way has come to its conclusion (see also Grawe's, 1998 and 2004, remarks on the pathogenic effects of inconsistency).

Thereby the limits of so-called *"anger-management"*- or *"anger-control"*-programs are defined — which is *no* reason *against* them; it only marks their risks and reaches.[43] The same applies to the strategies that have been proposed by integrative therapists, in part in reference to traditional martial arts:

Wherever undesirable forms of aggression come up ... they have to be cut off [!]; instead, *self-interruption* [!] and "active down-regulation" need to be immediately practiced to establish and reinforce *regulative competence*. Interruption alone is not enough! The derailing/derailed person not only must interrupt his excessive action, he also must ... fight the affect, suppress, and beat [!] it.... The person who is aggressively aroused must "practice mildness." The conqueror who is overwhelmed by the "flush of violence" has to exercise mercy, he has to force [!] himself

---

[43] See the outline of the structure of emotions from Holodynski (2006; see reference point 19), which we will present in the subsequent section on "appraisal." It demonstrates that control strategies can only interfer with the emotional process at a very late point in time (at the point of action planning), maybe even later (at the point of action performance).

with "mighty" exertion [!] to get back to calmness and prudence. (Bloem et al. 2004, p. 139 — italics and quotation marks in original; exclamation marks in brackets added).

In a different paper Petzold says basically the same: "*Peaceful narratives* can moderate and control *narratives of aggression* that are equally present" (2006, p. 56 — italics in original). During the conference we mentioned at the beginning of this paper, two integrative therapists presented this concept of aggression regulation in a workshop. A participant reports:

> In various dyadic exercises participants were trained to be aware of their aggressive impulses, to express them and then to interrupt the expression by means of a mental decision ("stop!"), before any harm was done. As an example, person A and person B were facing each other; A hits with his fist in the direction of B's nose and stops his strike an inch before B's nose. The presenters explained: through this practice a learning of impulse control takes place (which leads to new neural connections). The "aggressive competence" that is achieved in this manner must be understood as a "regulative competence." (W. Bock — personal communication, June 1, 2006)

A similar procedure is proposed by Storch (2006). Illustrating her approach she remembers how, driving to a psychoanalytic session, she was obstructed by another car — from her point of view, of course, without any justification. She reports:

> In the steaming bundle of rage that at this point in time sat in my little Honda only little was left of the capacity to think rationally and to act in reasonable ways. . . . "Fortunately," I thought, "I will have my analytical session now" — a good opportunity to talk it all over. From talking about it I most of all expected . . . to get rid of this

unpleasant emotion. ... In contrast to many other sessions in which the technique of talking about things and analyzing them had been very helpful, in this case the session did not help. (Storch 2006, p. 64)

The author does not explain why this was so; we do not want to speculate. From this experience she concludes:

> Today I would handle my rage differently. In order to get rid of it, I would choose an embodiment that is contrary to the embodiment of rage.... I would start by creating the embodiment that goes along with the mood of serene hilariousness.... In my case it would first be important to expand my chest widely and to transform my excited breath into regular and deep breathing. I would have to raise my head slightly and to let my gaze ramble in a broad angle. The arms had to stretch, the body had to move — a bit like when dancing Salsa —, and the legs would want to stretch just like after a round of jogging. By doing all of this my body would be able to let go of the anger step by step. (*ibid.*, pp. 64f.)

The example illustrates: Storch's procedure — as well as that of the integrative therapists — may be an efficient strategy for the regulation of anger that has already emerged and thus it may be useful to moderate and control that emotion. We have no objection against moderation, regulation, and control; in many life situations these coping strategies allow for a way of dealing with emotions, without which the everyday living together of people would hardly be manageable. Especially in the Gestalt therapy tradition such strategies have been pathologized and rejected as "deflections" or "retroflections" without justification much too frequently.

However, formulations such as the ones by Bloem et al. ("fight the affect, suppress, and beat it") clearly point at the problems which are associated with these strategies, which we have described above. It is interesting that even Honda-driver Storch, a few pages after she has described her angry experience as well as her subsequent consideration about the embodiment of serenity, makes the following remark:

> First a stressful state of mind is activated and then, in a second step, this state is called undesirable. First the respective neuronal network is activated, and then it is inhibited. From the viewpoint of energetic economy this is similar to the tactics of pushing the accelerator of a Ferrari and pulling the handbrake at the same time, if you want to stop. This may be a method for standing still, but there may be more economic alternatives. (2006, p. 68)[44]

In other words: as long as there are no better alternatives at hand, these strategies do have their value in spite of their well-known disadvantages. And even if there are alternatives without those disadvantages, control strategies can still remain an additional support for the client. Maybe in a larger societal context moderation and control are even the most realistic means for keeping aggression in check. Farther-reaching strategies such as meditation or therapy, which focus on the primary conditions for the emergence of aggression, may be available for a relatively small number of people only.

This will, however, not stop us from looking for a more radical approach. Let us briefly take stock at this point to build the ground for our further considerations.

---

[44] Strangely enough, it does not seem to occur to the author that her evaluation is in principle also applicable to smaller cars and will therefore also apply to the author in her little Honda as well as to other people who cannot or do not want to afford a noble Italian sportscar.

2.5. Between Scylla and Charybdis

We had to state that to "support" clients in acting out or in cathartically "abreacting" their aggressions, only increases aggressive tendencies instead of diminishing them. It also leads to a number of side effects. Thus this kind of "support" actually does not deserve that name; it should rather be called malpractice (see reference points 13, 16, 17). On the other hand, we must assume that inhibition of aggressiveness and self-control do have some (limited) efficacy, which is, however relatively unreliable and also associated with side effects that should not be trivialized (see reference point 18).

> [On the one hand,] it is far better to confront a person or situation than to hide our anger away, brood on it and nurture resentment in our hearts. Yet [on the other hand,] if we indiscriminately express negative thoughts and emotions simply on the grounds that they must be articulated, there is a strong possibility . . . that we will lose control and overreact. (Dalai Lama 2001, p. 103)

Both are not desirable. So where can the path between Scylla and Charybdis be found?

In order to come up to an approach to answer we would like to briefly illustrate the dilemma by means of an investigation which dealt with the correlation between heightened blood pressure on the one side and anger-related coping strategies on the other side. The question was: is it healthier (with respect to blood pressure), to express anger ("anger-out") or to hold it back ("anger-in")?

Spielberger et al. (1988) found a curvilinear, U-shaped connection, as we present it in the following sketch:

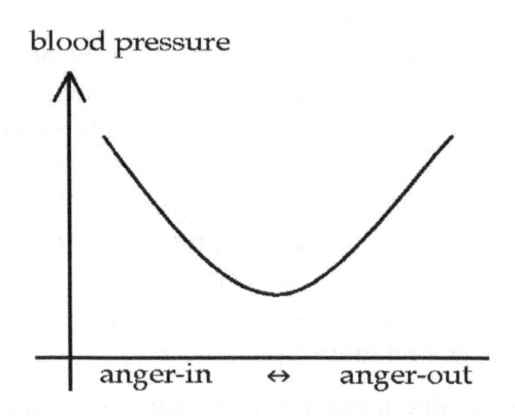

blood pressure

anger-in ↔ anger-out

see Spielberger at al. 1988

This curve can be read like this: the stronger a person's tendency to *hold back* anger a*nd* (!) the stronger a person's tendency to *express* anger, the higher their blood pressure goes, whereas in an intermediate zone *between anger-in* and *anger-out* the blood pressure remains normal. Thus, to express anger is as bad for your blood pressure as to withhold it. And that applies not only to blood pressure, but also to coronary heart disease: "... suppression of anger and the chronic full-blown expression of anger are *both* significant risk factors for cardiovascular disease..." (Power & Dalgleish 1997, p. 316 — italics added).

It is obvious: what *anger-in* and *anger-out* have in common, is *anger*. *Both* strategies to cope with anger are correlated with heightened blood pressure, *because they both presuppose anger*. Only *after* an angry emotion has been activated the question can come up whether to express it or to suppress it.

However, this question is *secondary* — both with respect to its systematic place in therapy and to its function in emotion regulation: the angry person finds herself in the situation to have to regulate an *already earlier activated* emotion, to moderate it or to control it or to act it out etc. Although she can do this more or less skillfully and efficiently and, thereby, exert an important influence on the way her relationships with other people will develop — whatever she does will be done *only after she has already become angry*. But at this point in time the *primary* alternative, i. e. to respond in non-aggressive ways, is no longer available, which brings about the afore mentioned consequence to health and social relationships.

> Having developed the wish that one would like to reduce one's hatred and anger and overcome them, if one simply wishes or prays that anger and hatred no longer arise, or simply prays that they just disappear, this will not make it happen. In addition, if one tries to do something when hatred or anger has already arisen it is unlikely to have much effect since at that moment one's mind is gripped by the intensity of anger and hatred. At that instant, to try to apply something to prevent that arousal is a bit foolish; one is already almost out of control.
>
> So, the best method is first of all to identify what factors normally give rise to anger and hatred. (Dalai Lama 1997, p. 18)

Since frequently even the anger that is held back is in one way or another conveyed to the other participants in the situation, it is not necessary for the angry person to obviously pout. In general people are empathic enough to already recognize the first physical clues of anger (the up-shooting arousal) as well as the accompanying subtle changes in the face of an angry person that show, even if she is trained in controlling her anger and tries to hide it (see Ekman & Friesen 1974; Ekman 2003a).

A more radical therapeutic approach to anger that aims at more than at its moderation and control will consequently have to turn to the conditions of the origination of anger themselves and must pose the *primary* question: how can it be possible to work in therapy in a way that helps the client not to activate anger in the first place, but to respond with *different* emotions that are more beneficial and maybe even enriching for the people involved as well as for their relationships?

Before we turn to this question, we will first deal with another question: are there certain situations or circumstances, in which anger and aggression are adequate and desirable responses in spite of their negative side effects?

2. 6. Can Anger and Aggression Ever Be Recommended?

One could reason as follows: the negative side effects of anger and aggression may have to be taken very seriously; however in certain situations they may be neglected if compared to their positive effects; in this perspective, that is, negative side effects would not provide a *general* argument against anger and aggression. To this reasoning we would like to respond with the question: are there situations conceivable in which anger and aggression yield so many advantages that their detrimental side effects have to be weighted as negligible and their experience and expression need to be recommended?

In our search of such situations we will look at a list of ten different forms of aggression proposed by Petzold (2006, p. 62):

1. *"Predatory aggression* (for instance, toward prey; HAG[45]: raids, prey, warfare for resources)" (*ibid.*) — If one finds it ethically (and, in some cases, also ecologically) justifiable to kill animals (for instance, for purposes of nutrition or the production of fur, this is a kind of aggression, the side effects of which do not belong to the realm we have discussed above. In our culture with its industrialized production of meat and the automated killing of animals one has to assume that this kind of predatory aggression does not go along with anger and its arousal and hence will not cause health problems. The fact that excessive consumption of meat increases the risk of bowel cancer cannot count as an argument in principle; it has been shown that to eat fish regularly fosters health. However, variants of predatory aggression that refer to human beings (raids, for instance) are a completely different matter; here the harmful effects are even much more serious than in the cases discussed before.

2. *"Competitive aggression* (competition for food, sexual mates, positions in hierarchies; HAG: dominance of one's ideologies, scientific, economic, political positions; economical warfare)" (*ibid.*) — This form of aggression is more than likely to bring about all the negative side effects that have been described under the categories of "Type-A" personality and of "hostility," respectively (see reference point 16). We do not need to point out in detail the manifold and disastrous consequences of economical warfare; in addition, its dynamics are outside of what is accessible within psychotherapy.

3. *"Defensive aggression* (fear-motivated, defensively oriented offensive behavior; HAG: armament, arms race, defense treaties, pre-emptive attacks)" (*ibid.*) — In immediate human relations this kind of aggression is called an "act of

---

[45] HAG = Human AGgression

self-defense"; fortunately, such situations are rare exceptions in everyday life. In principle, the justification of acts of self-defense must not be questioned; law also regulates them. The affected person does not cause the distress that a severe threat, which justifies an act of self-defense, brings about; it can be avoided only within certain limits. Nevertheless we find it remarkable in this context that in all sports of self-defense and martial arts that we know of, a determined, both centered and tactically astute and sober-minded approach is taught; in addition, letting one be guided by fear or rage is strongly discouraged. It appears to us that in these practices the assertive motivational system is addressed, whereas the aggressive is avoided. — Arms races and pre-emptive attacks etc. are situated outside of the psychotherapeutic realm with which we are concerned here. One can, however, imagine situations in which therapy clients need support in their attempt to act politically and with the necessary civil courage against the planning and pursuit of those military options by the authorities.

4. "*Irritation aggression* (as a reaction to external disturbance or to internal factors such as fatigue, disease, etc., including HAG)" (*ibid.*) — In these cases the negative consequences of enacted aggressiveness are presumably harmful. In general, it will be more advantageous to respond to disturbances from the outside with equanimous and peaceful activities that do not lead to additional distress for one's own psycho-biological system; this is even more true for internal factors such as illness. Some potentially irritating disturbances — for instance, heat (which has been demonstrated to increase humans' aggressive potential — see Baron 1976; Cassidy 1997) — can be influenced only to a small degree anyway and are best coped with by developing

the ability of accommodation. To resist or fight them is both useless and exhausting.[46]

5. "*Territorial aggression* (at the occasion of offences against the boundaries of the habitat; HAG: threats to one's interests, realms of influence, markets, scientific of ideological territories)" (*ibid.*) — To make a stance against a burglar is of course legitimate; however, it can be asked if an opposing action is not better taken in an assertive than in an aggressive manner. Anger can quickly result in an escalation. Many of the other mentioned occasions can again be attributed to "Type A" or "hostile" behavior; some others are outside of therapeutic scope.

6. "*Maternal and paternal protective aggression* (defense of offspring by the mother in the immediate surroundings and by the father at the border of the patch, sometimes including the chase of the offender; also in HAG)" (*ibid.*) — If children are attacked they doubtlessly deserve parental protection. However, we think that under our given life conditions this protection can in general be best provided in an assertive way — with respect to both its efficiency and its function as a role model. As parents we have had multiple opportunities to provide this experience.

7. "*Female and male or inter-group social aggression* (for instance, towards pups or animals of different groups; HAG: gender aggression, conflicts between generations, ethnic and religious conflicts)" (*ibid.*) — It appears almost unnecessary to us to mention that these kinds of conflicts between humans can be resolved much more easily and more lastingly in a non-aggressive fashion.

8. "*Sexuality-related aggression* (Aggression at the occasion of sexual rejection or frustration; HAG: offense against gender honor, societal sexual codes)" (*ibid.*) — We

---

[46] Political activities aiming at the reduction of global warming are a different (desirable) matter.

will extensively comment on non-aggressive possibilities for coping with the frustration of (sexual and other) needs as well as with experienced slights of pride and honor below (see reference points 14, 16).

9. *"Instrumental aggression* (habitualized aggressive behavior confirming one's capabilities and social positions even if no external triggers are present; HAG: acts of caprice; demonstrations of power by individuals or nations)" (*ibid.*) — These forms of aggression certainly do not justify any of their negative effects.

10. *"Dominance aggression* (aggression aiming at exerting power on other people out of various power interests — exclusively HAG)" (*ibid.*) — Here our opinion is the same as on the previous point.

Sometimes, and in addition to the ten points listed by Petzold, the reflexive signaling function of anger is mentioned as a reason for its justification. According to this argument anger is necessary and useful in that it alerts the respective person to the fact that what happens is not good for her. To us, this argument is not convincing. An *aversive* reaction fulfills the same function sufficiently, it does not have to be *aggressive*. Even if one has the impression that somebody else has violated one's rights, anger is not the best option. *Assertive* engagement for one's rights is more efficient in most cases as well as more desirable and in accordance with the rule of law — if one does not want to support vigilantism or lynch law.

As a last point we would like to mention the argument that anger — possibly in the shape of "righteous outrage" — may be helpful for maintaining one's dignity in the face of humiliating treatment. In our view, this can only be an intermediate solution in extreme situations, since in most cases outrage is nothing but ordinary insulted conceitedness, at which any support of anger is strictly contraindicated (see reference point 14):

> When angry, we may feel a sense of power, but this is false power because, fueled by aversion and blame, anger needs an enemy to exist. Genuine self-confidence, on the other hand, is open and lacks defensiveness. It is based on knowing our great human potential . . . (Chodron 2001, p. 34)

Sometimes aggressiveness in the shape of "just outrage" is advocated in larger contexts as a driving force of political resistance against the violation of human rights and oppressive societal structures. Indeed, again and again one has to witness hair raising instances of abusive and destructive maltreatments of individuals, ethnic groups, minorities (for instance, of sexual or religious orientations) or entire peoples, which make strong counter-measures desirable and urgently necessary. However, it must be doubted that *anger* is the most preferable motivation to deal with important ethical as well as with practical-political questions.

In our view, ethical and political decisions motivated by the commitment to human rights can more adequately be made on the basis of *compassion* with those whose maltreatment touches one's heart. Decisive espousal (assertion) of worthwhile values takes both heart and reason; hate (aggression) tends to make one blind and easily leads to terror and counter-terror.[47] In this context it is equally useful to clearly discern the respective motivational systems (see reference point 12).

---

[47] We say this although we know that it is part of the self-immunization strategies of those who hold power in this world to demand non-violence from those whom they deprive of self-determination and an adequate participation in power. A similar strategy consists in the denial of structural violence just "because" it is so far-reaching that for its maintenence physical force is no longer needed.

Thus we conclude that in the vast majority of situations that are thematized in psychotherapy it will be useful to support a developmental process that strengthens resilience and self-confidence, thereby reducing the likelihood of the emergence of anger and aggression in the first place.

There is, nevertheless, one exception to this rule of thumb: if a client has controlled, suppressed, or retroflected his anger, rage, or hostility in a way and to a degree that he is not aware of it anymore — which is not less problematic than the acting-out of anger (see reference point 18) —, there is no way around bringing awareness to these feelings and attitudes. This is a necessary precondition for subsequent therapeutic efforts that help the client not to activate those feelings anymore in the first place. What is not activated does not have to be suppressed or retroflected, nor does it need to be expressed or acted out.

This exception constitutes a kind of intermediate therapeutic step during which the salient experience of anger is transitionally useful. Because of the widely spread (false) belief in our culture that it is health-promoting to vent one's anger (see reference point 17), the therapist needs, however, to take care that the client does not misunderstand this intermediate step as the solution of his problem.

PART THREE

> What could it mean to deal appropriately with anger? We really don't want to be soulless creatures who remain thoroughly indifferent to what they come across, creatures whose appraisals consist only of cool, anemic judgments and nothing can shake them up because nothing really bothers them. Therefore, we can't seriously wish not to know the experience of anger and instead persist in an equanimity that wouldn't be distinguished from tedious insensibility. Anger also teaches us something about who we are. Therefore this is what I'd like to know: what can it mean to train ourselves in anger and imagine that we take advantage of its knowledge without being addicted to its poison?
>
> (Mercier 2008, p. 378)

3. 1. Appraisal

To approach an answer to this question it is useful to take a look at a branch of the psychology of emotions that has developed rapidly since the mid-1980's: *appraisal theory* (a good first overview is given by Roseman & Smith 2001).

To put it very simply, in essence appraisal theory holds that certain feelings are evoked by certain evaluations of situations or events (which do not always have to take place consciously) — a position that is pretty much in accordance with Perls et al.: "Experiencing the organism/environment field *under the aspect of value* is what constitutes *emotion*" (1951, 95 — italics in original). Even if two people *perceive* a situation in a similar fashion, their appraisals and thus their *feelings* may differ strongly. And today the same person may experience different feelings from, say, two months ago because of a change in the evaluation of the respective situations: the appraisal is decisive for both the quality and the intensity of the emerging feeling.

3. 1. 1. Personal Meanings in Social Context

"The same assumption is found in all appraisal theories claiming that emotions are generated by evaluation of events as they are relevant to a person's motives, goals, or concerns..." (Roseman & Smith 2001, p. 17). That implies that appraisal is a relational process that determines the way a person relates to her environment and to other people. Hence, in the section on catharsis, when criticizing the steam boiler model we have characterized emotions as "personal responses" and "as social processes in social situations."

It is no news for Gestalt therapists that there are not any supposedly "neutral" sensory stimuli that determine our emotional reactions; instead, the *meanings* that we attribute to those impressions are decisive for the kind of emotions we experience. This is also the opinion of one of the leading researchers in appraisal theory: "*Meaning*, or, better still, *relational meaning*, refers to the personal significance of information, which is constructed by the person. This is what gives an appraisal its emotional quality" (Lazarus 2001, p. 58 − italics in original).

> Hence, the quality of an emotion depends on the meaning which the individual attributes to the topical event with respect to the satisfaction of his motives. It leads to a certain relational interpretation ... and triggers an action tendency adequate to this relational interpretation. (Holodynski 2006, p. 18)

In other words, if I respond to two different events with the same feeling I must have appraised them in pretty much the same fashion. This is why appraisal theories assume that a common pattern of appraisals can be found in all situations in which the same feeling comes up, no matter how different these situations may be. Lazarus calls this pattern a "core relational theme"; we will return to this term soon.

3. 1. 2. Cognition and Feeling

Talking about "evaluations" and "appraisals" may sound rather cognitive. And indeed, one might understand the appraisal as the cognitive component of an emotion. As is the case with other cognitions (see Kihlstrom 1987; Perrig et al. 1993), this is of course not to say that these cognitions are or can become conscious always and in their entirety. To a minor degree they are based on innate patterns[48], and to a major degree on culturally given and learned patterns[49]: "... appraisals are the result of social experiences, and the social world is therefore an integral part of the appraisal process" (Manstead & Fischer 2001, p. 223). To be sure, frequently they are automatized and intuitively activated, thereby enabling the person to quickly find an emotional response to the ongoing situation without having to engage in a protracted rational analysis. The resulting feeling, however, is usually conscious and allows for a spontaneous reaction in terms of action.

---

[48] A typical example for an innate reaction pattern is the startle reflex that can be triggered by a sudden noise or the like. Some emotion researchers do not count such reflexes (brain stem responses) as emotions, since they are not mediated by appraisals in the strict sense of the term. It is all the more intersting that certain (meditative) practices can apparently enable a person to overcome the startle reflex, i. e. not only to control its physical expression, the flinch, but even to extinguish the relevant neuronal activations. This is what "the Lama in the lab," Öser, did when a pistol was fired off next to him while he was meditating (see Goleman 2003, pp. 15ff.).

[49] An "internalization model of emotional development" that tries to describe in detail the central function of cultural meaning systems as well as their influence on the development of the emotions is proposed by Holodynski (2006) in the style of Vygotskij (1978).

Among appraisal researchers there was and still is disagreement as to whether during the process of emotion emergence appraisal, i. e. the cognitive component, comes chronologically first or if the feeling component is primary (see Lazarus 1984 vs. Zanjonc 1984).[50] As time goes on, majority opinion seems to be evolving in favor of those who say appraisal comes first. Intuitively, this view is convincing: you first need to conceive (interpret and evaluate) a situation somehow, before you can then respond to it by way of a feeling (as well as expression and physical reaction) — as is shown in the following simplified sketch, which nevertheless, is sufficient for our purposes:

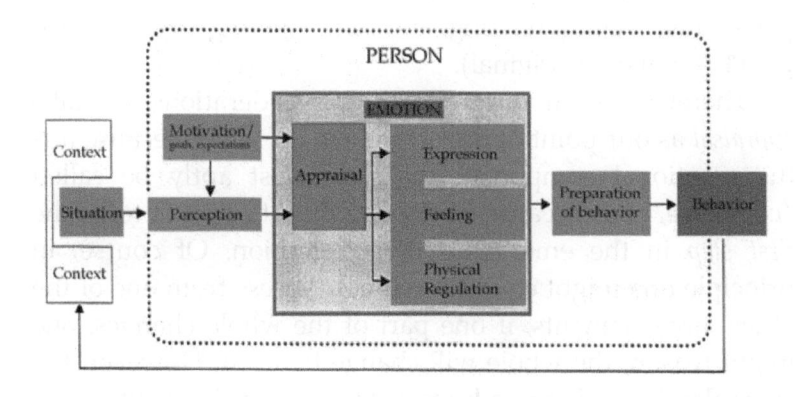

from Holodynski 2006, 45 (➲ 19)

---

[50] Depending on which particular emotion theory one draws on, there are varying numbers of additional components besides appraisal and feeling, but most of them mention physiological reactions and expressions — especially in the face (see Ekman 2003b); motivation and motor behavior or action, respectively, are in general seen as phases in the process of emotion generation that either precede or succeed emotion proper. In what follows we use the term "emotion," when we refer to the activity of all emotion components; we speak of "feeling," when we mean that single component.

For our discussion, however, the answer to the question of the exact chronological sequence of the emotional components is not significant in principle, since we regard the single components of an emotion as parts of a whole. That view does not permit us in a meaningful way to look at cognition and feeling as isolated from each other or to play off one against the other. From a modern point of view, emotions are "... interconnected networks of thoughts, memories, feelings, and expressive-motor reactions; ... the activation of any one of these components should activate the other components as well" (Berkowitz 1993, p. 101). "In other words, what we call 'emotion' is a dynamic and central function that integrates behavior, meaning, thinking, perceiving, feeling, relating, and remembering" (Siegel 2007, p. 211 — italics in original).

Therefore, if in our following considerations we take *appraisal* as our point of departure, we do so not because it is the emotional component that can most aptly be called "cognitive," but because of the fact that it appears to be the *first step* in the emergence of an emotion. Of course, in principle one might equally well gain access from one of the other three elements; if one part of the whole changes, one might reason, the whole will change by itself. However, the examples for such procedures as the ones we have discussed in the section on inhibition and control — the strike at another person's nose which is interrupted briefly before it hits its target; the purposefully non-angry embodiment of the irritated Honda-driver — are not persuasive if we want to replace anger with other feelings *from the very beginning* on.

Interestingly, if you look for the key word "emotion" in *Gestalt Therapy* you retrieve this definition: "An emotion is the *integrative* awareness of a relation between the organism and the environment" (1951, p. 407 — italics added).[51] And

---

[51] The parallels to Lazarus's "core relational theme" are distinctive.

among the relevant passages you will find a quote in which the cognitive component can easily be identified; nevertheless it is hardly possible to suspect the authors of one-sidedly emphasizing cognition. They write:

> The emotions are means of cognition. Far from being obstacles to thought, they are unique deliveries of the state of the organism/environment field and have no substitute; they are the way we become aware of the appropriateness of our concerns: the way the world is for us. As cognitions they are fallible, but are corrigible not by putting them out of court but by trying out whether they can develop into the more settled feelings accompanying deliberate orientation... (ibid., p. 409)

All aspects of an emotion together form a whole, and within this whole the various "... subsystems (and thus the components of emotion) are multiply and recursively interrelated (that is, changes in one component can lead directly to corresponding changes in others)" (Scherer 2001, p. 93).[52]

Subjectively, a figure-background shift in the experience of the components can of course always take place. Nevertheless, from a first person perspective the *feeling* is probably the one element of an emotion that is figural and most salient in most cases. It has a signaling function for the person that provides her with orientation in the situation and thereby enables the coordination of action. The feeling is the condensed and succinct manifestation of what Lazarus calls the "core relational theme"; it "... unifies the separate meaning components of appraising into a single, terse, holistic meaning that can instantly be grasped" (2001, p. 57).

---

[52] The illustration from Holodynski (2006, p. 45 — see reference point 19) can well be taken as an overview on the various possibilities to approach therapeutic work with anger and aggression: they begin with motivations that influence the perception of the situation, lead to the appraisal, and from there on to action.

In general, in order to be able to apprehend an everyday situation in the first place, a person does not necessarily need to be *conscious* of the operative appraisal. And frequently, even in the further course of events there is no imperative to become aware of the appraisal that has implicitly been activated — at least as long as one does not see a reason to change the emotional response to this kind of situation.

3. 1. 3. Cultural and Social Influences

Certainly, appraisals never are individual processes only, for they always take place in a cultural and social context. The particular culture provides the conventions not only as to what counts as infuriating and why, but also as to who is allowed to express anger, how may she or he express it, and towards whom; we have already given some examples in the section on the side effects of aggression (see reference point 13). Gender-specific cultural patterns are another example that is highly significant particularly in the context of aggression.[53]

The view beyond one's own nose, as we will take it below with regard to some Buddhist positions on aggression, can be more than interesting for therapists. It can also help them to remain independent in the face of clients' appraisals that are very much coined by cultural stereotypes and, thus, to maintain their freedom to challenge them, if appropriate.

It can be stated, however, that

> ... researchers have tended to study the way an isolated individual appraises an event and to pay little or no attention (1) to the fact that other persons are often involved implicitly or explicitly in the construction of appraisals or (2) to the possibility that others' reactions to

---

[53] A first survey of the recent state of research is given by Mesquita and Ellsworth (2001).

the emotional event are also appraised and thus play a significant role in the intensity, duration, and expression of emotion. In other words, appraisals are the result of social experiences, and the social world is therefore an integral part of the appraisal process. (Manstead & Fischer 2001, p. 223)

This social coconstruction of appraisals takes place both in the form of extended conversations, in which people discuss with others how to evaluate a certain situation and how to respond to it, and in the form of nonverbal microprocesses, by which people — sometimes in fractions of a second — scan the emotional reactions of others to the given situation and modify their own emotional responses accordingly.

How long and how loudly you laugh about certain jokes, for instance, depends very much on whether you are with somebody who joins in your laughter, or if you are with someone who finds the joke or your laughter embarrassing.

> In such a situation, the appraisal process seems to be mediated by an ongoing dialogue, in which emotional conclusions are reached via interpersonally distributed cognition, and neither person's separate cognitive processes can entirely explain the resulting coregulated reaction. (Parkinson 2001, p. 177)

Much more personally and closer to experience, Gendlin says the same:

> My sense of you, the listener, affects my experiencing as I speak, and your response partly determines my experiencing a moment later. What occurs to me, and how I live as we speak and interact, is vitally affected by every word and motion you make, and by every facial expression and attitude you show. (1962, p. 38)

This phenomenon that one might call "socially shared" or "interpersonally distributed" appraisal has been investtigated in developmental and social psychology under the label of "social referencing." This term denotes the process

> ... in which one person utilizes another person's interpretation of the situation to formulate her own interpretation of it... In referencing, one person serves as a base of information for another and, in so doing, facilitates the other's efforts to construct reality. (Feinman 1992, p. 4)

and this includes the reality of one's own feelings which, thereby, come under the influence of other participants in the joint situation.[54]

From our point of view this is an important fact in the therapeutic setting, since it means that therapists are involved in how clients appraise a situation they discuss and, as a consequence, which feelings clients activate in this situation. More precisely speaking, a therapist who welcomes dramatic expressions of his clients — maybe because he adheres to the catharsis model or maybe because he feels more alive himself, if in his sessions "things really take off," — reinforces his clients in a more or less subtle way to take those situations as occasions for aggressive responses.

3. 2. Anger Appraisal

To act aggressively *outwards* — through expression or behavior — is, however, only *one* possibility for coping with a problematic situation, as the following example is to show:

> For instance, annoyance about inattentive service in a restaurant may lead to a complaint to the manager in the hope that the service will improve.

---

[54] The notion of the "joint situation" has been developed by Schmitz (2002).

The attempt at coping with the situation, however, may as well be directed to one's own emotion and to a modification of one's appraisal.

Example: one might reinterpret one's irritation to the effect that the waiter probably has had a hard day and may deserve respect.

The result of this reevaluation would be that the annoyance would turn into compassion. So the quality of the emotion would change, although the external situation is still the same. (Holodynski 2006, p. 24)

If somebody is dissatisfied with the fact that he easily responds angrily and aggressively to many life situations and develops a desire for change, we are confronted with a genuinely therapeutic task. And here an understanding of appraisal processes opens up an immediate approach in therapy: the repetitive and continuous inclination to anger and aggression depends, as we have seen, on a certain repeatedly activated appraisal pattern that almost anybody knows from their own experience.

The basic structure of this pattern can be found in the manner in which people report their annoying experiences: first, there is another person's action that is seen as an impertinence, encroachment, insult, damage, attack, etc. Then there is the reaction of the person concerned who becomes angry or outraged and defends herself or looks for revenge. This narrative consists of a sequence of two events, whereas in each of them a different person plays the main part. However, the order is not optional; first there is always the experienced attack, and second is the reaction to it.

In this fixed succession another element of the narrative is hidden; it is not only about a temporal sequence, it is also about a *causal* link: typically, the first event is regarded as the *cause* for the second. Person A has acted unjustly upon person B, *therefore* person B reacts angrily. At the same time, this causal link is associated with the moral judgment (see Schrader 1973) that implies a kind of verdict — "guilty!" — on A's action ("attack") as well as a justification for B's *re*(!)-action ("defense"). This judgment also shows in the fact that the fierceness of the verdict on A's action depends on whether bad will and bad faith are attributed to A or if his behavior is interpreted as a result of carelessness and blunder. Accordingly, B is expected to modify her reaction: if A has been malicious, a harsher response is justified than if A has only been neglectful.

In our culture children are brought up in the spirit of this pattern. For instance, parents tend to encourage their children to "hit back" (="defend" themselves), if the parents have interpreted a previous action of another child as an attack; if the child does not resist the child might be depreceted as a wimp or coward.[55] Conversely, children are punished, if, from the perspective of their parents, they have been aggressive *first*. By these educational strategies parents convey the normative rule, "... that one needs to justify one's anger and aggression by reference to the other person's instigating act" (Miller & Sperry 1987, p. 28).

This social norm, then, is also valid in a slightly modified way: if I can convincingly present my aggressive action as a defense against a previous aggressive act by another person towards me, my own aggression will be justified. Under this norm, I *have* to define myself as the *victim* of a prior

---

[55] Other attitudes are also possible. The Buddha Shakyamuni taught:

Normally the weak have to bear the violence. In reality, the strength that comes from violence is the greater weakness. If you respond to a person full of anger by becoming angry yourself, things get only worse. The one who does not react with rage is the true winner. He acts to the benefit of everybody involved. Such a person will only be seen as a weakling by those who do not know the true ordinance of life. (in Köppler 2004, p. 165)

aggression against me, if my own aggressive action is to be morally accepted.

These are the sources from which the specific anger appraisal is drawn in our culture. It starts with the evaluation of another's action as an *attack* that is directly or indirectly aiming at oneself — and not at just anybody with whom one does not identify. In order for the other's action to be taken as an attack, first it is necessary to find it somehow *important*, to take it seriously or to see it as significant in some way; and second, one must regard this action as being directed *against* one's own needs, interests or aims.

In general, one's interests that have to be violated, if one is to be able to react aggressively, have to concern something which is of *personal* importance — what else could be important anyway? If somebody steals a used Kleenex from my garbage pail, I can indeed see it as a formal violation of my rights, but I am not very likely to get angry. In contrast, my reaction will be very different if my favorite book is stolen. Since it is close to my heart, I will somehow take the theft *personally*, for instance by evaluating it as a disrespect or defiance of what is important to me and, hence, of myself. Frequently, this personal level is experienced as an offence, an insult, or a disparaging of one's worth. It tends to be expressed in sentences such as, "Who do you think I am?"

All of these aspects of the typical anger appraisal are summed up by Lazarus in the "core relational theme" of anger, i. e. "*a demeaning offense against me or mine*" (Lazarus 1998, p. 359 — italics added).

The essential elements of the anger appraisal that are squeezed into this relational theme are subdivided in different groups (such as "primary" and "secondary appraise-l") by some theoreticians. For therapeutic purposes the following list of four aspects appears sufficient to us:

1. What is happening is *important* to me; something is at stake. (What is marginal to me does not bother me.) I am concerned as a *person*, i. e. with respect to my values, ideals, self-esteem or social reputation (see reference points 21, 22).

2. What is going on is *in contrast* to my needs, interests, and aims. (What fits with my needs, does not irritate me. – see reference point 26)

3. I hold the other(s) *responsible* for what is happening; maybe I even ascribe ill will to them; at least I attribute carelessness. (If there is nobody who I think is responsible, I do not get angry in general. If I think I am responsible myself, I may be angry with myself, but I will not attack others. – see reference point 30)

4. I do not have to tolerate this; I am *strong* (outraged[56]) enough to take action. (If I feel much weaker than, or inferior to, the one who triggered my anger, I do not dare to act aggressively against him; I may be afraid and withdraw. – see reference point 32)

Necessarily, these elements of the appraisal result in the construction of anger; their individual appearances vary only within narrow limits. Whenever as a therapist one has to deal with aggressive ways of experience and behavior of a client, one can therefore assume that he appraises the situations within which he gets angry in basically the same ways. This makes it possible to investigate – maybe with the help of therapeutic experiments – which of the elements bear which degrees of significance and which are the ones the client wants to change.

For this purpose, the relevant elements of the anger appraisal need to become conscious, of course. Often they are only partially conscious; all of them are, however, able to

---

[56] In the emotional tone of outrage the experienced violation of a social norm with which the person identifies is figural: she finds that "justice" or "morality" are on her side (see Bernhardt 2000).

become conscious in principle, although with differing degrees of ease.[57] Therefore, the first therapeutic step consists in working to enable the relevant anger appraisal to become conscious; this will make it possible for the appraisal to be de-automatized. This then serves as a precondition for subsequent therapeutic steps towards the development of alternative appraisals which, finally, because they are an integral part of the entire emotion, will lead to a change of the other components including the feeling.

3. 3. Case Example 1 (➲ 20)

We do not need to discuss therapeutic procedures of fostering awareness here; they are part and parcel of any comprehensive training in Gestalt therapy. However, to illustrate our approach we would like to report on a therapeutic session in which this approach has been successful after other strategies, among them cathartic ones, had failed to yield the desired results. It was just this

---

[57] "It is important to distinguish between unconscious appraising, which is based on casual inattentiveness, and defensive reappraising, which involves motivated self-deception..." (Lazarus 2001, p. 52). In the first case, one speaks of "cognitively unconscious" content, in the second case of "dynamically unconscious" material. "Reappraising" means: If a certain feeling has emerged in the context of a certain appraisal, e.g. anger, it can give rise to a problem for the person, for instance if she has developed the conviction, "I must not be angry." Now, in a secondary appraisal process, the first appraisal is reworked — and this process is called reappraisal —, maybe resulting in a repression or denial of the anger which hence becomes unconscious in the dynamic sense of the word. "Compared with the dynamic unconscious, the contents of the cognitive unconscious that are based on inattention should be relatively easy to make conscious by drawing attention to the conditions under which they occurred. Making the dynamic unconscious conscious, however, is another matter" (ibid., pp. 52f.) — a matter with which psychotherapists in general are capable to work with as well as with cognitively unconscious material.

therapeutic process that made it very clear to us again, why cathartic methods *inevitably* remain without positive effect: In these methods, the ways in which clients construe their experience so that anger arises (the relevant appraisal) is not picked out as a central theme — let alone worked on![58]

The client, whom for the sake of confidentiality we will call "Dieter," has not only been so kind as to provide us with his permission to publish the following vignette; moreover, he has himself importantly contributed to it by writing detailed minutes from his memory a few days after the session. We would like to take the opportunity to express our gratitude for his assistance. — We have supplemented his minutes with information from our own perspective and revised the style for the purpose of this publication.

3. 3. 1. Vignette

A week ago, Dieter had already discussed his problem with his therapist in an individual session and trusted in the therapist's affection. Nevertheless, he did not find it easy to share this topic with the therapy group now.

Dieter wants to work on his tendency to explode in temper tantrums. As he begins to describe his situation he feels increasingly constricted; he feels ashamed. By looking at the faces of the other group members he realizes that he is not despised and gains courage. He reports: if he feels misunderstood, not seen or abandoned in some other way by others, in particular by his partner, he easily loses control and becomes extremely furious. Sometimes he even turns violent.

As he gives his description, his predominant feeling is that he absolutely needs his partner. He expresses this with the sentence, "I need you!", while reaching out with his

---

[58] The same must of course be said of the above mentioned attempts at moderation and control (see reference point 18).

hands as if hugging and holding her tightly. At the same time he feels very small, and as he pays attention to this experience, he "sees" himself as an infant lying on his back with his arms extended. He has a fantasy of lying down like this on the carpet in the center of the group room, and experiences another wave of shame. He feels embarrassed about feeling so small and dependent on his partner in those situations, and he cries intensely.

Again, establishing eye contact with the members of the group proves to be helpful, and Dieter feels accepted with his dependency and shame. Now the therapist suggest imagining the face of his partner, against whom his tantrums are directed in most cases. As he does so, it becomes clear to him that he is caught in a transferential situation in which he feels pretty much the same as he used to feel towards his mother, and he realizes that he might lose control.

He takes the position of the infant lying on his back to experience his feelings more saliently. At first, the dependent feeling comes up again: "I need you!", he repeats. The therapist who has moved next to his head, suggests to him to stay with this feeling until the anger begins to emerge, but to let it become only as intense as it is still possible for him to regulate it and let it decrease again. Dieter concurs. He reaches out upwards with his hands, pulls up his legs and makes a soft, whining tone that sounds like the upbeat to a moaning scream.

The tone has barely begun, as Dieter interrupts is and looks at the therapist. Very swiftly, reality has started to become blurred, and things have turned black around him. The therapist acknowledges him for having interrupted his experience before it overwhelmed him and suggests he immerse himself in the experience again — just like before only until the edge of losing control, but this time to stay at this edge for a short while.

In his mind's eye Dieter sees something that he describes as "an energetic border," on which he stands. His hands make swinging movements, as if exploring what it is like to be a little bit in front and behind that border. He is able to develop a sense of how he could "explode," if he went clearly beyond the border; there the drama would take control, and the real world would be blurred.

As he tries to describe his experience of that border more precisely, his arms appear to move almost by themselves forming an arc in front of his chest; the fingertips of his two hands touch each other, and he suddenly has the experience of some new space having come into existence in front of him — some space of his own, in which he "still owns himself," in which he is still himself, without getting lost in anger. Within this space he has a clear sense of himself.

Now the therapist invites him to take a look from this space across the border to find out what the suction is like that emanates from the realm behind the border and that again and again prompts him to go beyond it. Dieter tries hard to get a sense of the suction and of the meaning that it has for him. At first he finds it difficult, but with some support and after a few attempts he realizes that within the space he perceives on his side of the border, he feels all alone — lonesome, lost, and sad. Out of this loneliness (in the twofold sense of "out of") he then transgresses the border in the angry attempt to force his partner to reestablish contact with him and to arrest his exposure to his seemingly unbearable solitude.

At this point in time, Dieter sits up from his lying position. At first he feels sad and cries; he has the feeling of having to remain lonely forever in his sadness about being abandoned. As he explores his actual situation with the support of the therapist he discovers that he just had had the choice to either stay on his own or to get angry. Although the loneliness is painful, right now he opts for it, since thereby he does not lose control and does not explode in rage. With increasing salience he has the sense that this is a good feeling to have, since it enables him to be in touch with himself and to care for himself. Moreover, it dawns on him that with his actual attitude it is much easier to reestablish contact with his partner. Although he still feels the sadness about having been left alone, a pleasant quietness and clarity spreads over him.

In the following week Dieter reports that he has been able to "see" and feel the new space in front of him again and again. There have been situations in which a quarrel with his partner could have taken place, but it did not happen. With increasing frequency he has had the feeling that it was not so bad for him to turn to himself in this new space and to console himself when he felt sad or alone.

3. 3. 2. Interpretation

Before the vignette we mentioned the four essential elements of the anger appraisal, which we will briefly repeat in what follows and complement them with comments about the vignette in order to highlight the parallels between appraisal theory and case example:

1. What is happening is important to me; I am concerned as a person; ego-involvement — key word: importance (see reference point 21)

Obviously something *important* is at stake for Dieter: the connectedness with his partner without the presence of whom he feels unbearably lonesome and sad as well as dependent and small (impaired in his self-esteem).

2. *What is going on is in contrast to my needs, interests, and aims* — key word: needs (see *reference point 26*)

If his partner does not understand him and stays at a distance, this is exactly *the opposite of what he desires*: understanding, closeness, connectedness, and appreciation of his significance.

3. *The other is responsible for what is happening* — key word: responsibility (see *reference point 30*)

Dieter sees his partner as the originator of the situation: *she* distances herself from him, *she* does not understand him, thereby denying him the satisfaction of essential needs.

4. *I do not have to tolerate this; I am strong enough to take action* — key word: power (see *reference point 32*)

In critical situations Dieter tries with his aggressive attitude to *force* his partner to provide him with what he wants; by doing so he sees a chance to avoid his feelings of abandonment and dependency and to reestablish the lost connection — if necessary by the use of physical power.

Essentially, the therapeutic work focused on the joint exploration of those decisive moments in which Dieter tended to become angry. The client accepted the therapist's offer of contact, and this contact provided him with the necessary support to take some not only cognitive but also emotionally involved steps on the narrow ridge between deautomatized aware experience and his tendency to "explode." At his "energetic border," as he called it, the anger appraisal becomes effective and leads to aggressive action — resulting not only in negative consequences for his partner and Dieter's relationship with her, but also for Dieter himself: "Feelings of embarrassment, shame, and guilt arise. Sometimes these feelings are experienced in parallel with the anger: unfriendly behavior is displayed, and *at the same time* the individual himself becomes aware of the inadequacy of his rage and feels uncomfortable about it" (Petzold 1995, p. 253 — italics in original), frequently leading to further self-devaluation and an experienced loss of dignity.

A first important element of the therapeutic procedure consists of the attempt at deautomatizing the client's entry into the anger. This is the purpose of experimenting with the approximation to the border in conjunction with the cautiousness for the client not to be "caught" by his anger and to "lose" himself. By doing so Dieter discovers his own options and freedom to make decisions: he can *choose* between feeling lost and being angry. At first this may look like the choice between two evils, but in the further course of the work he finds out that being alone is not as dire as he has expected: Dieter is able to a certain extent to care for himself.[59]

Therewith the forces are weakened that emanate from the four elements of the anger appraisal: if Dieter can look after himself, he is less dependent on his partner, and the importance (element 1) decreases that the critical situation has for him. If his partner does not understand him and/or distanced herself from him (element 2), this is in fact still in contrast to his wishes, but if he does not *have* to become angry and alienate his partner, there is a chance that the frequency and duration of the critical situations will lessen — along with the extent of his frustration.

Moreover, to the degree to which he can care for himself his frustration is reduced additionally. Dieter becomes more responsible for the satisfaction of his wishes (element 3) and, thereby, less dependent on his partner, which will also foster his self-esteem. In this context it will finally be possible for him to give up the attitude of the outraged victim (element 4) who with the seeming right of moral indignation demands what his ego considers it is naturally entitled to receive (element 1).

---

[59] This is a beautiful example of the "paradox of change" (Beisser 1970).

In spite of the fact that after this session Dieter already experienced a remarkable change in his everyday life, further changes of his anger appraisal are still imaginable, desirable, and possible.

Thus, in the subsequent sections of our paper we will turn to the four aspects of the anger appraisal pattern and discuss the question of which general options offer themselves for the therapeutic work on hostility that make it possible for emotions other than anger to emerge. We understand the dimensions we present in what follows as *suggestions* for possible departure points of the therapeutic work on anger. As always, of course the specific situation of the respective client has to be taken into account, and sometimes only one or two of the numerous existing possibilities will fit a certain client and will be promising in this case. Creative therapists will also discover additional options with their clients that are "custom tailored" to their specific conditions. We are not advocating finding as many options as possible, but out those which fit the individual client best under the given circumstances. Already the change in one *single* element of the anger appraisal may lead to a noticeable change in the hostility of the person concerned.

Maybe our following consideration can also be read as a contribution to the art of living (of clients and therapists as well as of people who are not involved in psychotherapy) — in the sense of what Schmid calls "pre-meditation." With this term he designates

> ... the exercise of thinking ahead that can become effective in three respects: It can induce a precocious *familiarization* with a possible situation and, hence, a composure; it can, if the expected situation itself cannot be avoided or changed, vary the *attitude* of the self, i. e. way in which it confronts the situation and makes use of it; and

finally, pre-meditation may be a kind of anticipating hermeneutics by which one interprets the *meaning* of what is to be expected, for instance by not attributing major significance to it... To assess the meaning of the situation at the moment when the affect is the strongest may be too late for a considerate reaction and does not leave much choice, whereas previously it can be appraised with tranquility and wisdom. (2000, 90f. – italics in original)

3. 4. Importance (➲ 21)

If what gets in my way is unimportant to me, I do not get angry. My anger lives on the significance that I attribute to the situation. Whatever somebody may do that contradicts my interests – it only annoys me if I take it *seriously*.[60] Apparently my own priorities are a decisive dimension in the formation of my anger. Only when a high priority meets a contrary situation, might anger arise. (Again, the already mentioned *relational* character of emotions is obvious.) Therefore, the Buddha Shakyamuni recommended:

> If you realize that you experience anger in relation to another person, you may develop the following attitude: Try to act friendly and affectionately towards that person, practice compassion, and look at her with equanimity. *Do not pay exaggerated attention* to that person and her behavior. (in Köppler 2004, 144 – italics added)

You can influence the significance that you ascribe to any particular event. On close inspection many occurrences may not be as important as they first appeared. How often one is irritated by an incident that turns out not to be worth the hassle. Sometimes a momentary pause is enough to become

---

[60] That is why humor is an effective antidote against anger (Baron 1976; Baron & Ball 1974; Landy & Mettee 1969).

aware that you take something much too seriously and spoil your own party (see also the subsequent section on needs — reference point 26).

However, people who tend to react aggressively are able to take all sorts of things as an occasion to become angry: it may be sufficient that another car in front of you is going slower than the speed limit permits and you cannot overtake it. Or you try to make a phone call and the line is busy repeatedly. Or the shirt you would like to dress in has not been ironed. Or your husband listens to the same music again. There is no end to those examples. Their number even multiplies if you add feelings such as impatience that are a preliminary stage to anger:

> Hugh Grant (46) is troubled by his impatience. "When I am at the post office and cueing behind one of those nice elderly ladies who take ages digging in their purse to find their wallet, I would like to grab her and knock her down," the actor (*Four Weddings and a Funeral*) admits to the magazine *Woman*. He is worried about his attacks of impatience: "That cannot be healthy." (Main-Post, March 7, 2007)

If such appraisals of importance rest upon habits only, then they can relatively easily be changed with attention. In those cases the respective person, for instance Hugh Grant, is usually ready to see that those occasions are in fact not important and that his anger does not bring about anything but distress for himself. Through a reevaluation of the occasions as "not significant," the trigger of the anger can be removed and composure be (re-)established.

3. 4. 1. Important Occasions

However, ultimately not all causes are insignificant. If survival is at stake, if water and food become scarce, things definitely are getting serious. It is not by accident that the factual, expected, or even erroneously assumed shortage of resources that threatens the fulfillment of essential needs is a frequent cause of aggression (see reference point 21). And doubtlessly even under conditions of good water and food supplies things might happen to you that impact your life in a very undesirable or detrimental way, and you cannot simply say this situation or event is insignificant. If you are exposed to bullying and mobbing by your boss or if your child is driven to desperation by an incompetent teacher you will not likely be able to correct your angry reaction by telling yourself to find things marginal — not to mention situations that may elicit fierce hate such as the homicide of close relatives in the course of unspeakable "ethnic cleansings."

In general, such feelings of anger and hate cannot be transformed by a change of the importance appraisal, even if the person has the sense of being cankered by her hate and is motivated to overcome it.[61] In these cases the modification of the appraisal has to be put forth in a different manner. — We will return to this question in the section on needs (see reference point 26).

Experiences with being treated in inhuman ways play an important role in trauma therapy, for instance with respect to the aftermath of sexual violence, with which almost any therapist is confronted at least occasionally. They all have in common that there is not only the impact of physically painful or harmful injury, but always also that of debasement, a denigration of the value and integrity of the

---

[61] Nevertheless, this option cannot entirely be negated. Sometimes in situations like that you can hear people say that in spite of all the suffering they are glad about having survived and that their relatives at least did not have to suffer for a long time. They relativize the ranking of the experienced stroke of fate by comparing it to a even higher priority, such as their own survival or the absence of an even harder lot.

person, the repercussions of which stay persistently with the survivors in many cases.

Among those repercussions, a very weak or at least labile self-esteem is pervasive. It shows its effects in many everyday situations, even if they bear no direct connection with the trauma. As we will demonstrate soon, the quality of self-esteem is an important dimension in the emergence of aggressive behavior. Therefore, focusing on self-esteem is an important approach to working with aggression. In the cases we have just discussed, however, this approach has only an *indirect* influence on the anger appraisal.

3. 4. 2. Self-Esteem and Slight (⊃ 22)

There are a great many different situations in which the therapeutic focus on self-esteem is intended to work on the anger appraisal *directly*. We are talking about all kinds of situations (and according to our experience they are the most frequent, which is why we will now turn to them more thoroughly), in which the importance that the anger-triggering event has for the person is not essentially related to the frustration of immediate needs. How else was one to understand that, for instance, that a traffic situation can elicit strong anger, although its effect on the immediate need of the driver to get back home soon can be measured in seconds? Or, to give a more serious example — how could we understand the worldwide furious protests of Muslims that took place in reaction to the "Mohammed caricatures?"

I (F.-M. St.) remember a client who once mistakenly came early to a session and rang the bell of our office. Since I had not yet expected her, the windows were open and the bells of the neighboring church were ringing loudly. I did not hear the door bell. Just before the prearranged appointment time, I closed the windows and took notice of the door bell that my client had rung again. I opened the door and let her in.

She was in a rage, refused to take her seat, and yelled at me: "Who do you think you are? Now you finally show your true face behind your empathic mask: there is nothing else behind it than in any other men. If you hoped I would get down on my knees to be let in and to be helped, you are damned wrong. You are a nuisance, you are no good! I will never return" — upon which she left, slamming the door.

One does not need extraordinary empathetic capabilities to understand that my client had felt insulted by me and had experienced herself as a mortified victim when I had not responded to the door-bell. In essence it was not a matter of the few minutes she had had to wait. The experienced humiliation, which of course I told her I felt sorry about since I had not intended it, formed the basis of the aggressive behavior she showed. The slight was the ground for the self-righteous outrage with which she accused me. The experienced offence provided her with an almost moral justification for her own aggressiveness.

The status of the victim, however, that may appear desirable because of its seemingly superior moral value, has its costs: it is accompanied by a feeling of powerlessness or, as in the case of this client, with an experienced humiliation that is very difficult to bear for most people: who likes to be a wimp who puts up with everything? And who wants to be seen by others as someone with whom they can do whatever they want?

The injured ego that has effortfully coddled itself up with the bonus of the victim, simultaneously undermines the ground on which it stands. It starts a forward escape and tries to turn its depressing passivity and helplessness into some hopefully liberating activity. It props itself up (is outraged) and (from its point of view of course morally justified) hits "back," sometimes experiencing helpless rage, sometimes murderous fury, but always with the righteous attitude of someone who "only" defends himself against the aggression of others. Pride, honor, self-respect, and action-ability must be reestablished at almost any cost, hence the restraining border to a merciless campaign of vengeance may easily be transgressed.

"If we examine how anger or hateful thoughts arise in us, we will find that, generally speaking, they arise when we feel hurt, when we feel that we have been unfairly treated by someone against our expectations" (Dalai Lama 1997, p. 9). Here we encounter what Lazarus calls *"ego-involvement"*: in all our examples (car driver, protesting Muslims, client) the *egos* of the persons were hurt. In this context, the term ego does not refer to the Freudian structure of the psyche; it also does not allude to the "ego" in the title of Perls's first book. It rather denotes what is meant in everyday parlance, when one says something such as, "He is only concerned with his ego," i. e. with his worth, pride, or individual importance.

Since at a later point we will also use this term in a somewhat different sense, it appears helpful to distinguish two aspects. The first aspect is the ". . . self-centered attitude, where one regards one's own interest as the only one worthy of consideration and remains quite oblivious or indifferent toward others' needs or feelings" (Dalai Lama 1997, p. 27). In contradistinction, there is a second aspect to this term about which we will say more in the section on "selflessness" (see reference point 25); it designates ". . . a belief in an enduring, permanent, concrete self or 'I'" (*ibid.*).

If a person feels attacked with regard to her ego (in the first sense), she typically experiences a slight.

> Slights are possible reactions to events, by which we feel psychically hurt. As a rule of thumb, these events that we find invalidating are criticism, rejection, denigration, exclusion or being ignored. The invalidation may pertain to our person, our actions or our significance for other

people. Invalidations directly touch our self-esteem, since we do not feel respected, appreciated or understood.... The experience of a slight and self-esteem are closely related and in part determine each other. First, slights are followed by a weakened self-esteem and are connected to self-doubts and uncertainty of one's identity. Second, people who easily feel hurt and of whom we think as "sensitive" frequently are people with a rather labile self-esteem. (Wardetzki 2000, p. 16)

A labile self-esteem in conjunction with an experienced slight is the most likely precondition for anger and aggression. As Gilligan reports about his moving conversations with violent criminals, "... the prison inmates I work with have told me repeatedly, when I asked them why they had assaulted someone, that it was because 'he disrespected me'..." (2000, p. 105), and he sums up:

> I have yet to see a serious act of violence that was not provoked by the experience of feeling shamed and humiliated, disrespected and ridiculed, and that did not represent the attempt to prevent or undo this "loss of face" — no matter how severe the punishment, even if it includes death. (*ibid.*, p. 110)[62]

At the end of his book the author concludes: "The social policies that would be most effective in preventing violence are those that would reduce the amount of shame." (*ibid.*, p. 236). Such a policy would need to counter humiliating social structures and shaming life conditions on the one

---

[62] Paradoxically, all too often, exactly in places where people are to be "resocialized" the general conduct and the institutional structures frequently take on forms that are likely to be experienced again as humiliating and shaming and hence to promote new violence. "... punishment stimulates shame and diminishes guilt, and shame stimulates violence, especially when it is not inhibited by guilt" (Gilligan 2000, p. 187 — see also Tangney et al. 1992).

hand and to try and stabilizes the labile self-esteem of many people on the other hand.

In this statement, the formulation "*labile* self-esteem" is important. Although the assumption that *low* self-esteem would be a frequent precondition to offence and anger is widely spread, it is demonstrably *false* (Kernis et al. 1989; Bushman & Baumeister 1998): in general, people with low self-esteem are not more aggressive than people with high self-esteem; if the long-term level of self-esteem plays a role at all, it is rather the self-ascription of high value that supports hostility.[63] This is, however, not the case because of this self-evaluation itself, but because of the fact that the more positive the self-evaluation, the more likely it is for a person to be confronted with a situation that challenges it.

Only if the (relatively) positive self-appraisal is *threatened* by a (relatively) negative external evaluation, is aggressive potential activated. "... violence is produced by a combination of favorable self-appraisals with situational and other factors. The most important situational factor that interacts with favorable self-appraisals to cause violence is an ego threat" (Baumeister et al. 1996, p. 26). However, an external evaluation that is negative in comparison to the person's self-appraisal only yields this threatening effect, if the self-appraisal is *labile*, i. e. easily influenceable: "... unstable high self-esteem individuals reported the highest tendency to experience anger..., stable high self-esteem individuals reported the lowest, and low self-esteem individuals scored between these two extremes" (Kernis et al. 1989, p. 1017).

---

[63] In the investigations to which we refer here low or high self-esteem is simply measured by the self-declaration of the participating individuals. For methodological and systematical reasons no distinction is made with respect to the question, for instance, of whether or not the self-ascription of high self-esteem appears to be authentic or inflated from an observer's point of view (see Baumeister et al. 1996, pp. 27f.).

Lability of self-esteem can have different causes. (1) Maybe the person has just valued herself in more favorable terms for the first time and has not yet integrated this valorization into her long-term self-image; this kind of lability might be dubbed *uncertainty*. (2) It is a different matter to talk about *unstable* self-esteem in the case of a person who because of enduring psychological conditions tends to experience gross fluctuations of her self-esteem; here we think of people who think of themselves as extraordinary the one day and find themselves disgusting the other day. (3) Lability may also be based on *inflated* self-esteem, i. e. an effortful attempt of the person at liking herself that lacks the resilience that would enable her to stay calm in the face of a challenge.

> ... when favorable views of self are confronted with unflattering external feedback, the person faces a choice point. The affective response will depend on which path is chosen. One path is to accept the external appraisal and revise one's self-esteem in a downward direction. Sadness, anxiety, and dejection might well result from such a course. In contrast, the other path is to reject the external appraisal and uphold one's more favorable self-appraisal.... In such a case, the person would infer that the external evaluation is mistaken and undeserved, and he or she may well develop anger or other negative affect toward the source of that evaluation... By focusing on his or her hostility toward the evaluators, the person avoids the dismal cycle of accepting the feedback, revising his or her self-concept, and experiencing the dejected feelings about the self... (Baumeister et al 1996, pp. 10f.)

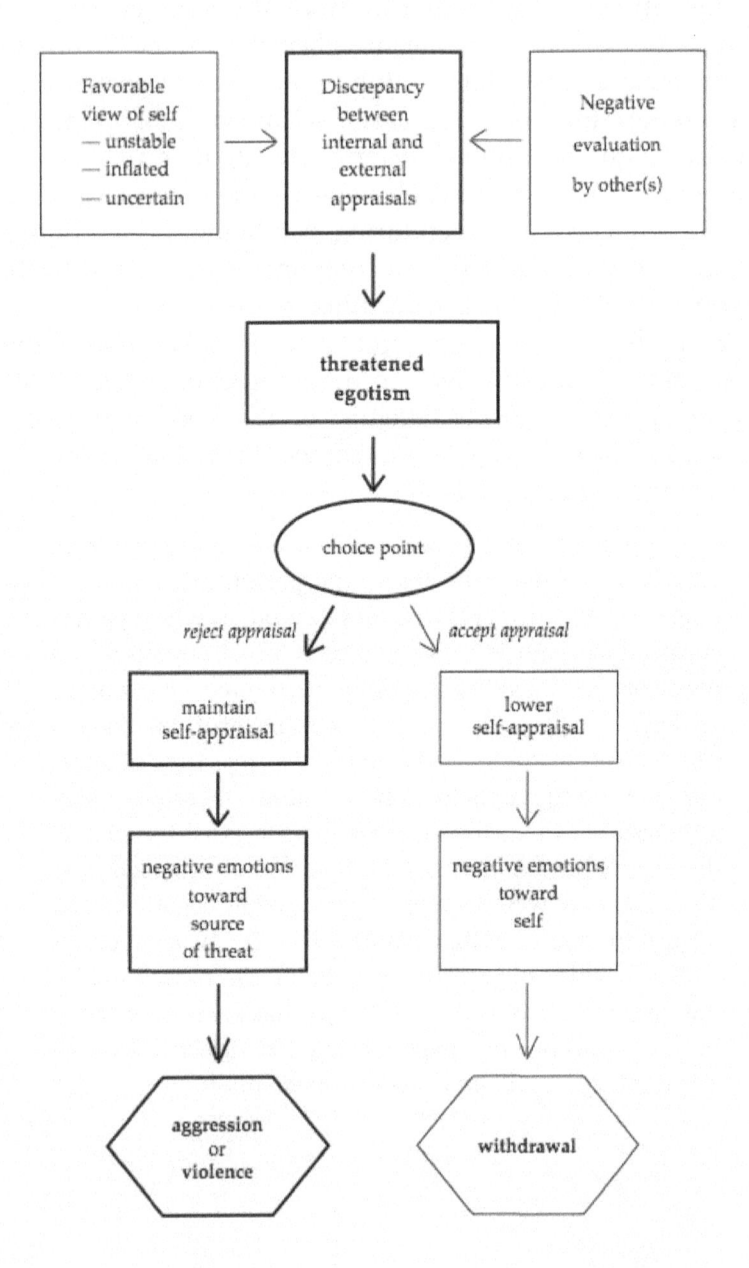

```
                    Favorable
                    view of self          Discrepancy
                    — unstable    →       between         ←    Negative
                    — inflated            internal and         evaluation
                    — uncertain           external             by other(s)
                                          appraisals

                                             ↓
                                       threatened
                                        egotism

                                             ↓
                                       choice point

                    reject appraisal ↙                    ↘ accept appraisal

                         maintain                              lower
                       self-appraisal                       self-appraisal

                             ↓                                   ↓

                      negative emotions                  negative emotions
                           toward                             toward
                           source                              self
                          of threat

                             ↓                                   ↓

                        aggression                          withdrawal
                            or
                         violence
```

from Baumeister et al. 1996, 12

So it becomes comprehensible why, in extreme cases, the execution of physical violence "... may even have an euphoric effect — just like a drug: temporarily, it turns the experience of humiliation, devaluation, and powerlessness into the triumph of physical superiority" (Dornes 2006, 346). Baumeister et al. (1996) illustrate these dynamics with the diagram on the preceding page (⊃ 23).

A good example of Baumeister's analysis is encapsulated in the following article that we read in our local newspaper. It is about a world-famous actor whose over all self-esteem is most likely not very low:

> Omar Sharif has been sentenced to two years prison with probation after a violent dispute with a parking attendant. Moreover, a judge in Beverly Hills pledged the "Doctor Zhivago"actor to take fifteen therapy sessions in order to achieve control over his temper tantrums. The argument started when Sharif got angry when his Porsche was not yet ready as he left a restaurant. (Main-Post 15. 2. 2007)

In the same newspaper we found another report that illustrates the same psychological dynamics, although with much more severe consequences:

> **Divorce Hurt Self-Esteem** ... yesterday the psychiatric expert delivered his medical estimate on the personality of a 33-year old who, in August 2005 ... strangled his wife and threw her corpse into the Main river. The psychiatrist had conducted several interviews with the defendant and had been present during the trial to collect further evidence.
>
> He was not able to diagnose the accused with a significant psychiatric disease. He found him normally intelligent, socially competent, and considerate in general.... The husband only has a slightly narcissistic person-

ality, however not to a pathologic degree. The failure of his marriage might have injured his self-esteem . . . (*ibid.*)

Both reports underline Wardetzki's assertion that "... the fact that we feel offended has more to do with ourselves than with the event itself" (2000, p. 26). This is exactly where a great potential for the therapeutic work on aggression is to be found.

We would like to illustrate this with a case example; we are grateful to the client who was so kind as to provide us with the respective pages of his diary.

3. 4. 3. *Case Example 2*

On my way to the therapy group weekend the following happened: weeks ago, L. and I agreed that L. would pick me up at the train station to give me a ride to the place where the workshop was to take place. When I arrived, L. was not on the platform. I was a little disappointed, but then I said to myself: "Certainly he is waiting for me in the hall, and if he is not there, he will be at the car park outside of the station." But L. was neither in the hall, which meant another disappointment for me, nor at the car park. I felt some irritation: "He promised to pick me up! If he could not make it, why didn't he give me a call?"

I took my luggage and went to where he lives. I rang the doorbell — no reply. Now a number of feelings came up at the same time: anger ("How can he let me down like this!?") and panic ("How will I make it to the workshop?"). However, I managed to calm down again by telling myself: "Maybe he was only late and is waiting at the station for me now." So I went back to the station, but to no avail. Now I became very agitated and angry about him not being there. A minute later my cell phone rang. It was L. who said: "Hi, I am very sorry. I fucked it up. I thought you'd arrive later. I will be there in a few minutes. Go and have a drink in the restaurant; I will pay for it."

In spite of L.'s excuse I was still mad at him. I thought: "By no means will I let him invite me for a drink. I am not corruptible! It is not as simple as he thinks: just to say "sorry" and everything is fine again . . . He cannot do this with me!" So instead of waiting for L. in the comfortable restaurant, I stood in the station hall. I was so furious that I was not able to imagine ever forgiving him. Even the idea that L. should apologize again honestly did not alleviate my anger. I experienced myself as a prisoner of my own implacability; I did not see any way out of it. In addition, I did not understand myself anymore. I knew I wouldn't want to spend the rest of my life in enmity with L.; that was important to me. Nevertheless, I had no idea how to leave my rage behind me. I also did not know what to make of all of my feelings; on the one hand, I thought: "Don't get into trouble! What happened to L., might also happen to yourself one day." On the other hand, I did not want to ignore my anger that I still experienced intensely. But what was I to think of my fury? Was it justified or was it just an expression of my vulnerability? — I did not know the answers to those questions.

L. was due to arrive any minute now. How should I greet him? (Along the way I remembered that I had experienced similar situations before when I felt mis-understood by my wife.) I did know this exorbitant wrath quite well, but that did not help me at the moment. (With my wife I used to fight for a while before I would give in; then I felt fine again) But how would such a fight take its course with L.? I didn't know what to do; I only knew that I was entirely confused. It was a terrible feeling to know that L. would show up soon and that I had no idea what to say to him: jovially forgive him ("No big deal.") or show him all my anger ("He shall see what he has done to me with his carelessness!")

Since my anger at L. had been so fierce and since I had experienced feelings like that before, I decided to work on them in the therapy group. First I described the situation at the train station. When I mentioned that I had understood L.'s behavior as indicating that I did not matter to him enough to keep his promise, the therapist alerted me to the fact that I had *interpreted* L.'s behavior in that fashion. I agreed that I had understood his absence as an attack on my worth. Then the therapist asked me if I knew what my vulnerable spot was that had matched that interpretation.

I responded, "I don't know. But I remember that I strongly wished to be joyously greeted by him." The therapist invited my to describe this wistful fantasy in more detail. Suddenly something happened: I realized that at once my compulsive anger vanished into thin air, and I began to feel affection for L. This happened entirely to my surprise. I had never experienced something like that before, but it felt unambiguous and sound. I imagined L. coming towards me, spreading his arms, and saying, "Nice that your are there. I am happy to see you." As I had this fantasy I felt a strong longing and began to cry.

My therapist gave me time. After a while he asked me what was going on in me. I told him that I had just thought of my elder brother, for whose acknowledgement I have been waiting all my life. I do not remember ever having heard any appreciative word from him. I am sure I could have a very successful career, but he wouldn't even acknowledge that. Whenever we meet, he puts himself on stage and talks to me vigorously about his accomplishments until I feel small and insignificant. My wife once said that he might be competing with me.

My therapist signaled that he understood and asked me to return to that wistful fantasy once more: "If you imagine L. greeting you joyously what would that give to you?" I reentered the fantasy and looked for a response to the question. "Maybe the feeling of being welcome... That it is good that I am there. Or that it is nice that I am in this world..." However, I realize that something is still missing, since I am glad to be in this world with him. That's it! "I would have had the feeling that it is nice to be in this world with you." In the words, "with you," there is joy about being connected. And that's exactly what I feel now. It just happened in *me*. I did not need something from outside. My self-esteem felt strong in a way that I hadn't known before. It emerged from myself without acknowledgement from somebody else.

My therapist alerted me to the fact that the words "value" or "worth" had not been spoken for a while. I realized that in a sense that was no longer the issue. What is more important is that I can feel happy about how nice it is to be in this world with L. and others. Then the therapist asked what my feelings were if I thought of my brother now. I imagined my brother doing his "dance" and said to him: "You don't need to do that. I love you anyway; you are my brother."

Then I turned to the group and looked at one face after the other. Whenever I looked at someone I thought, "It is nice to be in this world with you." Each time this sentence felt harmonious. I had a sense of a new, until-now unknown basis on which I can stand and be happy to be in this world with others.

It is difficult to find the right words. Words like "basis" or "a friendly home in me" come to my mind — a home that makes it possible to be glad about being in this world with other people. And in fact, I feel a certain independence from the way in which others might relate to me in specific situations. Even if I have the impression that somebody is not so well-disposed towards me, the feeling remains: "It is nice to be in this world *with you*." It's a great feeling!

3. 4. 4. Reduction of Importance

Any procedure that *a priori* reduces the importance of relatively negative external evaluations also reduces the aggressive potential. There is a great number of such measures, among them the following: first, awareness of the fact that an experienced slight to a large degree depends on oneself can help to relativize the significance of the event that triggered it and to put the lability of one's own self-esteem into the foreground of one's attention.

As the foregoing case example shows, the therapeutic exploration of the question how one's self-esteem can be so easily shattered enables a smaller liability to respective threats. Whenever a slight is experienced and (therapeutic) support is available, it is a good occasion to ask that question — if one does not prefer to go on dwelling in one's anger. Epstein reports:

> In the Tibetan tradition, according to the Buddhist scholar Robert Thurman, the best time to observe the self clearly is when we are in a state of *injured innocence*, when we have been insulted and think, "How could she do this to me? I don't deserve to be treated that way." (1995, p. 211 — italics in original).

Second, one can also contemplate the question of whether it is always better to reject the external evaluation in order to maintain the given self-appraisal. Maybe there is some truth about the external evaluation that is worthwhile including into one's self-evaluation. Moreover and third, frequently the "costs" of anger, aggression, and violence are higher than those of withdrawal, even if this may go along with feelings of sadness, shame or despondency. Maybe in the long run even a relatively lower self-esteem is more advantageous than an inflated one, since there will be fewer situations that challenge it.

Although it may distract a little from our central train of thought we find it useful to hint at the obvious connection that exists between the repeatedly mentioned individualistic ideology in our culture (➲ 24; see reference points 8, 15, 31) and the great significance that just this culture (as well as its prevalent psychology) attributes to the self-esteem of the individual.

> In Western psychological traditions, healthy development has meant becoming well individuated, not overly dependent on others, knowledgeable of one's own needs, and appropriately respectful of one's own boundaries, with a clear and stable sense of identity and a sense of self marked by cohesion and esteem. (Fulton & Siegel 2005, p. 39)

However, if it is the experienced threat to a relatively *high* self-esteem that, according to the above mentioned investigations, yields negative consequences in the form of a greater aggressive tendency, one cannot positively judge high self-esteem in general and without qualification. Its dark sides need to be taken into account too:

> An uncritical endorsement of the cultural value of high self-esteem may therefore be counterproductive and even dangerous. In principle it might become possible to inflate everyone's self-esteem, but it will almost certainly be impossible to insulate everyone against ego threats. In fact, as we have suggested, the higher (and especially the more inflated) the self-esteem, the greater the vulnerability to ego threats. Viewed in this light, the societal pursuit of

high self-esteem for everyone may literally end up doing considerable harm. (Baumeister et al. 1996, p. 29)[64]

Now we would like to return to the aspects of the importance appraisal that make it possible to reduce the significance of aversive situations and, thereby, to make the emergence of anger less likely. The fourth possibility lies in making it one's habit to assume that the other person "did not mean it" maliciously. The attribution of bad faith adds weight to any relational disturbance, especially to an experienced slight (see the following section on responsibility; reference point 30). Indeed, we think it is a matter of fact that many events that are opposed to one's needs happen for numerous reasons that can rarely be traced back to somebody's deliberate intention to cause harm. That is also true of insults, which in general do not take place out of malevolence, but rather out of inattention or a lack of knowledge about the "vulnerable spots" of the other.

As a fifth example we would like to point to the option of assuming an attitude that regards adversities as *normal* events in life — events that are as normal as rainy weather. One does not need to make them more important by seeing them as deviant from some ideal norm and, therefore, to pay extraordinary attention to them. Moreover, one does not have to look at oneself as the poor person who is haunted by some (of course, undeserved) bad fate, against which one has to revolt violently.

3. 4. 5. *Selflessness* (➲ **25**)

Another, much more basic possibility for reducing the significance of aversive events does not refer to those events themselves, but to the self that experiences them and feels

---

[64] Baumeister's et al. theory was thoroughly tested and confirmed in all essential aspects by Stucke (2000).

attacked. This possibility transcends even the above-mentioned focus on the self-esteem topic. Maybe this additional possibility is closer to the spiritual realm than to the psychotherapeutic and may not be adequate to all therapy clients; for some it may even be counter-indicated. However, we find it important enough to be noted here since in our view it bears resemblance to some central notions of Gestalt therapy; Mehrgardt & Mehrgardt (2001) have already called attention to it in their interesting book *Self and Selflessness: East and West as Reflected in Their Self Theories*.

These authors point to the traditions of the term "self" (sometimes also called "I" or, again with somewhat different connotations, "ego" [65]), the effects of which are omnipresent in our culture — a term of "self" that implies a reification of this self, as if it was an object, almost of material essence. However, this is an illusion:

> If one were to inspect the parts of which a person consists, one would nowhere find other parts than legs, muscles, blood vessels, the function of seeing as such, thoughts or the comprehension of meaning. But nothing of it all can be equated with the I, the self *per se*. (Mehrgardt & Mehrgardt 2001, p. 114)

For this reason Perls said: "In Gestalt Therapy we write the 'self' with lower case s, not capital S. Capital S is a relic from the time when we had a soul, or an ego, or something extra special" (1969b, p. 76). And at another place he adds: "Let us bear in mind that 'I' is not a real existing object or a part of the organism.... the 'I' is experienceable but has no fixity" (1975, p. 31). Of course, in the background of these statements the definition of the self stands as it was defined by Perls, Hefferline and Goodman: "Let us call the 'self' the

---

[65] Here we use the term "ego" in the second sense that we briefly mentioned in the section on Self-Esteem and Slight (see ref. point 22).

system of contacts at any moment. As such, the self is flexibly various, for it varies with the dominant organic needs and the ... environmental stimuli; it is the system of responses" (1951, p. 235).

This self (or "ego") is nothing persistent but something that comes into being anew from moment to moment; although it can always be symbolically *represented* by the same term, self, it *is* by no means always the same. Nevertheless, it is one of the properties of human consciousness to produce a "naïve realism" and the "illusion of givenness" (Metzinger 1993, p. 249) that makes it difficult for us "... to comprehend that even our I, the phenomenal center of the world, is no substance, but simply a mental model — although one of utmost complexity" (*ibid.*, p. 284).

Various meditative practices can be instrumental in looking through the illusion of givenness with respect to the self (as well as other phenomena) and to immediately grasp it as an illusion, to the effect that

> ... even our most cherished selves must be considered not to exist in the way we normally assume. Indeed, we find that if we search for the identity of the self analytically, its apparent solidity dissolves even more readily than that of the clay pot or that of the present moment. For whereas a pot is something concrete which we can actually point to, the self is more elusive: its identity as a construct quickly becomes evident. (Dalai Lama 2001, p. 42)

From this perspective the ego loses a large part of its significance, since "... we are forced to conclude that this precious thing which we take such care of, which we go to such lengths to protect and make comfortable, is, in the end, no more substantial than a rainbow in the summer sky" (*ibid.*, pp. 45f.). Depending on the range of the meditative insight, one may be led to ask the question whether it pays off to pursue such efforts. Or one may come to see with regret as well as with amusement[66] the absurdity with which one tries to maintain and to defend something so elusive.

Once the attachment to the perception of an ego has dissolved, there is no more chance for greed, hate, craving, and resentment to become manifest in the mind. No more longing for, or attachment to, the concept of the "I" will be experienced. One will no longer have the idea of not having to be considerate of others, of being spiteful or of wanting to get rid of them. (Khyentse 2002, p. 194)

This way slights will lose ground, and the angry attempt at counterbalancing the experienced challenge of one's importance with strenuous self-aggrandizement will no longer make sense. What will remain, however, is an independence of anything that might threaten the ego; a blithe equanimity towards the vicissitudes of life will emerge. "But that inner equanimity is neither apathy nor indifference. It's accompanied by inner jubilation, and by an openness of mind expressed as unfailing altruism" (Revel & Ricard 1999, p. 32).

By the way: the German word for "altruism" is "*Selbstlosigkeit*" ("selflessness"). It has *both* meanings: the absence of a continuous self *and* the engagement and compasssion for other people that are the attitudes that can be experienced once the ego lets go of being attached to itself and does not have to compulsively look after its own illusionary constancy.

As insight into the self-as-process grows, we begin to see the folly of accepting our naive adherence to the idea that the "I" as fixed, enduring, or even truly "mine." This insight greatly reduces our concerns for self-protection or

---

[66] We have mentioned the anti-aggressive effects of humor in an earlier footnote.

self-aggrandizement and allows us to respond compasssionately to others as we perceive our genuine interdependence with all of creation. (Fulton & Siegel 2005, p. 41)

3. 5. Needs (⊃ 26)

The experienced frustration of needs is the second essential element in the typical anger appraisal, to which we will turn now. Needs and their frustration, respectively, also play an important part in Gestalt therapy. Here it is remarkable that the way needs are understood in classical Gestalt therapy is closely linked to its theory of aggression (and to what we have called its "digestive psychology"). If hunger counts as the prototype of a need, as it frequently appears in the literature of Gestalt therapy, then already the title of Perls's (1947) first book, *Ego, Hunger and Aggression*, alludes to this close link between needs and aggression.

Let us briefly recapitulate.

3. 5. 1. The Function of Needs in Gestalt Therapy

"Well, the need is the primary thing. If you had no needs, you wouldn't do a thing" (Perls 1969b, p. 20). To perceive one's needs and to be able to care for their satisfaction forms the basis of "organismic self-regulation" (see Perls et al. 1951; Votsmeier-Röhr 2004) and, thus, of health. The process from the awareness of a need to the action that serves its fulfillment to the "assimilation" of what satisfies that need is described as the "contact cycle" (see reference point 10). Between physical and psychosocial needs no difference is made in principle; what is good for the satisfaction of any need, is assimilated either by physical metabolism or by "mental metabolism."

"The organism has psychological *contact* needs as well as physiological ones; these are felt every time the psychological equilibrium is disturbed, just as the physiological needs are felt every time the physiological equilibrium is disturbed." (Perls 1973, p. 6 — italics in original). Then the "organism" must activate its "healthy ad-gression" and "'step' toward the object of appetite" (Perls et al., 1951, p. 342; see reference point 5) or, in Dreitzel's words, it must make use of its "normal contact functions," if necessary, by "destructive rage" or by "annihilating hate" (Dreitzel 1995, p. 504; see reference point 3), in order to incorporate what it needs. To quote Perls again, "... from within, some figure emerges, comes to the surface, and then goes into the outside world, reaches out for what we want, and comes back, assimilates and receives" (Perls 1969b, pp. 21f.).

In principle, there can be two kinds of causes that may disturb this process and the satisfaction of the need. Either the course of the contact cycle is interrupted by psychological processes of the person, such as avoidances; in this case, these interruption must be overcome to (re-)establish the smooth function of organismic self-regulation. Or there are obstacles in the environment, in which case the person needs to intervene aggressively" and to "destroy" the "object of [her] hostility" in order to ensure successful need fulfillment.

However, in both cases awareness of the current need is necessary: "... first the therapist provides the person with the opportunity to discover what he needs..." (Perls 1969b, p. 37). In a second step, "for the individual to satisfy his needs, to close the gestalt, ... he must know how to manipulate himself and his environment" (Perls 1973, p. 8). Here the intensity of experience of the needs is critical: "The more intensely they are felt to be essential to continued life, the more closely we identify ourselves with them, the more intensely we will direct our activities towards satisfying them" (*ibid.*, p. 6).

To sum up these ideas about the satisfaction of needs in classical Gestalt therapy, one might compile the following list (➲ 27):

1. Salient awareness of, and unequivocal identification with, needs.
2. Overcoming of psychological hindrances and "aggressive" elimination of external obstacles.
3. Appropriation, incorporation, and assimilation of the "object of appetite."

We have already pointed out that the model of the contact cycle implies a very individualistic notion of the human condition (see reference point 10). If you look at it in its compressed form as presented in the list above, it appears egocentric, possessive, potentially abusive or even cannibalistic — at least if one does not ignore the category mistake (see reference point 7) and thinks of psychosocial needs, for the fulfillment of which other people and the quality of one's contact with them are essential (see reference point 32).

What we intend to underline in what follows is the way in which an idea of needs, as it is conceived of in classical Gestalt therapy — and also predominant in our consumer society! —, contributes to the emergence of aggression. Thereby, we hope to open other options regarding human needs, especially those options that provide human beings with the chance to respond to the possible frustration of their needs in other than angry ways.

3. 5. 2. *The Plasticity of Needs*

In order to get angry you do not only have to find important what happens, you also have to assume that it conflicts with at least one of your needs, interests or aims, if not with some of them. This statement is correct, but not complete. Since for you to get angry, you also need to *hold on* to that need, interest or aim and to insist on getting it satisfied, achieved, or reached. If, because of the frustration, you resign (in a negative sense) or let go (in a positive sense), you will not get annoyed.

The likelihood to let go or to resign, respectively, is related to the importance you attribute to that need; and some needs, especially if they concern survival, are and remain of highest significance for the person (see reference point 21).[67] However, for some people non-material aims such as the implementation of a certain worldview or of a political or religious vision can also acquire such a high value that under no conditions can they be dissuaded from pursuing them — including their own death.

These may be extreme situations that one normally does not have to deal with in psychotherapy. Nevertheless, in the normal course of therapy one can also see clients who by hook or by crook hold on to a certain need and/or the hope for its fulfillment and who, in spite of both great and futile efforts, never consider resigning or letting go. While the urgency and intensity of the felt need may be understood from within the patient's worldview, the experienced needs can, however, be relativized if clients are ready to self-critically explore the aggression that it brings about.

The first factor concerns the way needs are understood in our culture in general and in Gestalt therapy in particular. That hunger has to serve as an example again and again highlights this understanding and demonstrates once more the negative consequence of the category mistake (see ref. point 7). Since "in biologically-oriented approaches . . . needs

---

[67] And even in these cases there are different possibilities too; the idea that one will be reborn or to live with God after death, for instance, may qualify the significance of the wish for survival. The value the death of a "martyr" has for some terrorists is a terrible illustration of this fact. It also illustrates how the unconditional will to reach a certain goal may cause hate and violence.

designate such states of deprivation in the organism that in the long run can lead to damage or death of the individual (or extinction of a species)" (Drever & Fröhlich 1971, p. 60). From this perspective needs are "natural" events, and their satisfaction is more or less indispensable.

If this perspective is applied to the psychosocial realm without major modifications, sometimes a need whose fulfillment does not really have survival value may seem as important as if almost everything depends on its satisfaction. The strong identification with this desire (see reference point 27) — the Buddhists call it "attachment" — bestows the character of an addiction upon it, so that its fulfillment must be achieved at almost any cost, and if it cannot be achieved otherwise, must be aggressively eked out.

In the eighth century, the Buddhist sage Shantideva, who wrote extensively about anger and aggression, warned:

> Having found its fuel of mental unhappiness
> In the prevention of what I wish for
> And in the doing of what I do not want,
> Hatred increases and then destroys me.
>
> (in Dalai Lama 1997, p. 18)

The attachment to what is "prevented" soon becomes both inefficient and self-destructive (see Morgan & Morgan 2005, p. 75), as most of the needs that presuppose inter-human cooperation cannot be fulfilled in this way, and the attempt to enforce satisfaction by the use of aggressive means brings about all the risks we have described in the section on *The Everyday Side Effects of Aggression* (see reference point 13).

Perls once wrote:

> ... the patient comes for treatment because he feels that he is in an *existential crisis* — that is, he feels that the psychological needs with which he has identified himself,

and which are as vital to him as breath itself, are not being met by his present mode of life. The psychological needs that assume this life-or-death importance are as many and as varied as the patients themselves. To one, keeping up with the Jonses and surpassing them, if possible, is a dominant need. Such a person identifies his total existence with his social existence, and if his social position is threatened he is in an existential crisis. (1973. p. 44 – italics in original)

Given that Perls himself was a person to whom adaptation to external conditions such as social norms ("accommodation") did not have highest priority (see reference point 9), one can safely ascribe to him a certain critical distance with respect to the identification of this patient with the need to keep up with the Jonses – as well as with respect to the fact that for the patient this desire was "as vital as breath itself," with the result that its dissatisfaction threw him into an "existential crisis." However, Perls apparently did not notice how much his own understanding of needs was coined by the biological model and how he, in spite of his distance in the concrete case, was caught in the same paradigm as his patient – as are many other people in our culture.[68]

---

[68] The seeming life importance that in this train of thought is attached to the satisfaction of psychosocial needs yields strange results sometimes: whether or not the world or another person provides the fulfillment of the need is elevated to the status of a pseudo-ethical criterion: "... an event is judged as good if I desire it and bad if I do not.... The world becomes divided into good for me and bad for me" (Olendzki 2005, p. 251 – italics in original). Perls called this kind of evaluation the "morality of the organism" (1975, p. 29), which he explained thus: "Good and bad are responses of the organism. But the label 'good' or 'bad' is then unfortunately projected onto the stimulus; then, isolated, torn out of context, these labels are organized into codes of conduct, systems of morals..." (ibid. – italics in original).

Such people do not realize that most human needs are not at all manifestations of some physiological requirement (as are the needs for oxygen, water, and food). We propose to regard psychosocial needs rather as orientations and preferences in people's conduct of life, which within the framework of given cultural conditions are (inter-) subjectively construed. Therefore, maybe the term "wish" would be more appropriate; a wish is in no way predetermined, but is plastic and always open to modifications.

3. 5. 3. Basic Needs (⮕ 28)

Needs may be manifold, but they almost always can be assigned to one (or a combination) of a small number of dimensions that sometimes are called "basic needs" (Grawe 1999, pp. 383ff.). Grawe presents the following list; we paraphrase his descriptions with some amendments, shortenings, and small changes:

1. The need for *orientation and control*: every person develops a model of reality, a system of personal meanings into which to integrate her experiences; she tries to maintain this construction and, along with it, her self-image. She has a need to understand herself and her life situation in order to gain some control and influence on them (see *ibid.*, p. 385).

2. The need for *pleasure* and avoidance of dislike and pain: people aim at pleasurable experiences and try to avoid unpleasant and painful feelings (see *ibid.*, p. 393).

3. The need for *bonding* and relationship: people look for security, closeness, and for relationships that provide them with shelter and the feeling of belonging. They want to feel connected, understood, and intimate (see *ibid.*, pp. 395ff.).

4. The need for a stable and/or high *self-esteem*: people like to feel good about themselves. They have a wish to think of themselves a competent, valuable, and loveable. They strive to have a positive self-esteem and to heighten it, if

possible. This includes the need for appreciation by others. (We have already commented on the cultural bias of this need as well as on its perils — see reference points 22, 24)

Another way to define these basic dimensions of psychosocial needs can be found in the three factors which in Antonovsky's (1981; 1987) concept of salutogenesis make up what he calls the "sense of coherence" (SOC): (1) comprehensibility, (2) manageability, and (3) meaningfulness. These factors might also be interpreted as basic needs that to a large degree overlap with Grawe's list. They describe people's wishes that (1) the stimuli that during their lives arise from their own mind and from their environment be structured, predictable, and explicable; that (2) they have the resources and capabilities that are necessary for coping with those stimuli; and (3) that the demands of life be challenges that make sense and are worth some effort and engagement.

However one subdivides and names the basic dimensions of personal wishes, it may be evident that they are not independent of each other, but closely connected in many situations. For example, the sense of competence in coping with challenges will probably yield a positive impact on a person's self-esteem as well as her feeling of belonging and being loved. For many people the meaning of life consists in the experience of being connected to others. In turn, this may elicit pleasurable sensations.

We introduce these ways of defining basic needs because according to our therapeutic experience it can be very helpful for clients, who would like to loosen their attachment to certain, very concrete needs, if we support them in orienting their attention more to the respective basic dimension(s), from which their respective concrete desire springs. This helps them to let go and to engage in a creative search for other ways of fulfillment; sometimes it also opens their eyes to opportunities that in the attitude of attachment remain out of sight.

To say it with the words of William Blake:

> He who binds to himself a joy
> Does the winged life destroy;
> But he who kisses the joy as it flies
> Lives in eternity's sun rise.

One does not have to gain anything one has once dreamed of, and even if one does, it neither has to be in exactly the form one first imagined nor does it have to occur immediately. Sometimes without such compulsiveness one's view of life's opportunities is wider and there is a better chance to become aware of "the joy as it flies." *Carpe diem.*

This alleviative attitude of equanimity and liberty cannot always easily be assumed, especially in a society that is oriented to consumption, in which one is permanently indoctrinated not to get a sense of one's basic needs, but to run after the seeming satisfactions that are offered in the advertisements before one even knew of a corresponding wish. Paradoxically, in a life situation without hunger, such as the one we live in, people are seduced and pressed (and often act accordingly) to urgently provide themselves with goods — and, in recent years, increasingly with experiences (see Schulze 1992)[69] —, as if they were starving and were only able to avoid imminent death by immediate consumption, whatever the cost.

Pretty soon this amounts to a bustling and compulsive endeavor for the aspired satisfaction, suggesting that openly aggressive or at least ruthless procedures may be adequate

---

[69] Isn't it both surprising and appalling that values — or does one have to say: goods? — such as the intensity of immediate experience that formerly helped to make Gestalt therapy well-known, because they met a deficit, today are successfully sold (of course in a watered-down form)?

and justified. We have seen people who in certain circumstances justify those procedures with the weird ideology, "care for themselves." In this ideology, the alternative options of a patient postponement of gratification or even renunciation are only left to the stupid and penniless — and, of course, to those who are not able to activate sufficient "positive aggression" to be successful in the fight for survival; for those people these options just do not seem to exist as positive values and realistic avenues.

In this regard a therapeutic approach that wants to contribute to the decrease of aggressiveness may be helpful in that it supports awareness of the plasticity of human needs, including the possibility of voluntary surrender. Maybe in this context the individualistic ideal of independence can even be supportive at times.

3. 5. 4. Alteration of Referential Need

Another way to cope with dissatisfied desires in a flexible manner is to move that desire into a context within which it serves the satisfaction of a different desire. In this way the experience of frustration may be turned into the feeling of gratification.

To give you an example: one of our clients was again and again irritated by the behavior of a former friend who, since the end of their friendship did not seem to miss a chance to undermine the relationships of our client with other friends and acquaintances through the use of malicious gossip and similar intrigues.[70] The angry feelings of our client were based on her wishes for approval and love. They turned into amusement and gratitude when she discovered in therapy that the intrigues of her former friend were actually useful to

---

[70] This is an example of "relational aggression," which we have mentioned above and which in our culture is practiced by women more frequently than by men.

her in a certain way: from their respective effectiveness or ineffectiveness she was able to construe a more precise idea about which relationships were reliable and which were not. This satisfied her need to know her friends and acquaintances better and to find out if her relationships with them were resilient. She removed her experience with her former friend from the context of her need for acknowledgement and placed it in the context of a new referential need, i. e. her desire for orientation and connectedness.

The Dalai Lama practices a similar reframing. He states: "To learn patience, one needs adversaries. In this sense our enemies are extremely helpful" (2006, no pagination).

This kind of relocation of the reference to a frustrated need to another one that is being satisfied may also help to change the anger appraisal in much more severe cases: in the section on *Important Occasions* (see reference point 21) we have already referred to situations, the importance of which can hardly be relativized for those who are concerned (certainly not by outsiders!), for instance in the case of the murder of a loved one. However, for the bereaved the hate against the perpetrator may become a heavy burden, which they may want to leave behind after some time.

In the background of the hate is the longing that the loved one should be there — alive and available. Besides the necessary grieving and the processing of the pain of the loss, in those situations there is also the chance to connect the burdensome event with a different need. Some people do this by activating their compassion for the departed; they feel grateful and sometimes even glad that she "at least did not have to suffer very long." Others regard the loss as some sort of ordeal imposed on them by God in order to stimulate and to provoke their development. Again others manage to embed the painful experience into some other larger context and, thereby, to satisfy their desire for meaningfulness.

All of them may be supported by an insight that proves to be helpful in less dramatic situations too: to follow one's wish for revenge does not bring about a kind of satisfaction that is *peaceful*; to follow one's need for connectedness and to abandon vengeance promises a much more valuable gain.

3. 5. 5. Selfish Entitlement

Another way to support clients to free themselves from the slavery of their supposed needs and the corresponding aggressiveness consists of working on the sense of entitlement that can be found in many people. They think that if they "need" something, they automatically have a kind of right to "get" it. For them, their need appears to legitimatize some sort of enforceable demand for provision — a special kind of attachment. "For the modern person craving is . . . intense and even the suggestion that it might be set aside looks like an absurdity" (Crook & Low 1997, p. 106).

We recently saw a both regrettable and gross example of this attitude in a therapy session with a couple (➲ 29). The husband, very seriously and without any recognizable self-doubt, claimed that he "needed" sex with his wife each day for his general well-being. If she refused (which she did much more rarely than was her inclination because she was afraid of the consequences) he applied a rich arsenal of aggressive means of pressure and punishment, from offended pouting to insulting reproaches, to physical abuse (battering), to days of icy silence — without any pangs of con-science or feelings of remorse, not even in retrospect. Moreover, he held that "she did not deserve better," since he was much "worse off" than she, because with her refusal she would mortify him and ostensibly demonstrate to him in sadistic ways how humiliatingly dependent he was on her consent.[71]

The example illustrates a kind of righteous and self-centered entitlement that makes almost any aggression against people who are not ready to serve the posed demands, seem justified and justifiable. Frequently (but not always!) this kind of entitlement is part of a so-called narcissistic personality disorder "... that may foster tendencies toward sexual coercion, especially given the narcissistic propensity for self-serving interpretations, low empathy toward others, and inflated sense of entitlement" (Bushman et al. 2003, p. 1027). However, in its milder forms it can also be found in people who do not display the criteria for that diagnosis. Who does not know from one's own experience what it is like to insist stubbornly on the fulfillment of a wish while at the same time having a sense that one might well be able to live without it? "Sometimes it is necessary to admit to oneself that one *likes* to become angry.... Often situations in which I get mad include an element of self-importance: I want the others to concede that *they* are wrong" (Anantananda 2001, pp. 64f. − italics in original).

It is of course much easier to thematize this in therapy if a client displays these attitudes of entitlement and self-aggrandizement only occasionally rather than as part and parcel of a larger narcissistic issue. In any case, a successful dilution of entitlement leads to a decrease in a person's tendency for anger and aggression, since

---

[71] The absense of guilt and the presense of shame ("humiliation") is a frequent precondition to violence:

...in cases of interpersonal harm, the guilt-prone individual's response is likely to be modulated by interper-sonal empathy and concern, diffusing the potential for anger and hostility that is so prominent in the case of shame. (Tangney et al. 1992, p. 674)

... entitlement is linked to dismissing attachment (valuing the self but not others); decreased accommodation, particularly on active accommodating processes (entitlement is linked to less positive accommodating behaviors); lower empathy and perspective taking; less respect for the partner; and love associated primarily with game playing (ludus) and selfishness (less agape). (Campbell et al. 2004, p. 39)

In the investigation by Campbell et al. the attitude of entitlement was correlated with increased aggressiveness, *only in instances* in which the demanding person was somehow questioned, frustrated, or criticized — a result that is in accordance with the above mentioned investigations on labile self-esteem, slight, and aggressiveness.

Obviously, the attitude of entitlement is a typical example of an I-It-relationship (see Buber 1970). The other person is only perceived as a function of one's own need fulfillment and not as a person with her own autonomy, integrity, and dignity. Hence the therapeutic work on entitlement is never solely preventive work on aggressiveness, but always also work on the client's ability to relate to others in an I-Thou manner.

The numerous aspects of an I-Thou-relationship include the willingness to forgive the other if at times one has the impression that he has not fully lived up to one's expectations. This also has to do with the readiness to ponder the relative weights of the various factors that are involved; often it is much more appropriate to let a matter rest — we mean: to really let go of it, i. e. to also set aside a future utilization of the occurrence, maybe in the form of a polemic or of collected demands — and not to occupy oneself with it anymore. Sometimes this is the best way to cut one's losses.

> When things catch fire, you give maximum attention to putting it out, using all reasonable methods at your disposal to do so as quickly as possible. You do not first feel bitterly angry at the fire, shout and scream at it, curse its name and so on. You think of that as a waste of time and energy. So you need not bother to get angry with the unenlightened when they harm you, just make every effort to minimize or avoid the harm. (Thurman 2005, p. 85).

Thus forgiveness relates to entitlement as fire does to water: "... results strongly support our prediction that entitlement would be associated with an unforgiving stance" (Exline et al. 2004, p. 898). This does not come as a surprise, since after a frustration or offence has taken place, forgiveness means to "... humbly set aside hateful thoughts and vengeful fantasies that seem perfectly justified. To forgive means to cancel a debt, a debt for which one may fully deserve repayment" (*ibid.*, p. 910).

All in all, from the perspective of human relationships, the problem of entitlement underlines the humanely necessary relativity and plasticity of needs as a precondition for the sustainability of dialogue:

> Were a person to have definitive wants at the beginning of a relationship and insist that these wants be met without alteration, that person would be ignoring the actual relational nature of human functioning and would inherently be fostering connections of dominance and submission. (Lichtenberg & Gray 2006, p. 24 – see also reference points 29, 32)

3. 6. *Responsibility* (⟿ 30)

The third essential element in the anger appraisal is the attribution of responsibility. If there is nothing and nobody to whom I can ascribe responsibility for what triggered my anger, I will not become angry. If I lose my house in a flood that I interpret as *natural* disaster I will not be furious. However, if I hold any politicians responsible for not having been ready to spent money on the construction of causeways, I will get mad at them. Maybe I am also angry at a personal God who I think would have been powerful enough to prevent a natural disaster.

3. 6. 1. Agency and Control

The attribution of responsibility is tantamount to the ascription of agency and tacitly imputes at least a minimal degree of control over what happened to the agent. (If somebody runs amok in an bout of schizophrenic delusion, he is the agent of the harm done to other people, but he is not held responsible, because no control is insinuated.) The more control I attribute to the agent, the stronger my angry reaction to his deeds usually is.

Carelessness is a weaker form of control; in this case it is assumed that the agent did not really intend what he did, but just was not well informed or attentive enough to prevent what happened. In contrast, deliberateness is a stronger variant of control; here a conscious intent is assumed that was accompanied by the capacity to turn it into an action. However, it is still possible that the intent was not necessarily hostile; the harm that was inflicted may be accepted as an unavoidable side-effect of a more positive intent.[72] The most intense aggressive response will be evoked if bad faith is ascribed to the actor; in this case not only deliberateness is assumed, but also the conscious aim to inflict harm.

---

[72] Example: of course, one only aims at military targets and wants to treat civilians with care, but, alas, "collateral damage" cannot be avoided. — In the event that such reasoning does not appear plausible, it is easily interpreted as deception behind which ill will is surmised.

It is important to note that for my angry response it is *not* decisive that the other person acted deliberately, carelessly, or malevolently. It is critical which attitude *I* attribute to this person, and there may well be predispositions on *my* part that determine the kind of attitude I ascribe to the other.

> Anger indicates that important personal goals are being threatened, and also that this person tends to blame someone else for this, perhaps because of a vulnerable self-esteem that leads to assumptions of malevolence or insulting attitudes on the part of others. (Smith & Lazarus 1990, p. 630)

"He only did it to annoy me," you can sometimes hear people say. They reduce the event to a simple denominator, in which, tellingly, the event itself does not matter anymore. The illogical inference from one's own emotional reaction to the intention of others is a widely spread habit. Its curse is the implicit assumption of mandatory causality: "If the other does X, I have no alternative to becoming angry. As a result, the other is responsible for my anger."

Because of impaired acuteness of mind during anger, but even outside the heat of the battle, many people are not aware that between the action of an other and their own anger there is a series of steps, each of which is under their *own* influence (see the illustrations from Holodynski and Baumeister et al.; reference points 19 or 23). In their respective ways, both illustrations describe these steps, and concurrently, the responsibility of the one who gets mad, for his anger. For psychologists – when they think scientifically and are not emotionally involved –, this is an old adage that has been formulated by numerous authors in one way or the other many times before.

We would like to quote from two sources; we deliberately do not pick psychological texts, but ones from "natural" scientists, since they appear to enjoy special credibility (as the recent boom of the neurosciences proves anew). At the same time they are sometimes falsely thought to believe that human feeling and acting are highly predetermined.[73] In their classic book, *The Tree of Knowledge*, the biologists Maturana and Varela write: an "... interaction is not instructive, for it does not determine what its effects are going to be. Therefore, we have used the ex-pression 'to trigger' an effect" (1987, p. 96). The neuroscientist Jaak Panksepp also uses the word "trigger" and concurs:

> Other people do not cause our anger; they merely trigger certain emotional circuits into action. Ultimately, our feelings come from within, and perhaps only humans have a substantive opportunity, through emotional education or willpower, to choose which stimuli they allow to trigger their emotional circuits into full-blown arousal. (2005, p. 190)

Thus, even aroused "emotional circuits" do not absolve one from one's responsibility, the more so as they are plastic and can be changed through systematic practice. In other words, it appears to a reliable fact

> ... that the brain interweaves emotion and intellect — raising the possibility that the positive potential of this connectivity might allow us to bring more intelligence to emotional life. More particularly, the dictum ... that repeated experience modifies the brain raises the question of how we might best educate the emotions. (Goleman 2003, p. 205).

"So not only does the brain give rise to mental states, but the mental states must also be able to modify the brain condition. This is necessarily true" (Varela, in Goleman 2003, p. 207). However, when it comes to aggression, such insights

---

[73] Of course there are exceptions that contribute to that reputation. Roth (2003) appears to be one of them.

do not appear to be very popular, and if you promote them, you are likely to fall from grace. This happened to an author, Robert Solomon, who fervently proposed this point of view and received a lot of fierce criticism from some colleagues; here is what he wrote:

> ... emotions are judgments — normative and often moral judgments.... The (moral) judgment entailed by my anger is not a judgment about my anger... My anger is that judgment. If I do not believe that I have somehow been wronged, I cannot be angry. (1980, p. 257 — italics in original)

> If emotions are judgments and can be "defused" (and also instigated) by considerations of other judgments, it is clear how our emotions are in a sense our doing, and how we are responsible for them. Normative judgments can themselves be criticized, argued against, and refuted. ... if you should convince me that John has not wronged me, I do not simply conclude that my anger is unreasonable, unfair, or unbecoming. I cease to be angry.... Since normative judgments can be changed through influence, argument, and evidence, and since I can go about on my own seeking influence, provoking argument, and looking for evidence, I am as responsible for my emotions as I am for the judgments I make. My emotions are judgments I make (ibid., p. 261 — italics in original)[74]

One of the reasons for the lack in popularity of these insights can be found in the deep anchoring of the anger narrative in our culture (which we have described at the beginning of the section on *Anger Appraisal*). This cultural pattern in fact prescribes, "... that one needs to justify one's anger and aggression by reference to the other person's instigating act" (Miller & Sperry 1987, p. 28), because if you do not, you will be seen as the aggressor yourself. Hence, in

---

[74] Solomon speaks of "judgments;" the analogy to "appraisals" is obvious.

the kindergartens, but not only there, you can hear both sides of an aggressive exchange say: "*You* started this!"

The "emotional education" Panksepp calls on and that must be provided by any psychotherapy that wants to contribute to a reduction of human aggressiveness, will therefore have to support its clients to free themselves from their "illusion of irresponsibility" (see Staemmler & Bock 1998) and to discover the myriad ways they contribute to the emergence of anger instead of other feelings.

It goes without saying that the other remains responsible for what she or he has done to present a possible occasion for an angry response. However, the more or less naïve ascription of deliberate intent or even bad will which comes about through the false inference that only strengthens the angry response, can be therapeutically questioned and maybe dissolved with respect to its alleged automatic operation. By the way, in this context some research has been done that emphasizes "... that aggression can be reduced to the extent that the other's behaviour is interpreted as unavoidable or unintentional" (Krahé 2001, p. 217).

3. 6. 2. Freedom, Limitations and Interdependence

If this therapeutic step succeeds, it may in addition become clear that even in the case of actual[75] malevolence by the other, one's own irritation as well as the "counter"-aggression that may easily arise from it, are not imperative; rather, one remains free to interpret the experienced attack in ways which leave space for different emotions — maybe compassion for the other's emotional hardship, compassion for one who cannot support or regulate himself in better ways than by the inappropriate attempt to do harm to an-

---

[75] Such "facts" are difficult to prove, and they should always be subjected to careful and self-critical scrutiny. One can hardly ever be sure.

other person's physical well-being, to his material circumstances, or to his reputation in the eyes of third parties.

To be sure, if somebody does such things, she is the agent of this behavior in the sense we have discussed above; but does she really have full control? If indeed there is bad faith, does it not mean that this person at least in part has become a marionette of her own hostility? Is she still in control of herself and her feelings? This can be doubted if one assumes that all people actually have the wish to live together in peace and happiness.

"The appropriate response to someone who causes us to suffer ... is to recognize that in harming us, ultimately they lose their peace of mind, their inner balance and thereby their happiness" (Dalai Lama 2001, p. 112). Whoever is guided by their hate will have a hard time being peaceful and happy — not only because feelings of peace and happiness are incompatible to feelings of hostility, anger, and rage, but also because mostly anger arises from an experienced slight (see reference point 22).

> ... if this is the case even when a person inflicts harm on us, the harm that is inflicted is in some sense out of that person's control because he or she is compelled by other forces such as negative emotions, delusions, ill feelings, and so on. If we go even further, we find that even a very negative feeling such as ill will or hatred also comes about as a result of many factors and is the aggregation of many conditions which do not arise out of choice or deliberately. (Dalai Lama 1997, pp. 40f.)

One does not need much empathy (or recollection of similar experiences of one's own) to imagine how unfree, unquiet, and nasty it feels to be driven by hate against another person — to say nothing of the self-inflicted humiliation that is experienced by hostile people in their more light-hearted moments, when they sometimes (and always too late to avoid the humiliation) become aware of how little justice they have done to their own ethical values of tolerance, fairness, and respect toward the integrity of others, and how much they have harmed their own dignity after all.

The *so-called* malevolence — as we probably should call it after what we have said before — as well as the case of carelessness point to the limited range of human control over one's own motivations and actions. The fact that one is the agent of one's responses and behaviors never means that one can be conscious of all background factors and relevant information that may have an influence on the given situation and that might be useful to include into one's considerations and decisions: a great number of cognitive processes take place without ever becoming conscious, in part even without ever being *able* to become conscious at all (Kihlstrom 1987; Perrig et al. 1993).

> It is the rule of thumb among cognitive scientists that unconscious thought is 95 percent of all thought — and that may be a serious underestimate. Moreover, the 95 percent below the surface of conscious awareness shapes and structures all conscious thought. If the cognitive unconscious were not there doing this shaping, there could be no conscious thought. (Lakoff & Johnson 1999, p. 13)

Moreover, the structures of our mind are closely connected to the conditions of our bodies, from which we cannot escape (see *ibid.*; Gallagher 2005). And it is another characteristic of the human mind to always be bound to a certain subjective perspective, which again is influenced by cultural and subcultural preconditions that to a large extent exist in the format of *implicit* knowledge. As a conclusion from these facts it seems to be a matter of principle that a person's horizon is limited and that, therefore, even intellectual freedom can never be absolute, but is always a freedom within a given frame and its constraints.

So if you see people who are captive of their horizons and, for instance, are not able to act in other than hostile ways, this may be an occasion for a profound feeling of human connectedness and for a kind of compassion that lacks any arrogance since it derives from your clear awareness of your *own* narrowness. Supposedly, everybody knows this narrowness from their own life experience to a maybe painful but at any rate sufficient extent. This experience may even make it possible to forgive sometimes those who have attacked you with their hate and hostility.

Those who find it desirable for spiritual or other reasons to liberate themselves from their dependence on material success and public display may in the end even feel some gratitude towards the "wrongdoer," whose "malevolence" and aggressiveness may be a welcome impetus for their own development.

> I who am striving for freedom
> Do not need to be bound by material gain and honor.
> So why should I be angry
> With those who free me from this bondage?
> Those who wish to cause me suffering
> Are like Buddhas bestowing waves of blessing.
> As they open the door for my not going to an unfortunate realm,
> Why should I be angry with them?
>
> (Shantideva, in Dalai Lama 1997, pp. 94f.)

If you take a close look at the cultural context of the repeatedly used terms "agency" and "control," you will see how pervasively these terms are soaked in the cool mentality of individualism (➲ **31**; see reference points 8, 15, 24). They refer to the abilities of a more or less isolated individual who in the seclusion of his mind reflects upon the situations, by which he thinks he is *externally* surrounded — as if in fact he were separated from these situations by some substantial "boundary" and was able to confront them from an independent position (for a critique of the Gestalt therapy term of the "boundary" see Staemmler 1996; 2002a).

In the scheme of relational responsibility, however, this model is fundamentally critiqued and deconstructed. Instead, we envisage a world of relationships and interdependencies in which each individual is a nodal point of intersection and connection. Activity takes place within interrelationships and only has sense, meaning, and purpose within that context. Actions are always preceded by other actions, relationships by other relationships, and the individual self by the selves of others. There is no action taken by a rational consciousness in some mythical rarefied stratosphere above relationships and interdependencies. All actions take place in the context of other actions and within the realm of interconnections. Every act or practice is always preceded by other acts or made in connection with others. More often than not, individuals are in dialogue so that practice has a joint authorship. (Burkitt 1999, p. 72)

The individualist notion of responsibility denies our multiple interweavements with transindividual preconditions of our culture and language, impacts of the zeitgeist, constellations, reciprocities, fields, situations, atmospheres, loyalties, internalized relational patterns etc. which do not just surround us externally, but which *interpenetrate* us in to large degrees unnoticeable ways — in our speech, habitus, everyday practices and patterns of thought and behavior (see Staemmler 2005; 2006).

The individualist ideology that also manifests itself in the notion of responsibility in traditional Gestalt therapy[76]

---

[76] This term of responsibility, as it was coined by Perls ("... responsibility is really response-ability, the ability to choose one's

ignores or, to say the least, neglects these interdependencies and reduces them to marginal conditions. In therapeutic situations this ideology is apt to ascribe to our clients sole responsibility for their suffering and, hence, to expose them to a social isolation that is likely to enhance their distress rather than to alleviate it. Similarly, in non-therapeutic contexts the one-sided attribution of responsibility — and along with it that of guilt — becomes simple and usual, whereas considerations about one's own contributions to problematic situations becomes scarce.

The development of the idea of a "relational responsebility" is still in its infancy, as can easily be recognized from the reading of McNamee's and Gergen's (1999) book with the same title (a fact, to which the authors readily admit). "Once we accept that people do affect other people, then responsibility becomes more than an affirmation of self-as-source; it entails the obligation, duty, and responsibility we have *to* others" (Bindermann 1974, p. 287 — italics added[77]). This may also mean that the other's behavior may not only have causes within himself, but is motivated by numerous reasons including those that have to do with my own behavior. The more I acknowledge my co-agency of the given situation, the more influence I gain on it. I advance from a victim to a co-creator of the shared situation. And

---

reactions" — 1973, 78) has various shortcomings and is, from an ethical point of view, terribly shallow (see Staemmler 2001). According to this definition, an adult would act "responsibly, " if he passively observes a child crossing the street and being hit by a car, although he would have been able to intervene. All he had to do was "respond" — maybe by saying, "I did not want to bother." A meaningful notion of responsibility has to include much more than "the ability to respond;" it must define the "serious questions" (Böhme 1997) that need to be asked and it must set up clear criteria for the kind of answers that really count.

[77] The italics mean to point to the fact that this is not about taking responsibility for the other in the sense of taking personal responsibility away from him.

what is more, "if you see yourself as co-responsible for what happened to you, you strengthen your persuasion that events of this kind can be avoided in the future" (Montada 1988, p. 208).

As Gestalt therapists we can take these considerations as a stimulus to dedicate ourselves to the elaboration of a new term of responsibility, which — without throwing out the baby with the bath water, i. e. without denying the parallel existence of some relative individual responsibility — tends to overcome individualist thinking and which could be called "relational," "dialogic," or "field-theoretically based", maybe also "dialectical," since it would certainly be helpful for the elaboration of that term to draw on "dialectic constructivism" as it has been outlined by Mehrgardt (1994; 2005). To paraphrase one of Mehrgardt's central propositions, one would have to begin by acknowledging: I and Thou are related to each other in a dialectic reciprocity of responsibilities; they both construe and realize each other (see 1994, p. 452 — reference point 25).

Another concept might be useful for this project, i. e. that of the "joint situation" as proposed by new phenomenologist Hermann Schmitz:

> In fact, whenever people are together, from the very beginning a joint situation forms itself that cannot be divided into the individual parts that each individual contributes with his own character and perspective. This can be seen in the fact that, depending on which joint situation the person is found in, he can almost appear as a different person; by becoming part of an encompassing situation his personal situation turns into a dependent variable, and autonomy and heteronomy intermingle. (2002, p. 27)

McNamee and Gergen offer a concrete vision of how a relational understanding of responsibility might supplement the individualist one:

> Sometimes, we are faced with a person whose barbarity or hostility draws us into confrontation. We feel a strong urge, abetted by the joy of righteous indignation, to attack and correct. The result is reasonably predictable: Our effort only incites the other's antagonism. Realizing the rocky route on which we are now embarked and drawing on a repository of alternative voices, can we locate an alternative reaction to the other's failing? Could we in the face of attack, for example, imagine responding with a comment that constructs an image of the other as important, loved, respected, valued? Could we invite the other to work with us in creating an opportunity for his or her "success" in the present situation? Can we invite him or her to collaborate with us in a construction of ourselves as helpful, kind, concerned and himself or herself as important, respected, and so forth? (1999, p. 34)

Such an attitude might mean to take a caring and compasssionate stance toward the aggressive person and not see her as a troublemaker only. "Taking moral responsibility means not to consider the Other any more as a specimen of a species or a category, but as unique, and by so doing elevate oneself (making oneself 'chosen') to the dignity of uniqueness" (Bauman 1995, p. 60) — both unique and connected.

3. 7. Power (➲ 32)

"Power is any chance within a social relationship to succeed with one's own will, if necessary against opposition, no matter what this chance is based upon" (Weber 1985, p. 28). The fourth element of the anger appraisal refers to an evaluation of the respective situation that leads the angry person to trust that she will be able to get what she wants. Of course, frequently this element of the appraisal is not conscious when effective. However, if one did not see a chance to achieve what is at stake, one would not activate one's aggressive powers, but would accept or submit to the provocation or withdraw in some way (i. e. choose the pole within the aversive system that is opposed to aggressiveness; see reference point 12).

Sometimes the angry person decides to exert her power by applying physical force in order to remove what is in her way, sometimes she uses methods of verbal threatening or nonverbal intimidation (for instance by raising her voice or fists). Sometimes the attempted exertion of power also consists of the expression of moral reproaches and/or insulting curses. Many aspects of such behaviors resemble competitive fights for higher social status within hierarchies.

In moments in which one aggressively turns against others one exerts power. No matter if material needs are frustrated or one's self-esteem is challenged — if one gets angry or aggressive one tries to cause the person one holds responsible to change his behavior or to take back the insult, respectively. Simply becoming annoyed and letting it show can have the effect of a threat, especially if directed at people who are in a weaker position anyway.

To be sure, if rage is openly expressed, the effect may be even stronger, not only because of its greater intensity as compared to annoyance and anger, but also because of its implicit indication of a possible loss of control, by which the furious person nonverbally announces that soon her "hand will slip" or "she will not know what she does." Ostentatious displays of dominant behavior of this sort subserve the enforcement of the desired good, but also have symbolic meaning; they assign subordinate status to the other and, thereby, promote the restoration of the impaired self-esteem.

In addition, they function as punishments that are apt to reduce the likelihood of more frustrations or challenges in the future.

If according to Weber power is "*any* chance to succeed with one's own will *no matter what this chance is based upon,*" the combination of anger and aggression has to be understood as a *certain* way of exerting power. And that is exactly where the therapeutic work on this element of the anger appraisal can begin, since in Weber's view there is nothing wrong with power *per se*. It is legitimate to take one's chances in order to get what one wants; however, the *way* in which power is exerted, is essential. In other words, it depends on whether or not one tries to achieve one's need fulfillment by aggressive or other means.[78]

Asking for something, bidding for it or trying to convince the other, i. e. activating one's assertive motivational system in appropriate ways, is the first alternative to an aggressive exertion of power. For many clients it is helpful to discover that in most cases aggressive procedures in the pursuit of psychosocial wishes lead to exactly the opposite of what they aim at. The case example of Dieter (see reference point 20) is a good illustration for this. If you look for closeness and try to enforce it, you may achieve the other's conformance or submission; if you wish to be loved and file a suit for it, you will find it difficult to believe in the declarations of love you receive in return; if you would like to be respected and try to induce it by the use of threats and intimidations, you may merely activate anxious subjugation.

Sometimes our client in couples therapy, whom we mentioned above, would be "successful" with his aggressive strategies in the sense that his wife would make "love" with

---

[78] We have already discussed the possibility of relativizing the significance of needs (see reference point 21); we do not intend to repeat this now, but we would like to remind the reader of this important option.

him in order to avoid the expected trouble if she did not; however, his basic dissatisfaction about not feeling loved and desired remained unchanged. It was simply impossible to find the remedy in sexual encounters that were reached by coercion. The way in which he tried to get what he longed for was apt to prevent him from getting what he wanted; it even contributed to removing himself from it.[79]

The therapeutically acquired awareness of what Staemmler and Bock (1998; see also Staemmler 1993; 2000b) call the "theme" of a particular therapeutic process is a decisive step for the client to find out which of the methods with which he tries to satisfy his need, *in fact* have the character of avoidances that prevent the fulfillment of that need. Moreover, this work supports the client to discover how he can pursue his wishes with regard to other people within the framework of personal contact (see Staemmler 1993) as it is distinguished by an I-Thou-quality in the sense of Buber (1970). (From this point of view, therapy itself is an exercise in the activation of the explorative-assertive motivational system.)

The mobilization of aggressive motivation for the purpose of exerting power with the aim of the fulfillment of interhuman wishes is particularly doomed to failure *a priori*, when basic human needs are concerned (see reference point 28). Thus the therapeutic work must, first, support

---

[79] In this context in particular, we understand the effectiveness of the strategy of "nonviolent communication" (Rosenberg 2003) that has become quite popular in recent years. Although Rosenberg also takes into account other elements of the anger appraisal (e. g., the attribution of responsibility), his main approach consists in changing the manner in which power is exerted. However, we find it both remarkable and not convincing that he keeps on talking about the necessity of anger expression, for instance: "To articulate ourselves completely, we now open our mouths and enunciate our anger — that, however, has been transformed into needs and their corresponding feelings" (ibid., p. 146).

clients to understand this and, second, encourage the activation of their explorative motives to help them discover appropriate ways of pursuing their wishes for connectedness, enjoyment, and meaningfulness — as well as their ability to peacefully let go of these wishes, if to keep on pursuing them is bound to cause harm for themselves and for others.

Final Remarks

Without metaphors one can neither think complexly nor formulate theories (see Lakoff & Johnson 1980; 1999). But "one must learn where metaphor is useful to thought, where it is crucial to thought, and where it is misleading. Conceptual metaphor can be all three" (Lakoff & Johnson 1999, p. 73).

The result of our investigation is clear: the theory of aggression in classical Gestalt therapy, as was proposed in Perls's (1942; 1947) first book and later repeated with little variation, does not stand the test of thorough scrutiny. It is inconsistent and terminologically confused. Its basis is a misleading conceptual metaphor, the so-called "mental metabolism," the implicit category mistake of which has far reaching theoretical consequences (reductionism, one-sided emphasis on assimilation accompanied by ignorance of accommodation, etc.).

An especially profound consequence is the confounding of two entirely different motivational systems — the explorative-assertive system on the one hand and the aversive-aggressive system on the other hand — which leads to the misleading differentiation of "positive aggression" and aggression in the negative sense of the term. From this arises the illusion of a kind of aggression whose expression in everyday life and cathartic processing in therapy is supposed to be useful or even healthy.

However, there is vast evidence that the feeling and enactment of anger and aggression is supportive neither to the one who experiences or acts this way nor to the ones who are her or his addressees. On the contrary, the experience and expression of hostility is detrimental to the health of the individual herself or himself (blood pressure, coronary heart disease, social isolation, negative development of intellectual capacities, etc.). To say it in Gestalt therapy terms, to be *aware* of anger and to *express* it is harmful, but to be *conscious*[80] of it and to *relate* it *verbally* is not because it does not involve aggressive arousal (see Siegman 1993; 1994). Perhaps the only exception in which some aggressive expression might be necessary — at least as an intermediate step — is in the case of the client who has suppressed her aggressiveness to such a degree that it escapes her awareness.

In contrast to the tradition in Gestalt therapy, we maintain as a rule of thumb: to *talk about* anger (see Hariri et al. 2000; Ochsner et al. 2002), for instance with one's therapist, as well as to reflect on one's aggressiveness on one's own (e. g. writing a diary — see Pennebaker 1990, pp. 39f., 195) can be instrumental for reducing the readiness for anger and aggression.

However, the assumption that the cathartic expression of anger might have a lessening effect on possible subsequent aggressiveness has not only been disproved; additionally, it has been substantiated that catharsis *increases* subsequent aggression. This does not only result in a surge of the aforementioned damage to the physical and mental health of the individual, but also in a dramatic erosion of her or his social relationships. We urgently advise against the use of cathartic techniques in which another human being or only

---

[80] For the difference between awareness and consciousness see Staemmler and Bock (1998, pp. 47ff.).

the imagination of a person is implemented as the target of aggressive expression.

An extraordinarily disquieting outcome of our investigation has been the insight that not only the cathartic practice mentioned above but also certain aspects of classical Gestalt therapy *theory*, as they have first been formulated in *Ego, Hunger and Aggression*, are apt to foster and reinforce hostility. That is the case with respect to the confounding of different motivational systems. In addition, we are thinking of the individualistic ideology that shows up in many ways, for instance in the way in which self-esteem, satisfaction of individual needs, and the achievement of personal goals is overemphasized (see Wheeler 2000).

As a result of our analysis we have looked for an alternative therapeutic approach to hostility and aggression. Since the suppression and repression of existing aggressive tendencies yields harmful symptoms similar to those of their expression, we had to look for therapeutic ways that help to prevent the emergence of angry feelings from the very beginning. We have found a fertile point of departure for this approach in the psychology of emotions, more precisely in appraisal theory.

The constituent elements of the typical anger-appraisal (ascription of importance, ego-involvement, attachment to needs, blaming of others, exertion of power) can provide us with numerous toeholds for a therapeutic process that helps to dry out the ground on which aggression grows. For this work we present a long list of useful suggestions that have proven effective in our therapeutic work. By their implementation it becomes possible to support clients in developing other than angry feelings. Such emotional alternatives include modesty, humility, patience, sadness, joyfulness, humor, compassion, empathy, connectedness, equanimity, independence (based on interdependence), thankfulness, etc.

Working on the appraisal that leads to anger and aggression, therefore, does not only have a preventive function with respect to the negative consequences that result from it. At least equally important we find the fact that possible changes of this appraisal open up access to a number of emotions that are part of a happy and healthy life. There is evidence that "... positive emotions shorten the duration of cardiovascular arousal produced by negative emotions" (Fredrickson & Levenson 1998, p. 217); obviously positive emotions can counter the harmful effects of anger. "A cheerful heart is a good medicine" (*Bible, Proverbs* 17:22).

The therapeutic support of joy and happiness is at least as desirable as the alleviation of sorrow and pain. "The best therapists do not merely heal damage; they help people identify and build their strengths and their virtues" (Seligman 2002, p. xiv). Of these strengths and virtues Seneca speaks, with whose words we started our paper: "Man is born for mutual help ... Man desires union..."

We are convinced that this assertion provides us with a fruitful heuristic presumption — and maybe more. Since if we think

> ... that the basic nature of man is rather compassionate than aggressive, our relation to our world changes completely. If you see that other people are basically compassionate and if you do not regard them as hostile and egotistic beings, you will be relieved from many tensions and will experience confidence and a life of equanimity. In short, you will be much happier. (Dalai Lama, in Föllmi & Föllmi 2003, 5. 9.)

Empathy and compassion, however, are not only virtues in the sense of a positive attitude towards *others*. Moreover, there is neuroscientific evidence that "the very act of concern for others' well-being ... creates a greater state of well-being within *oneself*" (Goleman 2003, p. 12 — italics added).

Hence, the assertions of Seneca and the Dalai Lama do not only depict very useful heuristic presumptions, but they also make those who follow it the immediate beneficiaries. Of course you can sometimes be left stranded if you follow this advice. But in our experience the advantages prevail, and if you are sometimes stranded you will find it only half as bad, if you do not hold on to your wishes and, most of all, to your ego, but instead allow yourself to let go of those costly identifications at least in part or for some time.

As a supplement, it may be a good idea not only to follow the Dalai Lama's advice but to also assume also that other people may have similar experiences: many of them manage only in part or for some time to give up the attachment to their needs and ego; just like us it makes them vulnerable and, in consequence, sometimes angry.

One can support oneself by being attached to one's ego as little as possible. And one can support others by treating their egos as mindfully and respectfully as possible. Both are valuable contributions to prevent aggression and to give space to more beneficial emotions.

References

Als, H. (1979). Social interaction: Dynamic matrix for developing behavioral organisation. *New Directions for Child Development* 4, 21-39.

Anantananda, S. (2001). *Die Welt in meinem Kopf – Inspiration durch eine neue Wahrnehmung.* Telgte: Siddha Yoga.

Antonovsky, A. (1981). *Health, stress, and coping.* San Francisco & London: Jossey-Bass.

Antonovsky, A. (1987). *Unraveling the mystery of health: How people manage stress and stay well.* San Francisco & London: Jossey-Bass.

Asanger, R., & Wenninger, G. (Eds.) (2000). *Handwörterbuch psychologie – 2. Ausgabe, Digitale Bibliothek Band 23.* Berlin: Directmedia.

Averill, J. R. (1982). *Anger and aggression: An essay on emotion.* New York: Springer.
Averill, J. R. (1990). Inner feelings, works of the flesh, the beast within, diseases of the mind, driving force, and putting on a show: Six metaphors of emotion and their theoretical extensions. In D. E. Leary (Ed.), *Metaphors in the history of psychology* (pp. 104-132). Cambridge: Cambridge University Press.
Bakhtin, M. M. (1986). *Speech genres and other late essays* (C. Emerson & M. Holquist, Eds.). Austin: University of Texas Press.
Baron, R. A. (1976). The reduction of human aggression: A field study of the influence of incompatible reactions. *Journal of Applied Social Psychology 6/3,* 260-274.
Baron, R. A., & Ball, R. L. (1974). The aggression-inhibiting influence of nonhostile humor. *Journal of Experimental Social Psychology 10,* 23-33.
Baron, R. A., & Richardson, D. (1994). *Human aggression.* New York: Plenum.
Bauer, J. (2005). *Warum ich fühle, was du fühlst – Intuitive Kommunikation und das Geheimnis der Spiegelneurone.* Hamburg: Hoffmann & Campe.
Bauman, Z. (1995). *Life in fragments: Essays in postmodern morality.* Oxford: Blackwell.
Baumeister, R. F., Smart, L., & Boden, J. M. (1996). Relation of threatened egotism to violence and aggression: The dark side of high self-esteem. *Psychological Review 103/1,* 5-33.
Beisser, A. R. (1970). The paradoxical theory of change. In J. Fagan & I. L. Shepherd (Eds.), *Gestalt therapy now* (pp. 77-80). New York: Harper Colophon.
Berkowitz, L. (1993). *Aggression: Its causes, consequences, and control.* New York: McGraw-Hill.
Bernhardt, K. (2000). *Ein kognitives Trainingsprogramm zur Steuerung von Empörung.* Dissertation, Universität Trier.
Binderman, R. M. (1974). The issue of responsibility in Gestalt therapy. *Psychotherapy: Theory, Research and Practice 11/3,* 287-288.
Blankertz, S., & Doubrawa, E. (2005). *Lexikon der Gestalttherapie.* Wuppertal: Hammer.
Bloem, J., Moget, P., & Petzold, H. G. (2004). Aggressionsreduktion und psychosoziale Effekte: Faktum oder Fiktion? Forschung, Aggressionspsychologie, Neurobiologie. *Integrative Therapie 30/1-2,* 101-149.

Bloom, D. (2005). Laura Perls: The aesthetic of commitment. *Gestalttherapie (19/2,* 14-28.

Böhme, G. (1997). *Ethik im Kontext – Über den Umgang mit ernsten Fragen.* Frankfurt/M.: Suhrkamp.

Bower, G. H. (1981). Mood and memory. *American Psychologist 36,* 129-148.

Bräutigam, U., & Ribowski, A. (2003). *Farben der Sinne – Gelebte Rituale in Tibet / Colours of the senses: Living rituals in Tibet* (Buch mit DVD). Krefeld: Yarlung.

Buber, M. (1970). *I and Thou.* New York: Scribners.

Buck, R. (1994). The neuropsychology of communication: Spontaneous and symbolic aspects. *Journal of Pragmatics 22 3-4,* 265-278.

Burkitt, I. (1999). Relational moves and generative dances. In S. McNamee & K. J. Gergen (Eds.), *Relational responsibility: Resources for sustainable dialogue* (pp. 71-79). Thousand Oaks: Sage.

Bushman, B. J. (2002). Does venting anger feed or extinguish the flame? Catharsis, rumination, distraction, anger, and aggressive responding. *Personality and Social Psychology Bulletin 28/6,* 724-731.

Bushman, B. J., & Baumeister, R. F. (1998). Threatened egotism, narcissism, self-esteem, and direct and displaced aggression: Does self-love or self-hate lead to violence? *Journal of Personality and Social Psychology 75/1,* 219-229.

Bushman, B. J., Baumeister, R. F., & Stack, A. D. (1999). Cartharsis, aggression, and persuasive influence: Self-fulfilling or self-defeating prophecies? *Journal of Personality and Social Psychology 76/3,* 367-376.

Bushman, B. J., Baumeister, R. F., & Phillips, C. M. (2001). Do people aggress to improve their mood? Catharsis beliefs, affect regulation opportunity, and aggressive responding. *Journal of Personality and Social Psychology 81/1,* 17-32.

Bushman, B. J., Bonacci, A. M., van Dijk, M., & Baumeister R. F. (2003). Narcissism, sexual refusal, and aggression: Testing a narcissistic reactance model of sexual coercion. *Journal of Personality and Social Psychology 84/5,* 1027-1040.

Campbell, W. K., Bonacci, A. M., Shelton, J., Exline, J. J. & Bushman, B. J. (2004). Psychological entitlement: Interpersonal consequences and validation of a self-report measure. *Journal of Personality Assessment 83/1,* 29-45.

Cassidy, T. (1997). *Environmental psychology: Behaviour and experience in context*. Hove: Psychology Press.
Chodron, T. (2001). *Working with anger*. Ithaca, NY: Snow Lion.
Contrada, R. J., Leventhal, H., & O'Leary, A. (1990). Personality and health. In L. A. Pervin (Ed.), *Handbook of personality: Theory and research* (pp. 638-669). New York & London: Guilford Press.
Crick, N. R., & Grotpeter, J. K. (1995). Relational aggression, gender, and social-psychological adjustment. *Child Development 66/3*, 710-722.
Crook, J., & Low, J. (1997). *The Yogins of Ladakh: A pilgrimage among the hermits of the Buddhist Himalayas*. Delhi: Motilal Banarsidass.
Dalai Lama (1997). *Healing anger: The power of patience from a Buddhist perspective*. Ithaca, NY: Snow Lion Publications.
Dalai Lama (2001). *Ancient wisdom, modern world: Ethics for the new millennium*. London: Abacus.
Dalai Lama (2006). *Worte der Welshelt*. Kreuzlingen & München: Hugendubel & Diedrichs.
Darwin, C. (1898). *The expression of the emotions in man and animals*. New York: Appelton.
Davidson, R. J. (2000). Affective style, psychopathology, and resilience: Brain mechanisms and plasticity. *American Psychologist 55*, 1196-1214.
Dollard, J., Doob, L., Miller, N., Mowrer, O., & Sears, R. (1939). *Frustration and aggression*. New Haven: Yale University Press.
Dormann, C., Zapf, D., & Isic, A. (2002). Emotionale Arbeitsanforderungen und ihre Konsequenzen bei Call-Center-Arbeitsplätzen. *Zeitschrift für Arbeits- und Organisationspsychologie 46*, 201-215.
Dornes, M. (2006). *Die Seele des Kindes – Entstehung und Entwicklung*. Frankfurt/M.: Fischer.
Doubrawa, E., & Blankertz, S. (2000). *Einladung zur Gestalttherapie*. Wuppertal: Hammer.
Dreikurs Ferguson, E. (2000). *Motivation – A biosocial and cognitive integration of motivation and emotion*. New York & Oxford: Oxford University Press.
Dreitzel, H. P. (1995). Emotionen in der Gestalttherapie – Ihre Bedeutung und Handhabung im therapeutischen Prozess. In H. G. Petzold (Ed.), *Die Wiederentdeckung des Gefühls – Emotionen in der Psychotherapie und der menschlichen Entwicklung* (pp. 493-517). Paderborn: Junfermann.

Dreitzel, H. P. (2004). *Gestalt und Prozess – Eine psychotherapeutische Diagnostik oder: Der gesunde Mensch hat wenig Charakter* (unter Mitarbeit von Brigitte Stelzer). Bergisch Gladbach: Edition Humanistische Psychologie.

Drever, J., & Fröhlich, W. D. (1971). *Wörterbuch zur Psychologie.* München: dtv.

Ekman, P. (2003a). Darwin, deception, and facial expression. *Annals of the New York Adademy of Sciences 1000,* 205-221.

Ekman, P. (2003b). *Emotions revealed: Recognizing faces and feelings to improve communication and emotional life.* New York: Holt.

Ekman, P., & Friesen, W. V. (1974). Detecting deception from the body or face. *Journal of Personality and Social Psychology 29,* 288-298.

Epstein, M. (1995). *Thoughts without a thinker: Psychotherapy from a Buddhist perspective.* New York: Basic Books.

Esterling, B. A., Antoni, M. H., Kumar, M., & Schneiderman, N. (1990). Emotional repression, stress disclosure responses, and Epstein-Barr viral capsid antigen titers. *Psychosomatic Medicine 52/4,* 397-410.

Exline, J. J., Baumeister, R. F., Bushman, B. J., Campbell, W. K., & Finkel, E. J. (2004). Too proud to let go: Narcissistic entitlement as a barrier to forgiveness. *Journal of Personality and Social Psychology 87/6,* 894–912.

Eysenck, M. W. (1996). *Simply psychology.* Hove: Psychology Press.

Fackelmann, K. A. (1989). Child's aggression may foretell heart risk. *Science News, July 1, 1989,* p. 15.

Feinman, S. (1992). In the broad valley: An integrative look at social referencing. In S. Feinman (Ed.), *Social referencing and the social construction of reality in infancy* (pp. 3-13). New York & London: Plenum Press.

Fisher, A. (2002). *Radical ecopsychology: Psychology in the service of life.* Albany, NY: State University of New York Press.

Föllmi, D., & Föllmi, O. (Eds.) (2003). *Die Weisheit des Buddhismus Tag für Tag.* München: Knesebeck.

Ford, M. E. (1992). *Motivating humans: Goals, emotions, and personal agency beliefs.* Newbury Park, CA: Sage.

Frank, J. (1961). *Persuasion and healing: A comparative study of psychotherapy.* Baltimore & London: John Hopkins University Press.

Frech, H.-W. (2000). Gestalt im Feld – Theoretische und gesellschaftliche Herausforderungen. *Gestalttherapie 14/2,* 3-19.

Fredrickson, B. L., & Levenson, R. W. (1998). Positive emotions speed recovery from the cardiovascular sequelae of negative emotions. *Cognition and Emotion 12/2*, 197-220.
Fuhr, R., & Gremmler-Fuhr, M. (2001). Wachstum – Vom Beschwören eines Mythos zur Unterstützung von Qualität in der Gestalttherapie. In F.-M. Staemmler (Ed.), *Gestalttherapie im Umbruch – Von alten Begriffen zu neuen Ideen* (pp. 87-116). Köln: Edition Humanistische Psychologie.
Fulton, P. R., & Siegel, R. D. (2005). Buddhist and Western psychology: Seeking common ground. In C. K. Germer, R. D. Siegel & P. R. Fulton (Eds.), *Mindfulness in psychotherapy* (pp. 28-51). New York & London: Guilford.
Gaines, J. (1979). *Fritz Perls: Here and now*. Tiburon, CA: Integrated Press.
Gallagher, S. (2005). *How the body shapes the mind*. Oxford: Clarendon.
Geen, R. G., & Quanty, M. B. (1977). The catharsis of aggression: An evaluation of a hypothesis. In L. Berkowitz (Ed.), *Advances in experimental social psychology* (Vol. 10, pp. 1-37). New York: Academic Press.
Geen, R. G., Stonner, D., & Shope, G. L. (1975). The facilitation of aggression by aggresssion: Evidence angainst the catharsis hypothesis. *Journal of Personality and Social Psychology 31/4*, 721-726.
Geen, R. G. (2001). *Human aggression* (2nd edition). Buckingham & Philadelphia: Open University Press.
Gendlin, E. T. (1962). *Experiencing and the creation of meaning: A philosophical and psychological approach to the subjective*. New York: Free Press of Glencoe.
Gilligan, J. (2000). *Violence: Reflections on our deadliest epidemic*. London: Jessica Kingsley.
Goleman, D. (2003). *Destructive emotions and how we can overcome them: A dialogue with the Dalai Lama*. London: Bloomsbury.
Graumann, C. F. (1969). *Motivation*. Bern: Huber.
Grawe, K. (1998). *Psychologische Therapie*. Göttingen: Hogrefe.
Grawe, K. (2004). *Neuropsychotherapie*. Göttingen: Hogrefe.
Hafke, C. (1996). Nachdenken über den Opferbegriff. *Gestalttherapie 10/2*, 54-63.

Hansen, C. H., & Hansen, R. D. (1988). Finding the face in the crowd: An anger superiority effect. *Journal of Personality and Social Psychology 54/6*, 917-924.

Hariri, A. R., Bookheimer, S. Y., & Maziotta, J. C. (2000). Modulating emotional responses: Effects of a neocortical network on the limbic system. *Neuroreport for Rapid Communication of Neuroscience Research 11/1*, 43-48.

Harris, W. V. (2004). *Restraining rage: The ideology of anger control in classical antiquity*. Cambridge, MA: Harvard University Press.

Hicks, D. J. (1965). Imitation and retention of film-mediated aggressive peer and adult models. *Journal of Personality and Social Psychology 2/1*, 97-100.

Holodynski, M. (2006). *Emotionen – Entwicklung und Regulation* (Unter Mitarbeit von Wolfgang Friedlmeier). Heidelberg: Springer.

Houston, B. K., & Snyder, C. R. (Eds.) (1988). *Type A behavior pattern: Research, theory, and intervention*. New York: Wiley.

Huber, H. P., & Gramer, M. (1993). Cardiovasular reactivity and emotional control. In H. C. Traue & J. W. Pennebaker (Eds.), *Emotion, inhibition and health* (pp. (197-225). Seattle: Hogrefe & Huber.

Huesmann, L. R., Eron, L. D., & Yarmel, P. W. (1987). Intellectual functioning and aggression. *Journal of Personality and Social Psychology 52/1*, 232-240.

Kawachi, I., Sparrow, D., Spiro, A., Vokonas, P., & Weiss, S. T. (1996). A prospective study of anger and coronary heart disease: The normative aging study. *Circulation 94*, 2090-2095.

Kennedy, M., & Merten, R. (2006). Geld – Der Bruch eines der letzten gesellschaftlichen Tabus im Kontext von not-wendiger Selbstbehauptung und Zivilcourage. In F.-M. Staemmler & R. Merten (Eds.), *Aggression, Selbstbehauptung, Zivilcourage – Zwischen Destruktivität und engagierter Menschlichkeit* (pp. 138-158). Bergisch Gladbach: Edition Humanistische Psychologie.

Kepner, J. I. (2000). Gestalt approaches to body-oriented theory: An introduction. *Gestalt Review 4/4*, 262-266.

Kernis, M. H., Grannemann, B. D., & Barclay, L. C. (1989). Stability and level of self-esteem as predictors of anger arousal and hostility. *Journal of Personality and Social Psychology 56/6*, 1013-1022.

Khyentse, D. Rinpoche (2002). Shamatha,Vipashyana und die Natur des Geistes. In D. Wolter (Ed.), *Lebendiger Buddhismus heute* (pp. 189-(196). Bern: Scherz & Barth.
Kihlstrom, J. F. (1987). The cognitive unconscious. *Science 237*, 1445-1452.
Kitzler, R. (2006). The ontology of action: A place on which to stand for modern Gestalt therapy theory. *International Gestalt Journal 29/1*, 43-100.
Knights, W. A. (2002). *Pastoral couseling: A Gestalt approach*. New York: Haworth.
Kögler, H.-H. (1992). *Die Macht des Dialogs – Kritische Hermeneutik nach Gadamer, Foucault und Rorty*. Stuttgart: Metzler.
Köppler, P. H. (2004). *So spricht Buddha – Die schönsten und wichtigsten Lehrreden des Erwachten*. Frankfurt/M: Barth.
Kohut, H. (1972). Thoughts on narcissism and narcissistic rage. *The Psychoanalytic Study of the Child 27*, 360-400.
Krahé, B. (2001). *The social psychology of aggression*. Hove: Psychology Press.
Kubzansky, L. D., Sparrow, D., Jackson, B., Cohen, S., Weiss, S. T., & Wright, R. J. (2006). Angry breathing: A prospective study of hostility and lung function in the normative aging study. *Thorax 61*, 863-868.
Ladner, L. (2005). *Die verlorene Kunst des Mitgefühls – Psychologie und Buddhismus im Dialog*. München: Diamant.
Lakoff, J., & Johnson, M. (1980). *Metaphors we live by*. Chicago & London: University of Chicago Press.
Lakoff, G., & Johnson, M. (1999). *Philosophy in the flesh: The embodied mind and its challenge to Western thought*. New York: Basic Books.
Landy, D., & Mettee, D. (1969). Evaluation of an aggressor as a function of exposure to cartoon humor. *Journal of Personality and Social Psychology 12/1*, 66-71.
Lazarus, R. S. (1984). On the primacy of cognition. *American Psychologist 39/2*, 124-129.
Lazarus, R. S. (2001). Relational meaning and discrete emotions. In K. R. Scherer, A. Schorr & T. Johnstone (Eds.), *Appraisal processes in emotion: Theory, methods, research* (pp. 37-67). Oxford & New York: Oxford University Press.
Lee, J., & Stott, B. (1993). *Facing the fire: Experiencing and expressing anger appropriately*. New York: Bantam.

Lemerise, E. A., & Dodge, K. A. (2000). The development of anger and hostile interactions. In M. Lewis & J. M. Javiland-Jones (Eds.), *Handbook of emotions* (pp. 594-606). New York: Guilford.

Lempert, J. (2006). Gewaltberatung und Tätertherapie. In F.-M. Staemmler & R. Merten (Eds.), *Aggression, Selbstbehauptung, Zivilcourage – Zwischen Destruktivität und engagierter Menschlichkeit* (pp. (192-213). Bergisch Gladbach: Edition Humanistische Psychologie.

Lichtenberg, J. D. (1989). *Psychoanalysis and motivation*. Hillsdale, NJ: Analytic Press.

Lichtenberg, J. D., Lachmann, F. M., & Fosshage, J. L. (1992). *Self and motivational systems: Toward a theory of psychoanalytic technique*. Hillsdale, NJ: Analytic Press.

Lichtenberg, P., & Gray, C. (2006). Awareness, contacting and the promotion of democratic-egalitarian social life. *British Gestalt Journal 15/2*, 20-27.

Lorenz, K. (1967). *On aggression*. London: Methuen.

Mallick, S. K., & McCandless, B. R. (1966). A study of catharsis of aggression. *Journal of Personality and Social Psychology 4/6*, 591-596.

Manstead, A. S. R., & Fischer, A. H. (2001). Social appraisal: The social world as object of and influence on appraisal processes. In K. R. Scherer, A. Schorr, & T. Johnstone (Eds.), *Appraisal processes in emotion: Theory, methods, research* (pp. 221-232). Oxford & New York: Oxford University Press.

Manuck, S. B., Morrison, R. L., Bellack, A. S., & Polefrone, J. M. (1985). Behavioral factors in hypertension: Cardiovascular responsivity, anger, and social competence. In M. A. Chesney & R. H. Rosenman, R. H. (Eds.), *Anger and hostility in cardiovascular and behavioral disorders* (pp. 149-172). Washington, DC: Hemisphere.

Maturana, H. R., & Varela, F. J. (1987). *The tree of knowledge: The biological roots of human understanding*. Boston & London: Shambala.

McGinn, C. (1989). *Mental content*. Oxford & New York: Basil Blackwell.

McNamee, S., & Gergen, K. J. (Eds.) (1999). *Relational responsibility: Resources for sustainable dialogue*. Thousand Oaks: Sage.

Mead, G. H. (1934/(1963). *Mind, self and society – From the standpoint of a social behaviorist* (C. W. Morris, Ed.). Chicago: University of Chicago Press.

Meadows, D. L. (1972): *Die Grenzen des Wachstums – Bericht des Club of Rome zur Lage der Menschheit.* Stuttgart: Deutsche Verlags-Anstalt.

Meadows, D. H., Meadows, D. L., & Randers, J. (1993). *Die neuen Grenzen des Wachstums* Reinbek: Rowohlt.

Mehrgardt, M. (1994). *Erkenntnistheoretische Grundlegung der Gestalttherapie.* Münster & Hamburg: LIT.

Mehrgardt, M. (2005). Dialectic Constructivism: An epistemological critique of Gestalt therapy. *International Gestalt Journal 28/2*, 31-65.

Mehrgardt, M., & Mehrgardt, E.-M. (2001). *Selbst und Selbstlosigkeit – Ost und West im Spiegel ihrer Selbsttheorien.* Köln: Edition Humanistische Psychologie.

Mercier, P. (2008). *Night train to Lisbon.* London: Atlantic.

Merten, R. (2003). *Wachstum braucht Grenzen – Pädagogische, psychotherapeutische und gesellschaftliche Aspekte.* Unveröffentlichter Vortrag (Wien, 23. 5. 2003).

Mesquita, B., & Ellsworth P. C. (2001). The role of culture in appraisal. In K. R. Scherer, A. Schorr, & T. Johnstone (Eds.), *Appraisal processes in emotion: Theory, methods, research* (pp. 233-248). Oxford & New York: Oxford University Press.

Metzinger, T. (1993). *Subjekt und Selbstmodell – Die Perspektivität phänomenalen Bewußtseins vor dem Hintergrund einer naturalistischen Theorie mentaler Repräsentation.* Paderborn: Schöningh.

Miller, M. V. (1994). Elegiac reflections on Isadore From. *British Gestalt Journal 3/2*, 76-80.

Miller, P., & Sperry, L. L. (1987). The socialization of anger and aggression. *Merrill-Palmer Quarterly 33/1*, 1-31.

Miller, T. Q., Smith, T. W., Turner, C. W., Guijarro, M. L., & Hallet, A. J. (1996). A meta-analytic review of research on hostility and physical health. *Psychological Bulletin 1(19/2*, 322-348.

Montada, L. (1988). Die Bewältigung von "Schicksalsschlägen" — Erlebte Ungerechtigkeit und wahrgenommene Verantwortung. *Schweizerische Zeitschrift für Psychologie 47/2-3*, 203-216.

Morgan, W. D., & Morgan, S. T. (2005). Cultivating attention and empathy. In C. K. Germer, R. D. Siegel & P. R. Fulton (Eds.), *Mindfulness in psychotherapy* (pp. 73-90). New York & London: Guilford.

Müller, M. M. (Ed.) (1993). *Psychophysiologische Risikofaktoren bei Herz-/Kreislauferkrankungen – Grundlagen und Therapie*. Göttingen: Hogrefe.

Mummendey, A., Linneweber, V., & Löschper, G. (1984). Actor or victim of aggression: Divergent perspectives, divergent evaluations. *European Journal of Social Psychology 14/3*, 297-311.

Nell, V. (2006). Cruelty's rewards: The gratifications of perpetrators and spectators. *Behavioral and Brain Sciences 29*, 211-224.

Nichols, M. P., & Efran J. S. (1985). Catharsis in psychotherapy: A new perspective. *Psychotherapy: Theory, Research and Practice 22/1*, 46-58.

Ochsner, K. N., Bunge, S. A., Gross, J. J., & Gabrieli, J. D. E. (2002). Rethinking feeling: An fMRI study of the cognitive regulation of emotion. *Journal of Cognitive Neuroscience 14*, 1215-1229.

Olendzki, A. (2005). The roots of mindfulness. In C. K. Germer, R. D. Siegel & P. R. Fulton (Eds.), *Mindfulness in psychotherapy* (pp. 241-261). New York & London: Guilford.

Panksepp, J. (2005). *Affective neuroscience: The foundations of human and animal emotions*. New York: Oxford University Press.

Panksepp, J. (2006). The affective neuroeconomics of social brains: One man's cruelty is another's suffering. *Behavioral and Brain Sciences 29*, 234-235.

Parkinson, B. (2001). Putting appraisal in context. In K. R. Scherer, A. Schorr, & T. Johnstone (Eds.), *Appraisal processes in emotion: Theory, methods, research* (pp. 173-186). Oxford & New York: Oxford University Press.

Pennebaker, J. W. (1990). *Opening up: The healing power of expressing emotions*. New York & London: Guilford.

Perls, F. S. (1942). *Ego, hunger and aggression: A revision of Freud's theory and method*. Durban: Knox.

Perls, F. S. (1947). *Ego, hunger and aggression: A revision of Freud's theory and method*. London: Allen & Unwin.

Perls, F. S. (1969a). *Ego, hunger and aggression: The beginning of Gestalt therapy*. New York: Vintage.

Perls, F. S. (1969b). *Gestalt therapy verbatim*. Moab, UT: Real People Press.

Perls, F. S. (1973). *The Gestalt approach & Eye witness to therapy*. Palo Alto, CA: Science & Behavior Books.
Perls, F. S. (1975). Morality, ego boundary and aggression. In J. O. Stevens (Ed.), *Gestalt is* (pp. 27-37).
Perls, F. S. (1997). Gestalt therapy and cybernetics. *Gestalt 30*, 49-52.
Perls, F. S., & Baumgardner, P. (1975). *Gifts from Lake Cowichan: Legacy from Fritz*. Palo Alto, CA: Science and Behavior Books.
Perls, F. S., Hefferline, R. F., & Goodman, P. (1951). *Gestalt therapy: Excitement and growth in the human personality*. New York: The Julian Press.
Perls, L. (1992). *Living at the boundary: Collected works of Laura Perls* (J. Wysong, Ed.). Highland, NY: Gestalt Journal Press.
Perrig, W., Wippich, W., & Perrig-Chiello, P. (1993). *Unbewußte Informationsverarbeitung*. Bern: Huber.
Petzold, H. G. (1973). *Gestalttherapie und Psychodrama*. Kassel: Nicol.
Petzold, H. G. (1995). Das schulenübergreifende Emotionskonzept der "Integrativen Therapie" und seine Bedeutung für die Praxis "emotionaler Differenzierungsarbeit." In H. G. Petzold (Ed.), *Die Wiederentdeckung des Gefühls – Emotionen in der Psychotherapie und der menschlichen Entwicklung* (pp. (191-269). Paderborn: Junfermann.
Petzold, H. G. (2006). Aggressionsnarrative, Ideologie und Friedensarbeit – Integrative Perspektiven. In F.-M. Staemmler & R. Merten (Eds.), *Aggression, Selbstbehauptung, Zivilcourage – Zwischen Destruktivität und engagierter Menschlichkeit* (pp. 39-72). Bergisch Gladbach: Edition Humanistische Psychologie.
Petzold, H. G., Bloem, J., & Moget, P. (2004). Budokünste als "Weg" und therapeutisches Mittel in der körper- und bewegungsorientierten Psychotherapie, Gesundheitsförderung und Persönlichkeitsentwicklung – Transversale und integrative Perspektiven. *Integrative Therapie 30/1-2*, 24-100.
Philippson, P. (2006). Field theory: Mirrors and reflections. *British Gestalt Journal 15/2*, 59-63.
Piaget, J. (1971). *The psychology of intelligence*. London: Routledge.
Pieper, A. (2003). Individuum. In H. Krings, H. M. Baumgartner & C. Wild (Eds.), *Handbuch philosophischer Grundbegriffe* (pp. 61/1-61/8). Berlin: Xenomos.
Platon (1924). *Laches, Protagoras, Meno, Euthydemus*. London: Heinemann.

Power, M., & Dalgleish, T. (1997). *Cognition and emotion: From order to disorder.* Hove: Psychology Press.

Powers, W. T. (1973). *Behavior: The control of perception.* Chicago: Aldine.

Resnick, S. (1975). Gestalt therapy as a meditative practice. In J. O. Stevens (Ed.), *Gestalt is* (pp. 231-237). Moab, UT: Real People Press.

Revel, J.-F., & Ricard, M. (1999). *The monk and the philosopher: A father and son discuss the meaning of life.* New York: Shocken.

Roseman, I. J., & Smith, C. A. (2001). Appraisal theory: Overview, assumptions, varieties, controversies. In K. R. Scherer, A. Schorr & T. Johnstone (Eds.), *Appraisal processes in emotion: Theory, methods, research* (pp. 3-19). Oxford & New York: Oxford University Press.

Rosenberg, M. B. (2003). *Gewaltfreie Kommunikation – Aufrichtig und einfühlsam miteinander sprechen – Neue Wege in der Mediation und im Umgang mit Konflikten.* Paderborn: Junfermann.

Rosenblatt, D. (1998). Gestalt and homosexuality: A personal memoir. *British Gestalt Journal 7/1,* 8-17.

Rosenman, R. H., Brand, R. J., Jenkins, C. D., Friedman, M., Strauss, R., & Wurm, M. (1975). Coronary heart disease in the Western Collaborative Group Study: Final follow-up experience of 8.5 years. *Journal of the American Medical Association 233,* 872-877.

Roth, G. (2003). *Aus Sicht des Gehirns.* Frankfurt/M.: Suhrkamp.

Ryle, G. (1949). *The concept of mind.* New York et al.: Hutchinson.

Saner, R. (1989). Culture bias of Gestalt therapy: Made-in-U.S.A. *The Gestalt Journal 12/2,* 57-71.

Scheff, T. J. (1979). *Catharsis in healing, ritual, and drama.* Berkeley: University of California Press.

Scherer, K. R. (2001). Appraisal considered as a process of multi-level sequential checking. In K. R. Scherer, A. Schorr, & T. Johnstone (Eds.), *Appraisal processes in emotion: Theory, methods, research* (pp. 92-120). Oxford & New York: Oxford University Press.

Schmid, W. (2000). *Schönes Leben? – Einführung in die Lebenskunst.* Frankfurt/M.: Suhrkamp.

Schmitz, H. (2002). *Begriffene Erfahrung – Beiträge zur antireduktionistischen Phänomenologie.* Rostock: Koch.

Schrader, G. (1973). Anger and interpersonal communication. In D. Carr & E. S. Casey (Eds.), *Explorations in phenomenology: Papers of the Society for Phenomenology and Existential Philosophy* (pp. 331-350). The Hague: Nijhoff.
Schulze, G. (1992). *Die Erlebnis-Gesellschaft – Kultursoziologie der Gegenwart*. Frankfurt/M. & New York: Campus.
Selg, H. (1968). *Diagnostik der Aggressivität*. Göttingen: Hogrefe.
Selg, H. (1986). *Pornographie*. Bern: Huber.
Selg, H. (2000). Aggression. In R. Asanger & G. Wenniger (Eds.), *Handwörterbuch der Psychologie* (pp. 40-59). Berlin: Directmedia.
Seligman, M. E. (2002). *Authentic Happiness – Using the new positive psychology to realize your potential for lasting fulfillment*. New York: Free Press.
Seneca (1614). *The Workes of Lucius Annaeus Seneca*. London: Stansby.
Shekelle, R. B., Gale, M., Ostfeld, A.M., & Paul, O. (1983). Hostility, risk of coronary heart disease, and mortality. *Psychosomatic Medicine 45/2*, 109-114.
Siegel, D. J. (2007). *The mindful brain: Reflection and attunement in the cultivation of well-being*. New York: W. W. Norton.
Siegman, A. W. (1993). Cardiovascular consequences of expressing, experiencing, and repressing anger. *Journal of Behavioral Medicine 16/6*, 539-569.
Siegman, A. W. (1994). From type A to hostility to anger: Reflections on the history of coronary-prone behavior. Siegman, A. W., & Smith, T. W. (Eds.), *Anger, hostility and the heart* (pp. 1-21). Hillsdale NJ: Erlbaum.
Siegman, A. W., & Smith, T. W. (Eds.) (1994). *Anger, hostility and the heart*. Hillsdale NJ: Erlbaum.
Smith, T. W., Glazer, K., Ruiz, J. M., & Gallo, L. C. (2004). Hostility, anger, aggressiveness, and coronary heart disease: An interpersonal perspective on personality, emotion, and health. *Journal of Personality 72/6*, 1217-1270.
Smith, C. A., & Lazarus, R. S. (1990). Emotion and adaptation. In L. A. Pervin (Ed.), *Handbook of personality: Theory and research* (pp. 609-637). New York & London: Guilford Press.
Smuts, J. C. (1926/(1973). *Holism and evolution*. Westport, CT: Greenwood Press.

Solomon, R. C. (1980). Emotions and choice. In A. O. Rorty (Ed.), *Explaining emotions* (p. 251-281). Berkeley: University of California Press.

Spielberger, C. D., Krasner, S. S., & Solomon, E. P. (1988). The experience, expression, and control of anger. In M. P. Janisse (Ed.), *Individual differences, stress, and health psychology* (pp. 89-108). New York: Springer.

Staemmler, F.-M. (1993). *Therapeutische Beziehung und Diagnose – Gestalttherapeutische Antworten*. München: Pfeiffer.

Staemmler, F.-M. (1996). Grenze? – Welche Grenze? – Zur Problematik eines zentralen Gestalttherapeutischen Begriffs. *Integrative Therapie 22/1*, 36-55.

Staemmler, F.-M. (1997). Towards a theory of regressive processes in Gestalt therapy – On time perspective, developmental model and the wish to be understood. *The Gestalt Journal 20/1*, 49-120.

Staemmler, F.-M. (2001). Views from the clifftop. *Australian Gestalt Journal 5/1*, 67-75.

Staemmler, F.-M. (2002a). Realität und Wirklichkeit: Innen oder außen? – Zur Klärung einiger Verwirrungen an der Gestalttherapeutischen "Grenze." *Gestalt-Publikationen 37*. Würzburg: Zentrum für Gestalttherapie.

Staemmler, F.-M. (2002b). Dialogical diagnosis: Changing through understanding. *Australian Gestalt Journal 6/1*, 19-32.

Staemmler, F.-M. (2002c). "Simplistic approaches are inadequate": Book review of W. A. Knights, 2002. *International Gestalt Journal 25/2*, 135-142.

Staemmler, F.-M. (2005). Cultural field conditions: A hermeneutic study of consistency. *British Gestalt Journal 14/1*, 34-43.

Staemmler, F.-M. (2006). A Babylonian confusion?: On the uses and meanings of the term "field." *British Gestalt Journal 15/2*, 64-83.

Staemmler, F.-M., & Bock, W. (1998). *Ganzheitliche Veränderung in der Gestalttherapie* – Neuausgabe. Wuppertal: Hammer.

Staemmler, F.-M., & Merten, R. (Eds.) (2006). *Aggression, Selbstbehauptung, Zivilcourage – Zwischen Destruktivität und engagierter Menschlichkeit* [Aggression, self-assertion, and civil courage: Between destructiveness and engaged humanity]. Bergisch Gladbach: Edition Humanistische Psychologie.

Storch, M. (2006). Wie Embodiment in der Psychologie erforscht wurde. In M. Storch, B. Cantieni, G. Hüther & W. Tschacher, *Embodiment – Die Wechselwirkung von Körper und Psyche verstehen und nutzen* (pp. 35-72). Bern: Hans Huber.

Stucke, T. S. (2000). *Die Schattenseiten eines positiven Selbstbildes: Selbstwert, Selbstkonzeptklarheit und Narzißmus als Prädiktoren für negative Emotionen und Aggression nach Selbstwertbedrohungen.* Dissertation, Universität Gießen.

Tangney, J. P., Wagner, P., Fletcher, C., & Gramzow, R. (1992). Shamed into anger? The relation of shame and guilt to anger and self-reported aggression. *Journal of Personality and Social Psychology 62/4*, 669-675.

Tavris, C. (1988). Beyond cartoon killings: Comments on two overlooked effects of television. In S. Oskamp (Ed.), *Television as a social issue* (pp. 189-(197). Newbury Park, CA: Sage.

Taylor, C. (1992). *Sources of the self: The making of the modern identity.* Cambridge, MA: Cambridge University Press.

Thurman, R. A. F. (2005). *Anger.* Oxford: Oxford University Press.

Toch, H. (1983). The management of hostile aggression: Seneca as applied social psychologist. *American Psychologist 38*, 1022-1025.

Votsmeier-Röhr, A. (2004). Selbstregulierung in der Gestalttherapie. In P. Geißler (Ed.), *Was ist Selbstregulation? – Eine Standortbestimmung* (pp. 69-94). Gießen: Psychosozial.

Vygotsky, L. S. (1978). *Mind in society: The development of higher psychological processes* (M. Cole, V. John-Steiner, S. Scribner & E. Souberman, Eds.). Cambridge, MA, & London: Harvard University Press.

Walter, H.-J. P. (1999. What do Gestalt therapy and Gestalt theory have to do with each other? *The Gestalt Journal 22/1*, 45-68.

Wardetzki, B. (2000). *Ohrfeige für die Seele – Wie wir mit Kränkung und Zurückweisung besser umgehen können.* München: Kösel.

Warren, R., & Kuriychek, R. T. (1981). Treatment of maladaptive anger and aggression: Catharsis vs behavior therapy. *Corrective and Social Psychiatry and Journal of Behavior Technology, Methods and Therapy 27*, 135-139.

Weber, M. (1985). *Wirtschaft und Gesellschaft – Grundriß der verstehenden Soziologie*, Bd. 2. Tübingen: Mohr.

Werner, N. E., Bigbee, M. A., & Crick, N. R. (1999). Aggression und Viktimisierung in Schulen – "Chancengleichheit" für aggressive Mädchen. In M. Schäfer & D. Frey (Eds.), *Aggression und Gewalt unter Kindern und Jugendlichen* (pp. 153-177). Göttingen: Hogrefe.

Wertheimer, M. (1945). *Productive thinking*. New York & London: Harper & Brothers.

Wheeler, G. (1996). Characteristics of "The Cleveland School": A response to Peter Philippson. *British Gestalt Journal 5/2*, 130-132.

Wheeler, G. (2000). *Beyond individualism – Toward a new understanding of self, relationship, and experience*. Hillsdale, NJ: Analytic Press (Gestalt Press).

Wheeler, G. (2003). Contact and creativity: The Gestalt cycle in context. In M. Spagnuolo Lobb & N. Amendt-Lyon, *Creative license: The art of Gestalt therapy* (pp. 163-178). Wien & New York: Springer.

Wheeler, G. (2006). Die Zukunft der Aggression – Eine Gestalttherapeutische Meditation: Menschliche Natur, Theorie und Politik [The future of aggression: A Gestalt meditation – Human nature, theory, and politics. In F.-M. Staemmler & R. Merten (Eds.), *Aggression, Selbstbehauptung, Zivilcourage – Zwischen Destruktivität und engagierter Menschlichkeit* (pp. 14-38). Bergisch Gladbach: Edition Humanistische Psychologie.

Williams, M. A., & Mattingley, J. B. (2006). Do angry men get noticed? *Current Biology 16/11*, 402-404.

Williams, R. B., & Williams, V. P. (1993). *Anger kills: Seventeen strategies for controlling the hostility that can harm your health*. New York: Times Books.

Wirtz, U. (1989). *Seelenmord – Inzest und Therapie*. Zürich: Kreuz.

Wygotski, L. S. (1972). *Denken und Sprechen*. Frankfurt/M.: S. Fischer.

Yontef, G. M. (1991). Recent trends in Gestalt therapy in the United States and what we need to learn from them. *British Gestalt Journal 1/1*, 5-20.

Zajonc, R. B. (1984). On the primacy of affect. *American Psychologist 39/2*, 117-123.

Zinker, J. (1977). *Creative process in Gestalt therapy*. New York: Brunner/Mazel.

Zumkley, H. (1978). *Aggression und Katharsis*. Göttingen: Hogrefe.

Section 2
Time

2

The Here and Now is not What it Used to Be[1] –

The Tail of the Comet, the Face of *Janus*, and the Infinity of Possibilities

Frank-M. Staemmler

> Tempora "sunt" tria, praesens de traeteritis, praesens de presentibus, prasens de futuris.... praesens de praeteritis memoria, praesens de praesentibus contuitus, praesens de futuris expectatio.
>
> (Augustinus 1987, 640f.).[2]

---

[1] This title is a plagiarism (see Hendlin 1985), the subtitle and the subsequent text is not. I want to thank Werner Bock and Rolf Merten for their valuable remarks on previous version of the text, which was first published in Staemmler, 2001.

[2] "There 'are' three times: the present of the past, the present of the present, the present of the future.... the present of the past namely

... 187

The "here and now" is famous and infamous. Hardly any other catchword of classical Gestalt therapy has been used and misused so frequently; for many Gestalt therapists the phrase has gotten worn out to an extent that they would prefer not to use it any more. And Yontef states: "If the strict here and now were really adhered to as stated in the clichés, it would be closer to brain damage than enlightenment" (1993, 121). Ervin Polster (1985) calls the here and now a "dissociated situation" and warns not to enter the "prison of the present."[3] Petzold perceives the "here and now fixation" as a "denial strategy," which makes "classical Gestalt therapy attractive for those whose history is too bad to be looked at" (1993, 340). Gordon Wheeler criticizes the focus on the present as "figure-bound" and states "that psychotherapy (or any change induction process) is always a matter of reorganization of these structures of ground *over time* and not merely of contact figures of the moment" (1998, 3 — emphasis added).

For other more traditional colleagues[4] the here and now has central importance; some even perceive it as a "principle." The principle is: "Valuation of actuality: temporal (present versus past or future), spatial (present versus absent) and substantial (act versus symbol)" (Naranjo 1970, 50).[5] It seems reasonable to assume that the past, future and absence are undervalued in relation to the so formulated contrast. From this principle "rules" are deduced: "1. Live

---

memory; the present of the present namely immediate perception; the present of the future namely expectation."

[3] This formulation bears similarities to Sartres' "the islander ... who is locked up on the current island of his present" (1987, 165)

[4] Petzold and Orth also belong to the traditionalists in terms of their perception of Gestalt therapy. For them the here and now - be aware of the allusion to psychoanalysis: - is the "fundamental rule," which the clients in Gestalt therapy have to "submit" themselves to (1999, 17).

[5] Be aware of the repeatedly used word *"versus;"* I will return to this.

now. Be concerned with the present rather than with past or future. 2. Live here. Deal with what is present rather than with what is absent." (ibid., 49). In some places this principle still cannot be questioned with impunity. In one of my books I critically remarked on Naranjo's position that in Gestalt therapy "the here and now is sometimes confused with the be-all and end-all" (Staemmler 1993, 112), and one critic accused me of having "a somewhat disturbed relationship to the traditional concepts of Gestalt therapy" (Hahn 1995, 91).

The content of her statement of course was accurate, but not the intention of the accusation: certain traditions — including Gestalt theoretical ones — run the danger of turning into dogmas over time. One cannot continue the traditions unbroken, if one wants to acknowledge and take into account the development of one's personal experience and philosophical and scientific progress. Otherwise the traditions turn into unexamined ideology.[6] I will show in this article — in contrast to some traditions — how I understand the here and now today. For me the here and now is neither an expression of brain damage nor a principle written in stone. It contains a truth and value, which I do not want to miss, even though I believe, that both are hidden under a mountain of wrong interpretations and distortions. This mountain needs to be taken down first, before it becomes apparent what the purpose of the here and now was and still is ever since it found its way into Gestalt therapy through Jakob Moreno, through Gestalt psychology[7], and Kurt Lewin, but also Wilhelm Reich and Karen Horney (see Bocian 1992; Bock 2000; Petzold 1981). I

---

[6] Naranjo put his above quoted article in a later published book, which - on purpose or not - displays its ideological character. It is called: "Gestalt therapy — The attitude and practice of an *atheoretical* experientialism" (1993 — emphasis added).

[7] See Portele, 1999.

will also show that the here and now has gained in actuality and power through the latest psychotherapy research. But more about this later.

Misunderstandings

The "Out of Sight — Out of Mind" Misunderstanding

First I want to look at those misinterpretations and distortions Frederick Perls is often held responsible for which I do not necessarily agree with. He probably encouraged those misunderstandings through his simplifications and catchy phrases during his Esalen time. By looking at his whole work a different and more complex picture results. The gross distortions are mainly due to some of his desciples and some of his plagiarists, as one reads in Elten (1979). Elten was only able to stay in Poona, India, under great effort "completely relaxed in the here and now" with his Indian guru Shree Rajneesh. He made the here and now his motto: "Forget what happened, do not think about what will happen, live *now!*" (ibid., 208 — italics in original).

According to him he was able to follow this motto quite well when having an affair with an attractive woman. He found it more difficult to live this way when he did not have such pleasures at his disposal. So he returns from a stay in Germany to Poona for example and longs for his partner Astha who had stayed at home. He spends an evening with friends and "only after they had left I realized that they had not asked how Astha was. They are in the here and now. Those who are not here are simply not here" (ibid., 130).

I describe this incident because in it I see the first misunderstanding that I consider significant, of what the here and now can mean in a useful way. According to this interpretation it appears to mean "out of sight — out of mind": a person who is absent does not exist or count; inner connections or relationships, which go beyond the immediate contact are meaningless, superfluous or even disturbing. It reminds me of a song from that time by Crosby, Stills, Nash and Young: "If you can't be with the one you love, love the one you're with." Sometimes it may be quite nice if this becomes possible. But if this becomes a basic attitude or a goal, then this song from the hippie-time gets the questionable meaning of a sought after anterograde amnesia or a desired developmental disturbance. According to Piaget's (1971) research on "object permanence," infants learn in their first year, that an object, for example the dummy, still exists even if it is taken from their immediate perception; they start to look for it. One cannot simply "eliminate" it, by hiding it behind one's back.

But the above example is not about a simple thing, but about a human being. The "out of sight − out of mind" mentality gains particular weight in this context. The arbitrariness, vagueness, the lack of commitment to discussion, the lack of engagement with and the exchangeability of human beings, which comes across in such a stance, are to me in stark contrast to the understanding of the relationship in Gestalt therapy. Those who refer to Buber's (1958) idea of "I and Thou" or Lore Perls's (1986) "commitment," cannot mean the human - beings − disregarding carelessness and lack of respect of the so inter-preted "here and now," from which place one can neither send a penny to Africa, nor be a politically engaged opponent of nuclear power. No loving partnership can come into being nor persist on the basis of such a misinterpretation, neither can children be nourished and raised. Neither can a therapeutic relationship be maintained in this way through the inevitable and necessary crises (see Staemmler 1993).

Every real engagement, every commitment has a binding nature — one could speak of loyalty — meaning the clear decision to be available for the other person physically and psychically, not only in the given moment, but also tomorrow and the day after. Put differently, it means to be voluntarily and reliably committed, in some sense to be the same person tomorrow with the same attitudes, that I am today; in Marcels words:

> The engagement is only possible for someone who does not confuse himself with his immediate situation, who *acknowledges* the difference between himself and his situation.... A consistent phenomenology, which equates the I with his immediate present, would have to ... exclude the possibility of an engagement: How could I put someone under an obligation, who I by definition cannot know yet, because he does not yet exist? (1992, 180 — italics in original)

The "Nothing Exists Apart from the Here and Now" Misunderstanding

Another misinterpretation of the here and now with far reaching consequences, concerns the almost absurd attempt to flatly eliminate the past as well as the future by demanding concentration on the present; I remind you of the above cited quote from Naranjo: "Present *versus* past or future." Although Lore and Frederick Perls have emphasized again and again, that they especially did *not* mean this, some of their comments were time and again understood in this way. From this some almost comical situations ensued in some therapy sessions. In supervision I have seen some examples the quintessence of which I will illustrate in the following fictitious dialogue:

Client: Yesterday I met my ex-wife by accident. I did not feel good at all.
Therapist: And now?
Client: Well, she told me that she gets on well without me...
Therapist: That was yesterday. And what is happening now?
Client: Now I wanted to tell you this, because it preoccupied me the whole evening. After all we had been together for 8 years and I can't imagine that from now on I am just not important any more...
Therapist: You are still talking about yesterday. What are you noticing at the moment?
Client: I am confused, I do not know what to think about the situation...
Therapist: Formulate whole sentences, starting with "here and now I am aware..."
Client: Here and now I am aware that ... ah ... that I obviously am not important for my wife anymore...
Therapist: (interrupts) No, that is not what I mean. Please just describe what you are noticing, what you can hear, see and feel.
Client: What does this have to do with it? Well, if you think so. Well, I can hear the music next door, I see the picture at the wall, I feel that my right foot has gone to sleep.
Therapist: Okay, give your foot a voice. What is it saying?
Client: Can I say something else before? I really wanted to look at the situation with my ex-wife...

I have initially called this example "comical," because this is how *I* experience it. For the *client* such a therapy session could have been shaming, discouraging, offensive or simply useless — everything but therapeutic.

When it was applied in this reduced sense, the here and now took the shape of a denial and suppression of the issues that the client wanted to explore. This was at best ineffective, because as Erving Poster emphasized,

> the here-and-now emphasis was basically a dissociative instrument. It helped people to disconnect from the influences of their lives....By emphasizing the here and now, you get some of the same effects that hypnosis, brainwashing, and drugs do. They take you out of your context.... If you live dissociatedly by staying in the here and now, whatever advances you make may not be relevant to the situations where you would like those advances to have effect. (1990, 118f.)

By the way: many Gestalt therapists, to whom I also count myself, admit today that they have not always been supportive of their clients with such a restricted understanding of the here and now, but in some cases maybe even had a damaging effect. I believe it is appropriate within the framework of this article to express my regret about this.

Some colleagues – also here I include myself – have much too uncritically adopted certain attitudes for much too long, which we were taught by our Gestalt therapy teachers and "gurus." I believe it would be an interesting research project, to explore the motives for such lack of criticism particularly among psychotherapists. In the end zealous introjecting by abandoning one's own sensible thinking appears to be prevalent again and again also in Gestalt therapy circles. In recent years this has been particularly apparent in connection with Hellinger's "constellation work" and the connected at times naïve (see Beaumont 1998[8]), at times hair-raising, recently almost spiritistic ideology (see for example Gross and Hellinger 1999[9]; Linz and Hellinger

---

[8] Extract: "The soul is like a flower, which sometimes opens and sometimes closes itself" (ibid., 10).

[9] Extract: "The dead want to be seen, respected and then let go" (ibid., 17).

2000[10]; Mahr 1999[11]), whose intellectual level hardly presents itself as such anymore. The similarities between Perls and Hellinger regarding their pastoral-authoritarian disposition or their tendency to demagogically presented one-sidedness and simplifications is probably only one of many parallels which calls the same admirers (some of them on repeated occasion).[12] Now back to my example:

The following quote by Perls illustrates this kind of misleading thinking, which can lead to such comical practice:

> *Nothing exists except the here and now.* The *now* is the present, is the phenomenon, is what you are aware of, is that moment in which you carry around your so-called memories and your so-called anticipations. Whether you remember or anticipate, you do it *now*. The past is no more. The future is not yet. (1969, 41 − italics in original)

The beginning and end of this quote are obviously wrong. The terms "past" and "future" are put on the same logical level like the word "Martian." It would be right to say: "What is present, exists, what is past, does not exist

---

[10] Extract: "When the living turn towards them [the dead! − F.-M. St.], respect them in their dignity, ask them for their blessing, then the dead peoples' faces light up and they feel lighter" (ibid., 16).

[11] Extract: "Sometimes the living have to show the dead the consequences of their confused state of mind" (ibid., 11).

[12] In their book about "*The Myths of Psychotherapy,*" Petzold and Orth talk in this connection aptly about the "the continued effect of a 'crypto-religious' discourse of 'pastoral power'" and write: "Here also the apodictic interpretation templates of some 'systemic' approaches must be mentioned (see recently particularly Hellinger) ... , which presuppose a considerable amount of *religious zeal*, and which lack high regard for *common sense* (let alone general psychological knowledge and solid knowledge of philosophical and religious studies) as well as a *level-headed austerity*. Such phenomena must be viewed in their regressive quality: Higher authorities and powers − divine even − determine life, one entrusts oneself to them like a child and follows their impact and teachings" (1999, 219 − emphases in original).

anymore, what is in the future, does not exist yet" (Schmitz 1990, 247). However, just because an earlier *event* no longer exists and a later one has not yet occurred, one cannot dispute the past's and the future's existence as modes of time. This is exactly the flaw in Perls's reasoning. If one makes this mistake, one can also no longer speak of past or future events.

And yet time in its modes of past and present and future definitely exists. Otherwise it would not be possible here and now to remember the past and to anticipate the future. So one has to emphasize with Merleau-Ponty: "Every present includes in the end through its horizons of immediate past and nearest future the whole of all possible time" (1966, 109). Therefore the following is valid too:

> All *that is past* does no more exist, all *that's in the future* does not yet exist.... Thus we must *not* say: There *is* what existed in the past and what will exist in the future. By contrast, this is the right formulation: Some of what does not exist, belongs to the past ... and the future respectively. (Schmitz 1990, 248 — emphases added)

There is another reason why Perls's manner of speaking makes no sense. If there was only the present, if past and future did not exist, all three terms would be obsolete; there would not be any time at all. The term "time" makes sense only, if it includes[13] its three basic modi or at least the modalities of now and not-now and before and after (see Rammstedt 1975).

This may all sound like splitting hairs. But these distinctions are apparently necessary, if the afore-mentioned, regrettable misunderstandings are to be avoided: obviously

---

[13] "... in any case we can only discern present, past and future, by assuming that time *in* this difference forms a unity. In this sense the *unity* of time is the universal horizon for everything of which we can say, that it is, that it was and that it will be" (Picht 1980, 362 — original emphases).

the past and the future exist beside the here and now. The events of the past — or better: — the events of *my* past are not present *for me*[14], but I can imagine them, which means that I can remember them; the same applies to the future and the possibility of anticipation. This is indispensable for daily life because,

> the carrying out of an action plan, for example the making of a meal, would be almost impossible if one did not succeed in carrying out the separate steps in an order which helps to attain the goal. For that it is necessary to have *simultaneous awareness* of what *has* already *been done*, what *is being done* and what *will* need to *be done*. In other words: The completion of carrying out a step, the actuality of carrying out the following step and the expectation or intention to carry out the next step must be simultaneously in awareness for planned intended action to be possible. (Rusch 1991, 274 — italics in original)

The future already casts shadows on my needs, intentions, hopes, expectations, requests, questions, prayers, plans and projects[15], fears and goals, and the effects of my past are

---

[14] I correct myself here because what is past *for me* might still be present *for someone else* in this world: the car, which drove past me a few minutes ago and therefore belongs to the past for me, will for someone else who is a bit further down the road, become present right now. The modus of time in which something appears to me, also depends on the relationship that I have to the events and things (see Merleau-Ponty 1966, 468). One could talk of a psychological relativity theory: there is no absolute time. What is past for me, is present for someone else. And what is present for me, will belong to the past for my descendants. "All time, in nature as in society, seems to be specific to a given context: time is local" (Castells 1996, 429).

[15] Schmitz and Hauke aptly state: "We believe that the meaning of life is fundamentally conveyed in the experience of the surviving continuity of one's own action and the successful management of difficult situations in the framework of projects and developmental tasks. A project or plan is a system of connected actions, which are carried out throughout a certain

in fact even omnipresent. Actually my past not only exists in my reminiscences, but also in all that can be described in the broadest sense as my "memory." This entails not only the conscious and the unconscious results of psychological learning, but also for example, the adaptive achievements of my immune system or a considerable part of the "wiring" as well as the so-called synaptic weights in my nervous system (see Damasio 1994; Edelman 1987, 1989; Rosenfeld 1988).

Lore Perls (1977) attempted to say this in the following quotation from a talk she gave:

> ... emphasis on the Here and Now does not imply, as is so often assumed, that the past and the future are unimportant or nonexistent for Gestalt therapy. On the contrary, the past is ever-present in our total life experience, our memories . . . and particularly in our habits and our hang-ups ... The future is present in our preparations and beginnings, in expectation and hope, or dread and despair. (L. Perls 1992, 149f.)

In this declaration an argument repeats itself in a conspicuous way, which Kurt Lewin had already used 34 years earlier, in his 1943 paper about the "definition of the 'field at a given time.'" There he described his "principle of contemporaneity," which as it were represents the historical precursor of the "here and now." He wrote:

> One of the basic statements of psychological field theory can be formulated as follow: Any behavior or any other change in a psychological field depends only upon the psychological field *at that time*. This principle has been stressed by the field theorists from the beginning. It has been frequently misunderstood and interpreted to mean that field theorists are not interested in historical problems

---

time frame in a goal oriented way. Projects are the basis for the experienced structure of life in time" (1999, 46).

or in the effect of previous experiences. Nothing can be more mistaken. In fact, field theorists are most interested in developmental and historical problems. (1951, 45 — italics in original)

A few pages after this quote Lewin introduces the term "time perspective" with reference to Frank (1939). This term can, when looked at closely, clarify some of the misunderstandings about the here and now. Frank showed how through socialization in the course of development human behavior is integrated into new contexts with other behavior. But it is also integrated with for example values, and in this way human behavior again and again gets new meanings for the individual and society. Every stage of development has a specific "time perspective" i.e. a specific way for people to perceive themselves, their environment, their past and their future.[16] With every further day — strictly speaking even with every moment — the development proceeds and the given time perspective changes.

> In the perspective of the future the dimensions of the present are shaped by the focus of the future; but the dimensions of the past are shaped by the present which imposes upon previous events a perspective that is governed by the necessities and the values of the present. (Frank 1939, 301)

The respective present also provides the non-deceiveable as well as permanently changing perspective, through which a person views his surrounding world as well as the life behind him and ahead of him: "We stand astride time, as it

---

[16] In addition Frank discerns the different time perspectives which the same person can inhabit regarding different areas of life (like for example politics, religion, carreer, sex life, etc.) and which can extend more or less into the past and the future.

were, and, Janus-like, face[17] the future and the past, looking at once forward and backward and seeing events in both directions in a time perspective that is never fixed" (ibid., 303).

Figure 1: Janus's Head (on an ancient Roman coin)

Lewin called the concept of time perspective, which Frank had developed, the "principle of contemporaneity." The past as well as the future always exist in the way in which they appear to us from our momentary given

---

[17] Janus was, as one can look up in any encyclopedia, the classical Roman god of the public gates and passageways, of the entrances and the exits, who had, double-faced both directions in his view.

Recent studies ... cast great doubt on the primal connection with doors, and view those as derivative rather than original. Sol Altheim says: "Janus, regarded from the point of view of his linguistic formation, does not represent a concrete object, but is an abstraction. To put it more exactly, he represents a *'nomen actionis'*. Janus is the *'going.'*" (MacKay 1961, 158 — my emphases)

So Janus represents a process rather than a thing. According to the author further elaborating, he is also associated with the transitional stage from the waning to the waxing moon, with the change from the "old" to the "new" moon and then also more generally "with the notion of passage in general, especially *passage of crucial importance*" (ibid., 169 — my emphasis). The meaning of Janus contains in this respect a certain proximity to the meaning of the Greek term "*kairos*," which I will return to at the end of this article.

viewpoint and given the needs and conditions of our current situation. In this sense Lewin then formulates:

> It is important to realize that the psychological past and the psychological future are *simultaneous* parts of the psychological field existing at a given time t. the time perspective is continually changing. According to field theory, any type of behavior depends upon the total field, including the time perspective at that time, but not, in addition, upon any past or future field and its time perspectives (1951, 54 – emphasis added).

With my at any one time new, always present, time perspective my view of the past changes permanently as well as the meaning which I attribute to the future. So the present does not exist exclusively, but the present so to speak colors the other modes of time with its changing colors. From this results the only chance to change the past. The past cannot be changed as historical fact, but the interpretations and meanings which one attributes to it can be changed. (see Spence 1982). "Taking on the present, I comprehend my past differently and change it, I change its meaning and liberate myself and remove myself from it" (Merleau-Ponty 1966, 516).[18]

The Hedonistic Misunderstanding

I want only briefly to go into the third, hedonistic misunderstanding. It is about wrongly equating the intention to live *in* the here and now with the intention to only live *for* the here and now and doing this also picking the raisins out of the cake. This also has nothing to do with Gestalt therapy. In the

---

[18] Spinelli puts it like this: "*Any interpreted past event can be seen to be a means of defining both who one currently believes oneself to be as well as who one might wish to become at some future point in time*" (1996, 174 – italics in original).

introduction to "*Gestalt Therapy Verbatim*" Perls wrote specifically: "A release to spontaneity, to the support of our total personality — yes, yes, yes. The pseudo-spontaneity of the turner-onners as they become hedonistic — just, let's do something, let's take LSD, let's have instant joy, instant sensory awareness — *No*" (1969, 3 — italics in original).

Now I hope the most serious misunderstandings of the here and now have been outlined and disproved. So what does the here and now mean in a positive sense? I will try to find a new approach; while doing so the thoughts about Frank's time perspective will be useful.

Subjectivity

Talking about the here and now i.e., that in *this* moment and in *this* place something happens, means making — at first glance — a trivial statement: she or he determines a concrete point in the continuum of space and time. This occurs everyday and is nothing special, one might think. And still the here and now has not only in Gestalt therapy, but also in the history of mankind been given a special meaning again and again: lovers find happiness in it, people who meditate find eternity, those who want to forget find comfort, and those who are anxious find a moment of rest.

One can't help thinking: what do such definitely non-trivial feelings and experiences have to do with simple details about place and time? What predestines this particular place and moment to achieve such great importance?

One glance at a dictionary of linguistics helps to find a starting point to answer the question. The words "here" and "now" are so called "indexicalic" or rather "deictic" expressions — like for example the words "I" and "you." This means they are words where what they describe is completely dependent on who speaks them in what situation respectively: if I, while I am writing this text, write "I" or "you" or "here" or "now," I mean someone else and a different place and a different point in time than everybody else, who at another opportunity says the words "I" or "you" or "here" or "now." The words always stay the same, but their meaning differs so extremely as with hardly any other words (see Staemmler 1987). Although the "here and now" names something very concrete and unique at any one time, it belongs at the same time to the most abstract terms existing, because it never describes the same thing twice: the same now, the same time perspective never repeats itself, and whoever says "here," refers to a very specific place, for example to the country or the room in which he finds himself at that moment.

To carry out one of the classical exercises of Gestalt therapy, the so called "awareness continuum" (see Perls & Levitsky 1970), the client is told for a while not to do anything except describe what she or he notices from moment to moment in themselves and their environment, for example: "In this moment I feel my heart beating — now I hear a car go by — in this moment I see you laughing..." As one can see in these examples, the description of what happens at the given place does not even apply to what happens in the room in which the person is, but solely applies to what the person *experiences*, what *presents* itself to her in the respective present. In other words: the respective "here" is the place from which the awareness originates; so the "here" lies in the person herself, specifically in her nervous system or her subjective experience of where she localizes the virtual centre of her consciousness or that which she mostly calls her "I" in colloquial speech.

This center is experienced by different populations in different places. In some cultures it is put into the area of the solar plexus. The *hsin* of the Chinese, the heart of the spirit or the soul, is in the middle of the thorax. But most people in the west localize the I in their heads, onto which everything else is attached. The I sits somewhere behind the eyes and between the ears (see Watts 1980, 60).

For many people in our cultures the "here" in their experience is reduced as a rule to one place in their heads. Nevertheless, as the quotation shows, at closer examination the rest of the body is more or less included. And as — contrary to the sometimes differently used idiom in the psycho-scene — the head also belongs to the body, the respective Here is always in the body, in the "embodied mind"; it is always tied to the subjective experience of the living body — as the philosophers prefer to say in German: — tied to the *Leib*, the animated body.

The "here" refers to the respective physical self (see Waldenfels 2000) of the person who uses this word, to his specific perspective from which he perceives things, to his subjectivity. (And just like the body the subjectivity exists in time, which is why the respective perspective of the Here always also entails a time perspective; space and time are inseparably connected not only in modern physics.) The emphasis on the Here in therapy is therefore the emphasis on subjectivity, i.e. the completely unique, inimitable *way* in which the client is in the world, experiences the world and is pleasantly or unpleasantly immediately *affected* by the world. The emphasis on the here moves the "*subjective* facts" into the foreground, which Schmitz distinguishes from the "objective" depersonalized facts like this:

> Subjective facts are, so to speak, more real than objective facts; they come with the liveliness of a full-blooded and urgent realness, whereas the world, which is only constituted by objective facts, resembles a specimen, it is pale and good for stories in the third person, for a . . . life without love. (1990, 7)

But as objective facts ... are simple shadow pictures of subjective facts, the world in which I find myself as subject is rather the real world. (1997, 36)

It is in any case definitely the world which psychotherapy is aiming to research and change primarily, and the possible attempt to abstract from it in any way, is certainly not the suitable method (see Nagel 1984b) – quite the reverse, as I will explain later.

The afore-mentioned state of being personally affected, which is caused by the respective subjective facts, is *by definition* an immediately noticeable experience, which can only happen in the respective present. So I come to the "now."

Continuity

The "now" has often been interpreted as the short *point* in time between past and future, as the minimal fraction of a second. This interpretation has a catch. Because a point either extends under close scrutiny; then it is not a point anymore. The present would then not be a *point* in time but a *period* of time. Or it is an intellectual, mathematical abstraction of an infinitely small extension that tends to zero; then it does *de facto* not exist and there would also be no present.[19] The past would merge with the future. The time scientist Cramer states therefore: "This point does not exist. The assumption of a point is the biggest and most fundamental deception, even seduction of logical thinking. Insofar as there is also no point in time" (1996, 191).

---

[19] In connection with the above criticized claim that past and future do not (yet) exist (anymore), this assumption leads to absurdity which Minkowski gets to the heart of: "So the reality of time reduces itself to a nothing, which finds itself between two nothings" (1971, I, 28).

So we must imagine the present as extending. This also corresponds to our intuitive experience. The now is *lasting*. Bergson has described this very vividly:

> The real, concrete and experienced present, the present I mean when I talk about my momentary perception, necessarily lasts a certain duration. Where shall this duration be assumed? Is this duration to be found on this side of or beyond the mathematical point, which I define when I think about the present moment? It is clear that this duration is at the same time on this side and on the other side, and that what I call "my present" simultaneously meshes with my past and my future.... Therefore the psychological condition, which I call "my present" must at the same time be a perception of the immediate past and a determination of the immediate future. (1908, 139f)

In this context Husserl talks about "retention" and "protention" (1985).

What philosophers like Bergson and Husserl have long recognized has since been confirmed also empirically. The relevant research comes from Poeppel (1985). He researched the human experience of time and ascertained a kind of step sequence in which those modalities of time reoccur which I mentioned before under the keywords "now/not-now," "before/after" etc.:

> The hierarchy of the human experience of time is marked by the following elemental phenomena: experience of *simultaneity* in comparison with *non-simultaneity*, experience of *succession* or temporal *order*, experience of the *present* or the *now* and the experience of *duration*. Every later mentioned time experience pre-supposes the previously named time experience. (ibid., 17 — italics in original)

Unfortunately I do not have the space in this article to describe Poeppel's interesting experiments with this hierarchy. I can only refer to the result, which is important for my train of thought:

> The now has a temporal extension of maximum three seconds. The three seconds set the upper temporal limit. Of course contents of consciousness can also take a shorter time. This only means that we cannot exceed an upper temporal limit of the subjective present. It is probably obvious that there are individual differences for this limit. For one it may be two seconds, for the other four seconds may be the range within which the experienced appears present. As a rough average one can assume that approximately three seconds are the limit. (ibid., 63)

These approximately three seconds appear to be relatively constant interculturally because they are connected, as Poeppel suspects, to an innate timing of our nervous system.[20] One can observe this timing easily on oneself, if one for ex-ample changes between both views of an ambiguous figure:

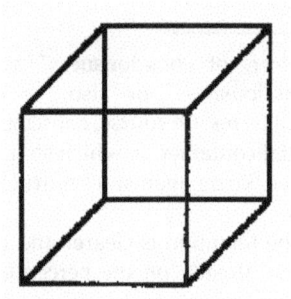

Figure 2: Necker's Dice

---

[20] The *whole* human organism with its different organs and organ systems can be perceived as a complex system of "inner clocks" (see Gooddy 1958/1959).

The range of these approximately three seconds long "windows of the present" which follow one another is not fragmented but flowing. Having seen one side of the ambiguous figure and changing to the other, the first side almost seems still present. Although it is moved into the background it has, so to speak, not yet completely disappeared. And also, with the experience of the change, the expectations develop quickly to see the second side of the figure again, while one still sees the first one. The three-seconds-now pulls a kind of "comet's tail" or a "shading" behind itself, as Husserl (1985) called it. On the other hand the respective now seems to lean, so to speak, towards the following now. One takes it for granted that it will come and under close observation one can find out that one also already roughly anticipates[21] a large part of the contents of consciousness that are expected for the near future[22].

---

[21] The term *"contents* of consciousness" as well as the wording something is *"in* consciousness" or also *"in* memory," have to be understood in colloquial terms. Of course, consciousness does not have the characteristics of a spatial container, *in* which some content can be just like food in the stomach. See Sartre against a "nutrition" or rather "digestion philosophy"(1997, 33f.).

[22] In many ways the retention is clearer and more extended than the protention; but there are already on the perception level examples for a reversed proportion:

> In typical subjects, reading text the size you are now reading [a ten point typeface — F.-M. St.], the attentional span is about 17-18 characters in width, and it is asymmetric about the point of fixation, with about 2-3 characters to the left of fixation and about 15 characters to the right. On the other hand, should you be reading Hebrew instead of English, and hence travelling from page right to page left, the attention span will be about 2-3 characters to the right and 15 to the left. (Churchland et al., 1994, 37f.).

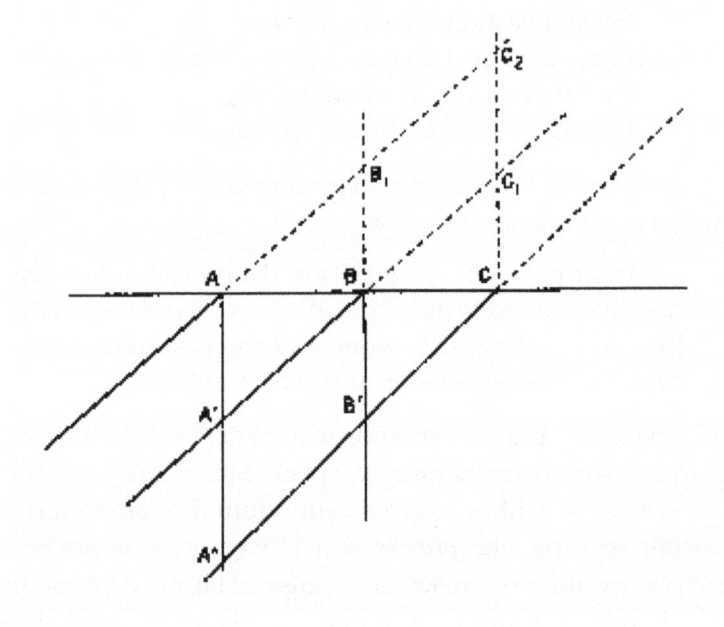

Figure 3: Husserl's Net of Time (from Lyotard 1993, 133)

The sequence of moments forms a continuity, which becomes clear with the example of listening to a tune. The individual phrases of a tune, which now are often composed in a way that they last approximately three seconds, do not remain isolated next to each other but link in consciousness to a whole and make one temporal gestalt [23] (see Staemmler 1994):

---

[23] The terms "temporal" and "non temporal" Gestalten go back to Christian von Ehrenfels. He wrote in 1890: "*Non temporal* Gestalt qualities are those whose basis can be completely provided in the concept of perception. With *temporal* Gestalt qualities subsequently only *one* element can exist in the concept of perception, while the others are available as memory pictures (or as expectations directed towards the future)" (in Weinhandl 1960, 22 — italics in original).

> Hey diddle diddle the cat and the fiddle,
> The cow jumped over the moon,
> The little dog laughed to see such fun
> And the dish ran away with the spoon.

Victor von Weizsaecker has summarized the occurances in this phenomenon as follows:

> What passes in ... time, is in the present to one half not anymore and to the other half not yet carried out. What lives in the present, is forming of the past towards the future — otherwise it is life that is not lived. (1960, 54)

The time and the stream of experience *flow*; in Gestalt therapy we correspondingly speak about the "awareness *continuum*."[24] Without such a continuum the central terms of Gestalt therapy like *process* and *change* or *development* and *growth* would not make any sense. The concept of time, which this continuum is based on, refers to Minkowski's (1971) "*continuity in becoming;*" he means a time, which not only "shades" itself backwards, but also *unfolds* forwards into the future, and nothing remains how it was or how it is at the moment (see Heraclitus, 1979: "everything flows."). In it the human being is, as Sartre says, "... nothing but his *design*, he exists only to the extent, in which he actualizes himself" (1969, 22 — my emphasis).

Erving Polster therefore suggested that "... if we replace our focus on the present with a focus of moving through time, we will be more accurate" (1985, 22). One could also say, that

---

[24] In the same sense Lewin states: "A 'situation at a given time' actually does not refer to a moment without time extension, but to a certain time-period. This fact is of great theoretical and methodological importance for psychology" (1951, 50). And: "Without altering the principle of contemporaneity as one of the basic propositions of field theory, we have to realize that ... we have to take into account in psychology ... a certain time-period" (1951, 52).

> there is an "inner time," which proceeds from the past to the future and in which the future and the past take part: the present contains contributions from the past and the near future, it is so to speak a transitional layer between the past and the future. (Florey 1991, 178)

The current moment therefore still has the privileged status of a *figure* within awareness because of its salience, but it is not "dissociated" from its connection with its predecessors and its descendants as Polster deplored. Moreover, the current moment is embedded in the back-ground of the temporal continuum in which it exists and without which it would have no meaning. Because the figure of the given moment only obtains its meaning in relation to the background of the temporal continuum.[25]

This continuum includes all modes of time — also the future, which in my view sometimes does not receive enough attention in Gestalt therapy literature. In one way or another human beings always live in expectation of the future.[26] When that is not the case anymore death results, as Heidegger in connection with his term "care" has so convincingly demonstrated. He sees it as a "structure of care,"

> in Dasein there is always something still outstanding, which, as a potentiality-for-Being for Dasein itself, has not yet become "actual". . . . But as soon as Dasein "exists" in such a way that absolutely nothing more is still

---

[25] In this context I believe Perls et al. suggested definition of "therapy as Gestalt-analysis" has its place: "The therapy, then, consists in analyzing the internal structure of the actual experience . . . By working on the unity and disunity of this structure of the experience here and now, it is possible to remake the dynamic relations of the figure and ground until the contact is heightened, the awareness is brightened and the behavior is energized" (1951, 232).

[26] Even "hopelessness, for instance, does not tear Dasein away from its possibilities, but is only one of its own modes of *Being towards* these possibilities" (Heidegger 1962, 279).

outstanding in it, then it has already for this very reason become "no-longer-Being-there" ... Its Being is annihilated when what is still outstanding in its Being has been liquidated. (1962, 279f.)

But the experience of a temporal continuum is only possible with the help of memory, which connects the respective moments with each other.

Memory

The continuity of our experience is ensured in that there is a connection regarding content, a semantic integration of the different contents of consciousness. What is respectively represented in one "window of the present," and what is represented in the next, depend on each other in terms of content (Poeppel, 1989, 15).[27]

This semantic integration though would not be possible without memory, whose status in the here and now I will characterize in the following:

Our memory belongs to the most complex and to a great extent not yet researched cognitive structures. What I can say about this here is furthermore necessarily extremely simplified and geared to the purpose I follow. Roughly speaking the memory has different levels, which can keep information of differing complexity available for varying lengths of time. "For example, each sensory system has one or more temporary buffers. These aid in perception, allowing the system

---

[27] The so-called formal disturbances of thinking, which can be observed in the course of a psychosis, suggest a decay of this integration (see Heimann 1989). Luis Bunuel, said once: "One must lose one's memory once, and be it only in little portions, to realize that the memory determines our life. Life without memory is no life. . . . Our memory is our coherence, our rationality, our emotion and even our action. Without it we are nothing" (quoted from Schmidt 1991, 7).

to compare what it is seeing or hearing now to what it saw or heard a moment ago" (LeDoux 1996, 270).

This is the first step of the "semantic connection"[28] which Poeppel mentions, but this is not all. The buffers are a kind of ultra-short-term memory; they are connected with the working memory (also called short term memory), by "containing"

> the stuff we are currently thinking about or paying attention to. But working memory is not a pure product of the here and now. It also depends on what we know and what kinds of experiences we've had in the past. In other words, it depends on long-term memory. (LeDoux 1996, 270)

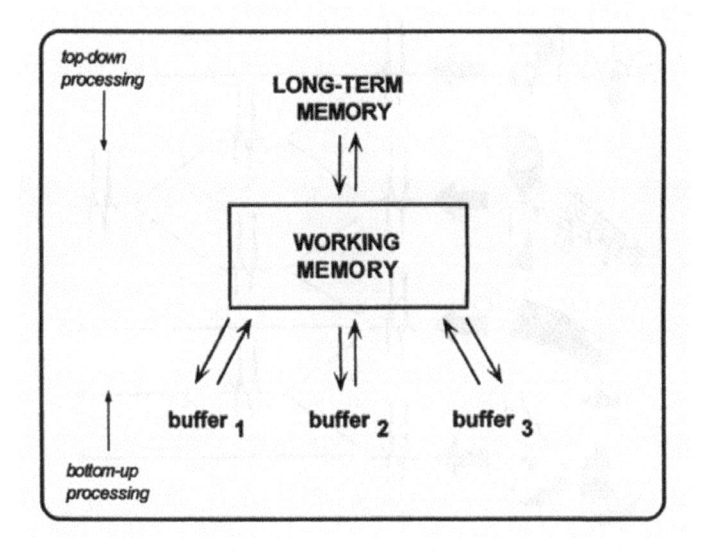

Figure 4 (from Ledoux 1996, 273)

---

[28] If *semantic* processes are necessary for the production of continuity of experience then that means that already on this level the term *meaning* becomes relevant (see Ruhnau 1996, 205; Staemmler 1999c).

Without the comparison between working- and long-term memory we could not *discern*, what we perceive, and we also could not *name* it. Because to recognize something means, to perceive it *as* something (see Heidegger 1962), and this in turn means to perceive it as part of a certain type or category.[29] Therefore "recognizing ... only happens, when the 'sensory impressions' are tied together with contents of memory" (Florey 1991, 171). And one can only name the recognized if the belonging word from the language memory is activated.

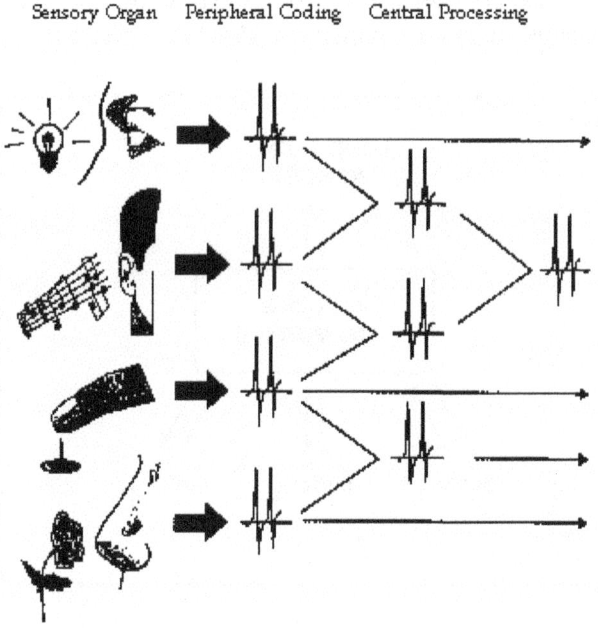

Figure 5: Neutrality of Neural Code (from Roth 1995, 81)

---

[29] Schmitz emphasizes, "that the phenomenologist not only has to take notice of something, but also has to acknowledge something *as* something, as a case of something from a certain point of view, and that this presupposes categories, under which the phenomena can be subsumed" (1997, 19 — italics in original).

Perception is therefore not a process that in the literal sense can be viewed as "depiction" of an outer reality in the mind. Perception is rather a *hermeneutic*, an interpretative and meaning giving process (Heelan 1983; Heidegger 1953; Roth 1991a, 1991b; Scheurle 1984), during which the excitations delivered from the sense organs are several times transformed by the nervous system and considerably expanded and enhanced. Many people do not know what the physiology of the senses has taught for a long time: our different sense organs all transmit the *same* kind of information to our brain, namely certain electrical impulses, which look the same on the nerves behind the ears and on the nerves behind the eyes; this is called the "neutrality of the neural code" (See Figure 5).

The signals, which come from the sense organs, "are partly separately passed on in the brain, partly processed together. From the composition of the neuronal signals alone their meaning can not be concluded" (Roth 1995, 81). The meanings develop only in the further mental processes and assume a range of additional information. These enhancements of course originate from what the brain has available in terms of information, i.e. from the memory. In his book with the characteristic title *The Interpreted World* Spinelli wrote:

> Phenomenologists point out a basic *invariant* relationship that exists between the real world and our conscious experience of it. Unable to bracket this relationship, we are forced to acknowledge, through it, the undeniable role of interpretation, which lies at the heart of all our mental experience. (1989, 12 − italics in original)

The enhancements and interpretations, which are part of every perception process prove to be extremely useful. Without them life could be hardly coped with, because our cognitive system would otherwise have to do work again and again which would hardly leave it capacity for the many other requirements of daily life (see Hejl 1991, 302). "Perception is itself an extremely knowledge-rich cognitive skill, which evolves through development and through experience" (McClelland 1995, 141); those who have looked at an ultrasound picture once without the necessary experience and only saw undefined shadows know what is being talked about.[30] A complementary example provides the futile attempt of an experienced reader to *see* a text without *reading* it. Two well-known cognitive researchers have once reduced this to a concise common denominator: "What you see, if you see something, depends on what kind of thing it is, that you see. But as what you see, it depends on what you know about the thing that you see" (Fodor & Pylyshyn 1981, 189).

In daily life one does not have a realistic idea of how quantitatively the input coming from the environment relates to the added input from one's own brain within the perception process. The brain researcher from Bremen Gerhard Roth calculated the following:

> For every neuron which processes primary sensory data, about one hundred thousand neurons process this "information" further, compare it with past experience and use it to construct cognitive reality. We can say without exaggerating that the *memory is our most important sense organ*. (1987, 280 — my emphasis; see also 1995, 111)

In view of such facts Nobel prize-winning neuro-scientist Gerald Edelman even named one of his books *The Remembered Presence* (1989). In addition to this there is also the fact that this mental process of perception naturally takes

---

[30] Also intercultural comparisons can illustrate this: in some cultures for example things or living beings depicted on photographs are not recognized as such, in other cultures depicted living beings are despite their two-dimensionality taken as being alive (see Deregowski 1973).

time − approximately 0.5 to 1 second (see Libet et al. 1983), which means, "that the present aware perception has as content a past event and that the whole perceived world belongs to the past which does not exist (any more) in the moment of the subjective present" (Florey 1991, 176).

So from the assumption of an isolated here and now and the naïve realistic[31] idealization of the pure "immaculate perception"[32] (Nietzsche), still to be found in Gestalt therapy writings, hardly anything remains. And under close observation this is right, as without the interpretation processes between sensory input and behavior reaction we would not have any freedom but would be pure stimulus-response-machines. And this would mean, "we would surely be tyrannized by the here and now − imprisoned by what is" (Gregory 1973, 63).

But this is fortunately not the case. Because we can also *choose* what we want to pay attention to and this leads to

---

[31] Tholey (1986) has shown with important reference to Bischof (1966) that a critical-realistic position fits better to a phenomenological as well as Gestalt theoretical thinking. This *epistemological* position does of course not contradict people *in their day to day awareness* behaving like naïve realists: "Mental presentations are being activated so fast and reliably, that the meta-representational function which represents them and makes them *contents of consciousness,* does not grasp their construction process anymore. [Footnote: It may also be that this meta-representational registration does not succeed because it is already not 'planned for' in the functional archi-tecture of the brain.] Therefore presentations (but also other mental states produced by very fast operations) are embedded not as *constructs,* but as *objects* or 'objective' characteristics in the current model of reality. This rep-resentational characteristic of human nervous systems produces a psycho-logical feature which could be described as *naïve realism of experience* or *illusion of actuality*" (Metzinger, 1993, 249 − original emphases).

[32] Alluding to Kant, Churchland et al. phrase "A critique of the pure vision" and ascertain: "The idea of 'pure vision' is a fiction ... that obscures some of the most important computational strategies used by the brain" (1994, 23).

another important connection between current experience and memory: imagine you drive your car to work. As long as traffic is normal, you are in a state of consciousness which can almost be described as a light trance. Maybe you think of your imminent schedule or you are humming a tune from the radio. But no sooner than the car in front of you makes an *unexpected* move you will be wide-awake and react with full concentration. The car in front has deviated from the expectations of "normal behavior," which have built up in your memory during the previous minutes or even during your whole life as a driver. With your swift reaction to the critical traffic situation you have also not only activated and applied a whole range of previously acquired knowledge about how cars accelerate and slow down, but you also activated and applied complex motor movement patterns from your memory. Now traffic is normal again and you look at your clock on the dashboard of your car. This you can also only do because your memory gives you the information that there is a clock in your car at all and where it is (see Desimone et al. 1994, 75f).

The sequence of such examples could be continued endlessly. They all show one thing very clearly: sayings like "lose you mind and come to your senses" (Perls, 1969, 69) are unrealistic and unrealizable nonsense. Their value lies solely in that they present with embarrassing clarity what happens if you try to follow them.

One has to therefore stress that one could not do very much with "pure" sensory stimuli in the here and now without the experience from the past stored in the memory. Phrasing it like this I must immediately add: really one cannot say that the past in the usual sense of the word is "stored" in memory. Because the human memory, or rather the human brain, does not work like a computer, on whose hard disc certain data is put down physically and can be recalled when needed in the same form in which it was once stored. One cannot even apply the often-used differentiation between hardware and software:

> The brain is not just the hardware; the brain is the hardware *and* the software. In fact, it is almost impossible to separate the two.... The brain is clearly not programmed by lists of instructions. The fact is that most of the things we do are carried out by routines that we have learned by experience. (Sejnowski 1995, 217 — italics in original)

These "routines" are in connection with Bartlett (1932/1995), also called "schemata"[33] by many researchers. These are only different descriptions for the habitual behavior-, experience and thinking patterns, which everybody knows about themselves and which when they become unproductive for the person in connection to their needs are the subject matter of therapeutic work. For therapy it is of utmost importance that one is not dealing with computer-like beings, but with human beings who are just not "programmed by lists of instructions," whose parts one could change when required. The memory contents or schemata are not put down in some solid shape, even if their existence depends partly on the grown connections of nerve fibres.[34] One could almost say on the contrary: they are not "put down" anywhere, because they are based on neuronal patterns of consciousness which do not exist as long as they are not currently *produced*. So Iran-Nejad and Homaifar define a schema expressively as "a living pattern of consciousness ..., which can only exist as long as it is

---

[33] Bartlett himself did not like this term very much (see ibid., 200f.).
[34] But these are changeable up into old age (see Damasio 1994, 160; Edelmann 1987; Gehde & Emrich 1998, 984)!

produced by the respective activity of the brain and maintained as a whole" (1991, 228).

Process Activation[35]

This means: "In fact, if we consider evidence rather than presupposition, remembering appears to be far more decisively an affair of construction rather than one of mere reproduction" (Bartlett 1932/1995, 205). And: "Memories exist in no other place and at no other time than *now* in the cognitive system" (Schmidt 1991, 35 — italics in original). This has far-reaching consequences. Because if a memory depends on the current production of a specific neuronal pattern of excitation, so it is under no circumstances independent of the situation in which the remembering person just is, because this situation is also represented in the shape of neuronal patterns of excitations. The different patterns of excitation subsequently overlie and influence one another mutually. Grawe has summarized the facts succinctly:

> The contents of memory do not exist in the shape of fixed, invariant structures, but they are ... being (re)constructed respectively newly under the influence of the current conditions of the context, i.e. simultaneously activated other patterns of excitation (perception, ideas, moods). Also, remembering is to be understood as an active construction process ... remembering is not a true depiction of what has been, but remembering is both a product of what was initially perceived and the influences of the current situation in which remembering happens.... What a patient tells us about his life story would have to be viewed as ... a threefold transformation of the actual initial event:

---

[35] I gave a more detailed description of this "effective factor" somewhere else (see Staemmler 1999b).

– It would be transformed by the subjective interpretation of the event at the original point in time, which does not have to coincide with the "objective" event;
   – it would be influenced by the function which his present account has in the framework of his self description with the therapist,
   – and it would be transformed by the influence of his memory through the present context. (1998, 230)

I do not know whether you have noticed already: the here and now, the quantitative meaning of which as compared to memory we had to qualify so strongly before, has now, by talking about memory – virtually through the neuro-scientific back door – come back to the forefront. Lewin's position, "that the psychological field which exists at a given time contains also the views of that individual about his future and past" (1951, 53), finds a similarly clear confirmation in modern research as some of Perls's phrasing, like for example this one:

   For me, the present includes a childhood experience, if it is vividly remembered now; it includes a noise on the street, an itch on my cheek, the concepts of Freud and the poems of Rilke, and millions of more experiences whenever and to whatever degree they spring into existence, into *my* existence in the moment. (1975, 57 – italics in original)[36]

It is important to take the following psychological facts into account, if one intends to exert therapeutic influence on those schemata, which are dissatisfying for the client: the human memory consists so to speak of different

---

[36] If one takes this seriously, important consequences result for dealing with regressive processes or the understanding of so called "early disturbances;" I have talked about this in other places (see Staemmler 1997; 2000).

"departments" (see for example Goschke 1996). One of the most important distinctions is between "explicit" and "implicit" memory, which I will look at as an example. From the explicit memory the contents that a person can talk about explicitly can be recalled, like the name says. With the implicit — sometimes also called "procedural" — memory this is not the case. But particularly these contents are often decisive for those habitual ways of behavior and experience, the schemata, which are the central subject of therapeutic work. In Neisser's words: "In procedural memory the past modulates what we do in the present without standing apart from it" (1988, 47).

As shown before, memory contents do not "exist" in the narrow sense, as long as the respective patterns of excitation are not activated. This has an obvious as well as a momentous consequence: *a schema can only be influenced when it is activated.* This does not just happen if a person talks about it explicitly, because in talking the person primarily activates her *explicit* memory contents.

> But one can resurrect the past. One can experience a situation from the past in the same brightness as if it happened in the here and now; this means one can recreate the past, revive it ... As far as this is possible the past stops being past, it *is* the here and now. One can also experience the future as if it was the here and now. This happens when a future situation is so completely anticipated in one's consciousness that it only "objectively" belongs to the future, i.e. as an outer fact, not in the subjective experience. (Fromm 1979, 125 — italics in original)

Therefore what psychotherapy researcher Grawe emphasizes as his most important results is valid:

The conclusion that comes to light is something of a paradox: As a therapist one has to evoke what one wants to remove, to be able to remove it or to change it (1998, 242).[37]

Conversations about psychological processes or problems, which remain pure contents and are not transformed in process events do not effect any change (ibid., 128).

However, "process events" are nothing but the "events in the here and now," the "immediate subjective experience" or "awareness," as we say in Gestalt therapy. We foster this awareness by understanding the non-verbal and para-verbal expressions of our clients, which they are generally not even aware of, but they are "implicit" and thus provide access to the existing schemata. Further we then direct our clients' attention to them with suitable replies and feedback, and we try to elucidate and influence them in their awareness by suggesting certain activities (for example "experiments" or "home work" — see Staemmler 1999a).[38]

Exactly this therapeutic strategy has been thoroughly empirically researched under the name "experiential confrontation":

> In a meta-analysis of all so far researched process-outcome-connections of Orlinksy, Grawe and Parks (1994) "experiential confrontation" was found to be one of the most effective therapeutic interventions in general. Here the therapist confronts the client with his presently happening experience and behaviour. He directs attention onto what is being procedurally activated and turns it into content. There is a lot to be said for this being the most

---

[37] Which Gestalt therapist does not feel reminded of Beisser's "paradoxical theory of change" (see Beisser 1970)?

[38] I do not need to elaborate that this influence is not supposed to happen in a lecturing or manipulative way.

effective way to create new consciousness[39] for the patient's experience and behavior. (Grawe 1998, 132)

I think it has become clear that it cannot be about playing out the past and the future against the present and vice versa. Rather for effective psychotherapy it is important to support clients to perceive and experience what they talk about and what they currently experience holistically as much as possible. And for this it is useful to take seriously those psychological contents, which are represented in the actual psychological field of the client and which refer to the past and the future — so seriously that one supports the clients to imagine them in their whole present meaning, to bring them into the here and now. In this sense I cite Perls once again:

> By no means do I deny that everything has its origin in the past and tends to further development, but what I want to bring home is, that past and future take their bearings continuously from the present and have to be related to it. Without the reference to the present they become meaningless. (1947, 93)

Kairos

Those knowing Gestalt therapeutic work will know what sometimes surprising moments can take place in the course of a therapeutic process accompanied in this way: unexpected, intensive feelings can develop, past events can appear in a new light and so far undiscovered future perspectives can open up. These are the moments that Balint (1968) calls the "new beginning." The ancient Greeks named these moments *kairos*. They meant that favorable moment of fateful consequence in which the person finds himself mostly

---

[39] In Gestalt therapy one mainly talks about awareness.

unexpectedly, and which he must recognize as an important chance for his future life and use spontaneously without much hesitating and vacillating. In such moments he can and must decide what to do or not to do. Only

> in the respective present one can make a beginning, to give life a new direction and to begin with the realization of possibilities. The present alone is the time of change, and yet she is also the bottleneck of time, because the possibilities must go through this *eye of a needle* of time to become reality. (Schmid 1998, 357 – italics in original)

The "eye of a needle" is the present, the current moment, in which one can decide and act. The person, who Sartre defines as "an infinity of possibilities" (1987, 190) regarding his respective future, must choose, which of those is right for him now. And he must put them into action. Often "… it is not enough … to simply decide to be what one is anyway or what one has become" (Boehme 1997, 116). Moreover it is often necessary to take the risk of failure and to look towards the future not only with anxiety but also with courage.

This is similarly true in human encounters – "I and thou, here and now" – should get a chance to succeed: it takes "work and courage" (Staemmler 1985). Because "the present is the time to be met" (Haeffner 1996, 26), and "the real and fulfilled (present) exists only in so far as there is presence, meeting and relationship" (Buber 1958, 16):

> He who cannot … stand on the threshold of the moment, who cannot stand in one place like a goddess of victory without dizziness and fear, he will never know what happiness is, and worse: He will never do what makes others happy. (Nietzsche 1930, 103)

References

Augustinus (1987). *Bekenntnisse* — Zweisprachige Ausgabe. Frankfurt/M.: Insel.
Balint, M. (1968). *The basic fault: Therapeutic aspects of regression.* London: Tavistock Publications.
Bartlett, F. C. (1932/1995). *Remembering: A study in experimental and social psychology.* Cambridge: Cambridge University Press.
Beaumont, H. (1998). Die Entbindung der Mütter. *ZIST-Programm* Januar-Juni 1999.
Beisser, A. R. (1970). The paradoxical theory of change. In J. Fagan & I. L. Shepherd (Eds.), *Gestalt therapy now* (pp. 77-80). New York: Harper Colophon.
Bergson, H. (1908). *Materie und Gedächtnis — Essays zur Beziehung zwischen Körper und Geist.* Jena: Diederichs.
Bischof, N. (1966). Erkenntnistheoretische Grundlagenprobleme der Wahrnehmungspsychologie. In W. Metzger (Ed.), *Handbuch der Psychologie in 12 Bänden, Vol. I/1: Allgemeine Psychologie: Der Aufbau des Erkennens: Wahrnehmung und Bewußtsein* (pp. 27-78). Göttingen: Hogrefe.
Bocian, B. (1992). Karen Horney — Eine Skizze zu Leben, Werk und zur Bedeutung fur die Gestalttherapie. *Gestalttherapie* 6/1, 5-14.
Bock, W. (2000). Der Glanz in den Augen — Wilhelm Reich als ein Wegbereiter der Gestalttherapie. In B. Bocian & F.-M. Staemmler (Eds.), *Gestalttherapie und Psychoanalyse — Berührungspunkte — Grenzen — Verknüpfungen* (pp. 109-141). Göttingen: Vandenhoeck & Ruprecht.
Böhme, G. (1997). *Ethik im Kontext — Über den Umgang mit ernsten Fragen.* Frankfurt/M.: Suhrkamp.
Buber, M. (1958). *I and thou.* New York: Scribner & Sons.
Castells, M. (1996). *The information age — Economy, society and culture, Vol. 1: The rise of the network society.* Malden, MA, & Oxford: Blackwell.
Cramer, F. (1996). *Grundlegung einer allgemeinen Zeittheorie.* Frankfurt/M.: Insel.
Churchland, P. S., Ramachandran, V. S., & Sejnowski, T. J. (1994). A critique of pure vision. In: C. Koch & J. L. Davis, J. L. (Eds.), *Large-scale neuronal theories of the brain* (pp. 23-60). Cambridge, MA, & London: Bradford & MIT Press.

Damasio, A. R. (1994). *Descartes' error: Emotion, reason and the human brain*. New York: Putnam's Son.
Deregowski, J. B. (1973). Illusion and culture. In R. L. Gregory & E. H. Gombrick (Eds.), *Illusion in nature and art* (pp. 160-191). London: Duckworth.
Desimone, R., Miller, E. K., & Chelazzi, L. (1994). The interaction of neural systems for attention and memory. In: C. Koch & J. L. Davis, J. L. (Eds.), *Large-scale neuronal theories of the brain* (pp. 75-91). Cambridge, MA, & London: Bradford & MIT Press.
Edelman, G. M. (1987). *Neural Darwinism: The theory of neuronal group selection*. New York: Basic Books.
Edelman, G. M. (1989). *The remembered present − A biological theory of consciousness*. New York: Basic Books.
Elten, J. A. (Swami Satyananda) (1979). *Ganz entspannt im Hier und Jetzt − Tagebuch über mein Leben mit Bhagwan in Poona*. Reinbek: Rowohlt.
Florey, E. (1991). Gehirn und Zeit. In S. J. Schmidt (Ed.), *Gedächtnis − Probleme und Perspektiven der interdisziplinären Gedächtnisforschung* (pp. 170-189). Frankfurt/M.: Suhrkamp.
Fodor, J. A., & Pylyshyn, Z. W. (1981). How direct is visual perception? Some reflections on Gibson's "ecological approach," *Cognition 9*, 139-196.
Frank, L. K. (1939). Time perspectives. *Journal of Social Philosophy 4*, 293-312.
Fromm, E. (1979). *Haben oder Sein − Die seelischen Grundlagen einer neuen Gesellschaft*. Munchen: DTV.
Gehde, E., & Emrich, H. M. (1998). Kontext und Bedeutung − Psychobiologie der Subjektivität im Hinblick auf psychoanalytische Theoriebildungen. *Psyche 52/9-10*, 963-1003.
Gooddy, W. (1958/1959). Time and the nervous system − The brain as a clock − Parts 1/2. *The Lancet* 31. 5. 1958, 1139-1144; 26. 12. 1959, 1155-1156.
Goschke, T. (1996). Lernen und Gedächtnis − Mentale Prozesse und Gehirnfunktionen. In G. Roth & W. Prinz (Eds.) (1996), *Kopf-Arbeit − Gehirnfunktionen und kognitive Leistungen* (pp. 359-410). Heidelberg: Spektrum.
Grawe, K. (1998). *Psychologische Therapie*. Göttingen: Hogrefe.
Gregory, R. L. (1973). The confounded eye. In R. L. Gregory & E. H. Gombrick (Eds.), *Illusion in nature and art* (pp. 49-96). London: Duckworth.

Gross, B., & Hellinger, B. (1999). Opfer und Täter. *Praxis der Systemaufstellung 1*, 15-21.
Häffner, G. (1996). *In der Gegenwart leben – Auf der Spur eines Urphänomens*. Stuttgart: Kohlhammer.
Hahn, A. (1995). Rezension von Frank-M. Staemmler: Therapeutische Beziehung und Diagnose – Gestalttherapeutische Antworten. *Gestalttherapie 9/2*, 91-92.
Heelan, P. A. (1983). Perception as a hermeneutical act. *Review of Metaphysics 37*, 61-75.
Heidegger, M. (1962). *Being and time*. Oxford: Basil Blackwell.
Heimann, H. (1989). Zerfall des Bewußtseins in der Psychose. In E. Pöppel (Ed.), *Gehirn und Bewusstsein* (pp. 33-43). Weinheim: VCH.
Hejl, P. M. (1991). Wie Gesellschaften Erfahrungen machen oder Was Gesellschaftstheorie zum Verständnis des Gedächtnisproblems beitragen kann. In S. J. Schmidt (Ed.), *Gedächtnis – Probleme und Perspektiven der interdisziplinären Gedächtnisforschung* (pp. 293-336). Frankfurt/M.: Suhrkamp.
Hendlin, S. J. (1985, unpublished). *Gestalt therapy – The here and now is not what it used to be*.
Heraclitus (1979). *The art and thought of Heraclitus – An edition of the fragments with translation and commentary* (C. H. Kahr, Ed.). Cambridge: Cambridge University Press.
Husserl, E. (1985). *Texte zur Phänomenologie des inneren Zeitbewußtseins (1893-1917)* – Herausgegeben und eingeleitet von R. Bernet. Hamburg: Meiner.
Iran-Nejad, A., & Homaifar, A. (1991). Assoziative und nichtassoziative Theorien des verteilten Lernens und Erinnerns. In S. J. Schmidt (Ed.), *Gedächtnis – Probleme und Perspektiven der interdisziplinären Gedächtnisforschung* (pp. 206-249). Frankfurt/M.: Suhrkamp.
LeDoux, J. E. (1996). *The emotional brain: The mysterious underpinnings of emotional life*. New York, NY: Simon & Schuster.
Lewin, K. (1951). *Field theory in social science*. New York: Harper & Brothers.
Libet, B., Gleason, C. A., Wright, E. W., & Pearl, D. (1983). Time of conscious intention to act in relation to onset of cerebral activity (readiness-potential) – The unconscious initiation of a freely voluntary act. *Brain 106*, 623-642.

Linz, N., & Hellinger, B. (2000). Der Schaffensprozess – Blick in die Werkstatt zum 75. Geburtstag von Bert Hellinger, nachgefragt von Norbert Linz. *Praxis der Systemaufstellung* 2, 11-18.
Lyotard, J.-F. (1993). *Die Phänomenologie.* Hamburg: Junius.
MacKay, L. A. (1961). Janus. *University of California Publications in Classical Philology* 15, 157-181.
Mahr, A. (1999). Wie Lebende und Tote einander heilen können. *Praxis der Systemaufstellung* 1, 8-14.
Marcel, G. (1992). *Metaphysisches Tagebuch 1915-1943 –* Ausgewählt und herausgegeben von Siegfried Fölz. Paderborn: Schöningh.
McClelland, J. L. (1995). Toward a pragmatic connectionism. In P. Baumgartner & S. Payr (Eds.), *Speaking minds: Interviews with twenty eminent cognitive scientists* (pp. 131-144). Princeton, NJ: Princeton University Press.
Merleau-Ponty, M. (1966). *Phänomenologie der Wahrnehmung.* Berlin: de Gruyter.
Minkowski, E. (1971). *Die gelebte Zeit, Vol. 1: Über den zeitlichen Aspekt des Lebens; Vol. 2: Über den zeitlichen Aspekt psychopathologischer Phänomene.* Salzburg: Otto Müller.
Nagel, T. (1984a). *Über das Leben, die Seele und den Tod.* Königstein/Ts.: Hain.
Nagel, T. (1984b). Subjektiv und Objektiv. In: T. Nagel, *Über das Leben, die Seele und den Tod.* Königstein/Ts.: Hain.
Naranjo, C. (1970). Present-centeredness: Technique, prescription, and ideal. In J. Fagan & I. L. Shepherd (Eds.), *Gestalt therapy now* (pp. 47-69). New York: Harper Colophon.
Naranjo, C. (1993). *Gestalt therapy – The attitude and practice of an atheoretical experientialism.* Nevada City, CA: Gateways.
Neisser, U. (1988). Five kinds of self-knowledge. *Philosophical Psychology* 1/1, 35-59.
Nietzsche, F. (1930). *Unzeitgemäße Betrachtungen.* Stuttgart: Kröner.
Orlinsky, D. E., Grawe, K., Parks, B. K. (1994). Process and outcome in psychotherapy – Noch einmal. In A. E. Bergin & S. L. Garfield (Eds.), *Handbook of psychotherapy and behavior change,* 4th edition (pp. 270-376). New York: John Wiley & Sons.
Perls, F. S. (1947). *Ego, hunger and aggression.* London: Allen & Unwin.
Perls, F. S. (1969). *Gestalt therapy verbatim.* Moab, UT: Real People Press.

Perls, F. S. (1975). Theory and technique of personality integration. In J. O. Stevens (Ed.), *Gestalt is* (pp. 45-68). Moab, UT: Real People Press.

Perls, F. S., Hefferline, R. F., & Goodman, P. (1951). *Gestalt therapy – Excitement and growth in the human personality*. New York: Julian Press.

Perls, F. S., & Levitsky, A. (1970). The rules and games of Gestalt therapy. In J. Fagan, & I. L. Shepherd (Eds.), *Gestalt therapy now* (pp. 140-149). New York: Harper Colophon.

Perls, L. (1986). Commitment – Opening address, 8th annual conference on the theory and practice of gestalt therapy, May 17, 1985. *The Gestalt Journal 9/1*, 12-15.

Perls, L. (1992). *Living at the boundary* (J. Wysong, Ed.). Highland, NY: Gestalt Journal Press.

Petzold, H. G. (1981). Das Hier-und-Jetzt-Prinzip und die Dimension der Zeit in der psychologischen Gruppenarbeit. In C. H. Bachmann (Ed.), *Kritik der Gruppendynamik – Grenzen und Möglichkeiten sozialen Lernens* (pp. 214-299). Frankfurt/M.: Fischer.

Petzold, H. G. (1993). Zeit, Zeitqualitäten, Identitätsarbeit und biographische Narration – Chronosophische Überlegungen. In H. G. Petzold, *Integrative Therapie – Modelle, Theorien und Methoden fur eine schulenübergreifende Psychotherapie – 1. Klinische Philosophie* (pp. 333-395). Paderborn: Junfermann.

Petzold, H. G., & Orth, I. (1999). *Die Mythen der Psychotherapie – Ideologien, Machtstrukturen und Wege kritischer Praxis*. Paderborn: Junfermann.

Piaget, J. (1971). *Psychologie der Intelligenz*. Olten & Freiburg: Walter.

Picht, G. (1980). *Hier und Jetzt – Philosophieren nach Auschwitz und Hiroshima*, Bd. I. Stuttgart: Klett-Cotta.

Pöppel, E. (1985). *Grenzen des Bewußtseins – Über Wirklichkeit und Welterfahrung*. Stuttgart: DVA.

Pöppel, E. (1989). Gegenwart – psychologisch gesehen. In R. Wendorff (Ed.), *Im Netz der Zeit – Menschliches Zeiterleben interdisziplinär* (pp. 11-16). Stuttgart: Hirzel.

Polster, E. (1985). Imprisoned in the present. *The Gestalt Journal 8/1*, 5-22.

Polster, E. (1990). Erving Polster. In R. Harman (Ed.), *Gestalt therapy discussions with the masters* (pp. 111-128). Springfield, IL: Thomas.

Portele, G. H. (1999). Gestaltpsychologische Wurzeln der Gestalttherapie. In R. Fuhr, M. Sreckovic & M. Gremmler-Fuhr (Eds.), *Handbuch der Gestalttherapie* (pp. 263-278). Göttingen: Hogrefe.
Rammstedt, O. (1975). Alltagsbewußtsein von Zeit. *Kölner Zeitschrift fur Soziologie und Sozialpsychologie 27*, 47-64.
Rosenfeld, I. (1988). *The invention of memory – A new view of the brain*. New York: Basic Books.
Roth, G. (1987). Autopoiese und Kognition – Die Theorie H. R. Maturanas und die Notwendigkeit ihrer Weiterentwicklung. In S. J. Schmidt (Ed.), *Der Diskurs des Radikalen Konstruktivismus* (pp. 256-286). Frankfurt/M.: Suhrkamp.
Roth, G. (1991a). Neuronale Grundlagen des Lernens und des Gedächtnisses. In S. J. Schmidt (Ed.), *Gedächtnis – Probleme und Perspektiven der interdisziplinären Gedächtnisforschung* (pp. 127-158). Frankfurt/M.: Suhrkamp.
Roth, G. (1991b). Die Konstitution von Bedeutung im Gehirn. In S. J. Schmidt (Ed.), *Gedächtnis – Probleme und Perspektiven der interdisziplinären Gedächtnisforschung* (pp. 360-370). Frankfurt/M.: Suhrkamp.
Roth, G. (1995). *Das Gehirn und seine Wirklichkeit – Kognitive Neurobiologie und ihre philosophischen Konsequenzen*. Frankfurt/M.: Suhrkamp.
Roth, G., & Prinz, W. (Eds.) (1996). *Kopf-Arbeit – Gehirnfunktionen und kognitive Leistungen*. Heidelberg: Spektrum.
Ruhnau, E. (1996). Zeit-Gestalt und Beobachter – Betrachtungen zum tertium datur des Bewußtseins. In T. Metzinger (Ed.), *Bewußtsein – Beiträge aus der Gegenwartsphilosophie* (pp. 201-220). Paderborn: Schöningh.
Rusch, G. (1991). Erinnerungen aus der Gegenwart. In S. J. Schmidt (Ed.), *Gedächtnis – Probleme und Perspektiven der interdisziplinären Gedächtnisforschung* (pp. 267-292). Frankfurt/M.: Suhrkamp.
Sartre, J.-P. (1969). *Drei Essays*. Frankfurt/M. & Berlin: Ullstein.
Sartre, J.-P. (1987). *Das Sein und das Nichts – Versuch einer phänomenologischen Ontologie*. Reinbek: Rowohlt.
Sartre, J.-P. (1997). *Die Transzendenz des Ego – Philosophische Essays 1931-1939*. Reinbek: Rowohlt.
Scheurle, H. J. (1984). *Die Gesamtorganisation – Überwindung der Subjekt-Objekt-Spaltung in der Sinneslehre – Phänomenologische und erkenntnistheoretische Grundlagen der allgemeinen Sinnesphysiologie*. Stuttgart & New York: Thieme.

Schmid, W. (1998). *Philosophie der Lebenskunst — Eine Grundlegung*. Frankfurt/M.: Suhrkamp.
Schmidt, S. J. (1991). Gedächtnisforschungen — Positionen, Probleme, Perspektiven. In S. J. Schmidt (Ed.), *Gedächtnis — Probleme und Perspektiven der interdisziplinären Gedächtnisforschung* (pp. 9-55). Frankfurt/M.: Suhrkamp.
Schmidt, S. J. (Ed.) (1991). *Gedächtnis — Probleme und Perspektiven der interdisziplinären Gedächtnisforschung*. Frankfurt/M.: Suhrkamp.
Schmitz, E., & Hauke, G. (1999). Sinnerfahrung, innere Langweile und die Modi der Stressverarbeitung. *Integrative Therapie 25/1*, 42-63.
Schmitz, H. (1990). *Der unerschöpfliche Gegenstand — Grundzüge der Philosophie*. Bonn: Bouvier.
Schmitz, H. (1997). *Höhlengänge — Über die gegenwärtige Aufgabe der Philosophie*. Berlin: Akademie.
Sejnowski, T. J. (1995). The hardware really matters. In P. Baumgartner & S. Payr (Eds.), *Speaking minds: Interviews with twenty eminent cognitive scientists* (pp. 215-230). Princeton, NJ: Princeton University Press.
Spence, D. P. (1982). *Narrative truth and historical truth — Meaning and interpretation in psychoanalysis*. New York & London: Norton.
Spinelli, E. (1989). *The interpreted world — An introduction to phenomenological psychology*. London: Sage.
Spinelli, E. (1996). *Demystifying therapy*. London: Constable.
Staemmler, F.-M. (1985). Arbeit und Mut — Über Sexualität, Kontakt und Nähe. *Gestalt-Publikationen 1*. Würzburg: Zentrum für Gestalttherapie.
Staemmler, F.-M. (1987). Jenseits von Wörtern und Zeit — Über Inhalt und Prozeß in der Gestalttherapie. *Gestalt-Publikationen 4*. Würzburg: Zentrum für Gestalttherapie.
Staemmler, F.-M. (1993). *Therapeutische Beziehung und Diagnose — Gestalttherapeutische Antworten*. Munchen: Pfeiffer.
Staemmler, F.-M. (1994). Gleichzeitigkeit und Gestalt. *Gestalttherapie 8/2*, 75-77.
Staemmler, F.-M. (1997). Towards a theory of regressive processes in gestalt therapy: On time perspective, developmental model and the wish to be understood. *The Gestalt Journal 20/1*, 49-120.
Staemmler, F.-M. (1999a). Der Geist der Gestalttherapie in Aktion — Methoden und Techniken. In R. Fuhr, M. Sreckovic & M. Gremmler-Fuhr (Eds.), *Handbuch der Gestalttherapie* (pp. 439-460). Göttingen: Hogrefe.

Staemmler, F.-M. (1999b). Déjà vu?: Klaus Grawes "Psychologische Therapie" — Eine Rezension und Evaluation aus gestalttherapeutischer Sicht. *Gestalttherapie 13/2*, 86-124.

Staemmler, F.-M. (1999c). Hermeneutische Ansätze in der klassischen Gestalttherapie. *Gestalt 36*, 43-60.

Staemmler, F.-M. (2000). Der schiefe Turm von Pisa — oder: Das unstimmige Konzept der "frühen Störung" — Plädoyer für die Abschaffung eines generell irreführenden und speziell in der Gestalttherapie unbrauchbaren Begriffs. *Integrative Therapie 26/1*, 64-95.

Staemmler, F.-M. (Ed.) (2001). *Gestalttherapie im Umbruch — Von alten Begriffen zu neuen Ideen*. Köln: Edition Humanistische Psychologie.

Tholey, P. (1986). Deshalb Phänomenologie! — Anmerkungen zur phänomenologisch-experimentellen Methode. *Gestalt Theory 8/2*, 144-163.

Waldenfels, B. (2000). *Das leibliche Selbst — Vorlesungen zur Phänomenologie des Leibes*. Frankfurt/M.: Suhrkamp.

Watts, A. (1980). *Die Illusion des Ich — Westliche Wissenschaft und Zivilisation in der Krise — Versuch einer Neuorientierung*. München: Koesel.

Weinhandl, F. (Ed.) (1960). *Gestalthaftes Sehen — Ergebnisse und Aufgaben der Morphologie*. Darmstadt: Wissenschaftliche Buchgesellschaft.

Weizsäcker, V. von (1960). *Gestalt und Zeit*. Göttingen: Vandenhoeck & Ruprecht.

Wheeler, G. (1998). *Gestalt reconsidered: A new approach to contact and resistance*, 2nd edition. Cambridge, MA: GIC Press.

Yontef, G. M. (1993). *Awareness, dialogue, and process: Essays on gestalt therapy*. Highland, NY: Gestalt Journal Press.

3

Towards a Theory of Regressive Processes in Gestalt Therapy –

On Time Perspective, Developmental Model, and the Wish to Be Understood

Frank-M. Staemmler

And the seasons they go round and round,
And the painted ponies go up and down.
We're captive on the carousel of time.
We can't return, we can only look behind
From where we came
And go round and round and round
In the circle game.

(J. Mitchell)

Once and for all we have to recognize the fact that the first wish of a patient is to be understood.

(M. Balint)

In the course of my development as a therapist I have gone through a number of phases in which my opinions on important therapeutic concepts have changed, extended and refined. One of these concepts has been concerned with the treatment of regressive processes in my clients. In my Gestalt therapy training, I was not taught about these processes. The word "regression" was used only occasionally. Later, when I searched for Gestalt therapy literature on this topic, I did not find more than a few incidental comments. Only recently was an article published by Philippson (1993).

Lacking a clear orientation I vacillated between two poles: working with the apparently necessary regressions of clients to allow them to progress in therapy and alternately thinking such episodes — "... a long detour, leading back over... earliest childhood" (Freud 1914/1957, p. 10) — more or less superfluous or even unproductive. Looking back on this I can see that I did not have a rational justification for either point of view.

Over the years, I have been repeatedly confronted with my practical and theoretical uncertainty. Recently, through clinical experiences with some of my clients which to me seem to be more severely disturbed than others, I have been reminded of Balint's work which I had read many years ago:

> ... patients in this state apparently lose a good deal of their drive to get better, of their wish, and even their ability, to change. Parallel with this, their expectations from the analyst grow out of proportion to anything realistic, both in a positive sense, in the form of sympathy, understanding, attention, small gifts, and other signs of affection, and in a negative sense, in the form of fierce attacks, merciless retaliation, ice-cold indifference, and extreme cruelty. (1968, p. 85)

Clinical experiences similar to those described by Balint prompted my ambition to clarify my position on regressive processes. In this article, I want to share the results to date. I will especially refer to Kurt Lewin, Daniel Stern, Tilman Moser (a German body-oriented psychoanalyst) and Michael Balint. Their thoughts have proved to be very helpful to me and deserve acknowledgment and appreciation.

The synthesis which has evolved first led me to challenge some of the traditional modes of thinking about regression and then led me to let go of them. As the temporary result a new view on regressive processes has emerged which at present looks fertile to me. I hope that my colleagues, be they of *Gestalt therapy* or other therapeutic orientation, will benefit from this work.

The Psychoanalytic Term of "Regression" – A Brief Explanation and Some Critical Comments

"Applied to a psychical process having a determinate course or evolution, 'regression' means a return from a point already reached to an earlier one" (Laplanche & Pontalis 1988, p. 386). With this description, *The Language of Psycho-Analysis* assigns the term "regression" to an experience in psychological development oriented to the course of time. Thus, the reference to developmental psychology plays an important part in what is to follow.

The authors above further refine their definition by discussing three aspects of regression, the topical, the temporal, and the formal. For the purpose of my discussion, only the temporal and the formal are relevant:

> In *temporal* terms, regression implies the existence of a genetic[1] succession and denotes the subject's reversion to past phases of his development ... In the *formal* sense,

---

[1] The word "genetic" here refers to the personal history of the individual, not to her or his hereditary outfit.

regression means the transition to modes of expression that are on a lower level as regards complexity, structure and differentiation. (ibid. — italics in original; see also Freud 1900/1958, p. 548)

The temporal aspect picks up the developmental line of thought and makes it more precise in that it points to a given "genetic succession" which consists of some "phases." The assumption is that each phase ensues from the previous one and is superseded by the following phase: "What happens, then, to the previous phases, to the earlier world views? Either they are eclipsed and drop out or ... they remain dormant but become integrated into the emergent organization and thereby lose much of their previous character" *(Stern 1985, p. 29).*

Regression in this sense can be understood as an actualization of a previous developmental level by the individual, while the later level, at least for a certain period of time, is given up. Anna Freud even conceived of regression as a "principle in mental development," which takes "two steps forward and one backward" (1963, p. 131).

As a rule of thumb, the mental development of human beings can be seen as a process of slowly increasing variability, differentiation and integration. Therefore, it is possible to relate the temporal form of regression to the "formal" one, i. e. a step back on one or a few of the three dimensions mentioned above. If such a step back in quality is observed, it is called "regression," as well. In terms of the formal aspect, the emphasis is on the fact that the behavior in question exhibits an "inferior" or "more primitive" level than can be observed under normal circumstances. Goldstein, one of the 'ancestors' of Gestalt therapy, describes regression on the basis of his investigations with brain-damaged people as a disintegration which "... *proceeds from the highly differentiated and articulated state to a more amorphous total behavior"* (1939, p. 31 — italics in original).

In psychoanalytic literature the temporal and the formal aspects of regression are regarded as so closely connected that either they are hardly individuated or *both* are implied, when the word "regression" is used. In contrast Lewin (1952), another "ancestor" of Gestalt therapy, viewed the distinction between the two aspects to be so important that he introduced a separate word, "retrogression," for the temporal aspect; he reserved "regression" for the formal aspect alone. He opposed the contentions of Freud (1900/1958, p. 548) in *Interpretation of Dreams* and pointed to several research findings which suggested: "It is frequently true that retrogression will also have the character of regression, and vice versa. However, this does not need to be the case" (Lewin 1952, p. 94). Unfortunately, Lewin's delineation has not been sustained.

The quasi-equation of the two aspects takes place almost by itself, if one thinks within a frame of a developmental model in which several phases of increasing levels of differentiation follow each other in a more or less linear way and thereby *replace* each other. Figure 4 illustrates a simplified schematic paradigm.

Many older developmental models in psychology and psychoanalysis either implicitly or explicitly follow this pattern. Sometimes they don't, but even then they generally are interpreted this way. One example can be found in Freud's model of psycho-sexual development of the child (oral, anal and phallic phases). Very often they have been understood in terms of the paradigm shown in *Figure 1* — in spite of Freud's warning: "It would be a mistake to suppose that these three phases succeed one another in a clear-cut fashion. One may appear in addition to another; they may overlap one another, may be present alongside one another" (1953/1964, p. 155).

degree of psychological complexity and differentiation

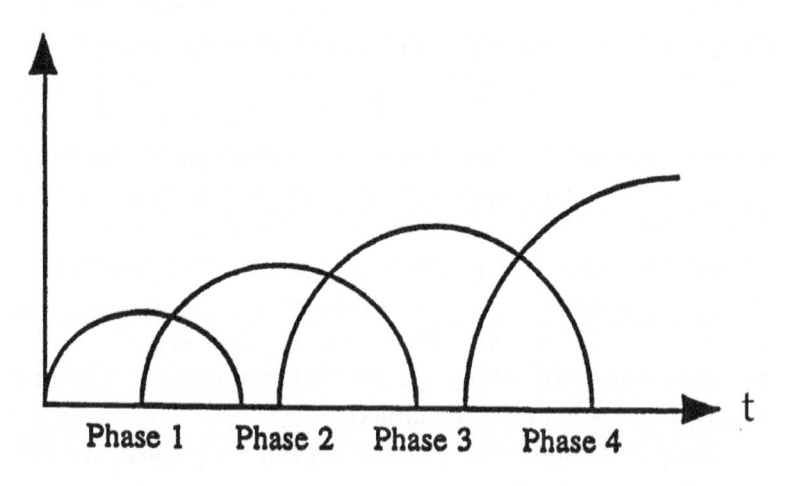

Phase 1   Phase 2   Phase 3   Phase 4   t

Figure 1: Classical Developmental Model in Psychoanalysis

Another well-known example is Margaret Mahler's theory on the infant's process of separation-individuation. To be fair in her case, too, one has to take notice of her qualifying remark: "Like any intrapsychic process, this one reverberates throughout the life cycle. It is never finished; it remains always active; new phases of the life cycle see new derivatives of the earliest processes still at work" (Mahler et al. 1975, p. 3).

It would be easy to continue this list of examples.

Further discussion of the fact that Freud, Mahler et al. and others have contributed to their own warnings not being heeded is not necessary here. More important is how the concept of regression within the above paradigm has obvious consequences: for instance, a person who according to her or his age is located in phase 4 and has developed the appropriate behavior and experience is *regressed* by definition, if her or his behavior and experience are dominated by characteristics which are attributable to one of the three earlier phases.

In psychoanalytic thinking, this view has normalized the concept that relatively frequent behaviors of adults are regressive as soon as they are based on cognitive ("primary process") patterns which in "healthy" adults are supposed to have been replaced by different ("secondary process") patterns for the most part. This is especially the case, if the behavior in question (like that of playing games, artistic activity, or dreams) resembles a behavior that children still display with greater frequency. Objections to this inflationary use of the term regression were raised already long ago: "... I hold ... that they [the psychoanalysts] give to the principle of regression too wide an application" (McDougall 1926, p. 293).

The psychophysical functions form a hierarchy, but not every instance of functioning of the lower levels should be called regression. I suggest that the term should be restricted to those instances only in which the morbid nature of the process is revealed by the fact that, *when circumstances call for the higher modes of functioning*, the patient is unable to respond with those higher modes ... (ibid., p. 297f. – italics added)

In my way of thinking, this excessively extended term of regression creates a gloomy image of humankind. In this image, the ability to surrender selflessly, to play cheerfully, and to explore creatively does not fit appropriately into adulthood. According to the underlying developmental model, this behavior can only appear in the adult person if s/he has regressed ... mentally returning to childhood and leaving some part of her/his adult competencies behind.[2] One mode of experience only becomes available at the expense of the other, a regrettable either/or choice. Concepts like the "regression in the service of the ego" by Kris (1977) try to soften the rigidity of this false alternative and thus try to reconnect what has been divided by the underlying paradigm. Former Gestalt therapist Petzold, who now calls himself an "integrative therapist," holds the same opinion:

> The *ability to regress* is a central capacity of a healthy ego; it becomes a goal of therapy, since love, sexuality, joy, play, creativity require the ability to regress benignly, to immerse in the experience without losing oneself and to come up again in a stable condition. (1989, p. 71 — italics in original)

In that view, love, sexuality, joy, creativity, immersion in the experience, etc. all seem to require *childlike* capacities. Who are the "adults" described implicitly as lacking these forms of spontaneous responsiveness?

More important to and directly relevant for the practice of psychotherapy is the correlation between regression and psychopathology. Psychopathology is most often seen as an expression of regression to an earlier stage of development, momentarily or chronically, with the quality of "fixation" inherent in the behavior. Accordingly, what appears to be "neurotic" or even "psychotic" in the adult is related to certain "normal" stages in the development of the infant. The more frequently and the longer the regressive periods occur, and the earlier the stages of development to which a person regresses, the more this person is thought to be mentally disturbed.

---

[2] Indeed, some adults don't dare surrender to playing and the like, just because this behavior is thought to be childlike or even childish.

> The belief in the correlation between phases of development and specific pathology seems to have led to a general acceptance by many psychoanalysts of the idea that it is possible to establish a chronological developmental timetable of etiological phase specificity for the various psychotic illnesses, borderline states, and neurotic disorders. (Willick 1990, p. 1050)

Today the probably best known proponent of this view is Kernberg, who in his books and articles writes similar comments as:

> Mahler's proposed timetable for the normal sequence of development thus permits us to link borderline pathology to a stage of development that covers, broadly speaking, the period from the first half of the second year to the second half of the third year of life. (1985, p. 14)

I am aware that this presentation is simplified. Many psychoanalysts have warned against such a wide-spread point of view that is too simple. One of the first to challenge the equation of an "early" disturbance to a "deep" or severe disturbance was Winnicott who said: "... a human infant must travel some distance from early in order to have the maturity to be deep" (1965, p. 114). And Alexander insisted: "... antiquity is not always equivalent to depth from the point of view of pathogenesis" (1956, p. 184). Particularly during the last two decades such criticism has gained additional support in the wake of modern research on the psychological development of infants (see Dornes 1993; Lichtenberg 1983; Stern 1985). These research results show clearly that the infant's development takes quite a different course than had been assumed by traditional psychoanalytic theory.

Prior to this theoretical breakthrough, there were many voices that challenged several aspects of the concept of regression and the related theories of the "clinical infant"

(Stern) holding that this reconstructed infant "... is made up of memories, present reenactments in the transference, and theoretically guided interpretations" (Stern 1985, p. 14). Some writers (such as Peterfreund 1978 or Willick 1990) questioned the theory because of its inherent logic ("adultomorphization"), others contradicted it on the basis of clinical material: "We also concluded that we cannot reconstruct a rigid chronological timetable ... from the regressive behavior and symptomatology of disturbed patients." And "... we found that the conceptualization of a single phase-specific determinant for the pathology of these patients and a therapeutic approach geared to such a hypothesis were at variance with our views of the complexity and individuality of our patients" (Abend et al. 1953, pp. 171, 198). Modell, also an analyst like those quoted before, puts it even more harshly: "... our customary way of thinking about regression and developmental arrests in psychoanalysis may simply be muddled and wrongheaded" (1984, p. 108).

These positions received solid support from independent longitudinal investigations into the correspondence between effects of the various negative *and* positive influences to which children, youngsters, and adults are exposed in the normal course of their lives and the psychological disturbances that they will display later on ... or just *don't* display: "It became clear that people changed a good deal over the course of development and that the outcome following early adversities was quite diverse, with long-term effects heavily dependent on the nature of subsequent life experiences" (Rutter 1989, p. 24).

A survey on such investigations is given by Petzold et al. (1993). Their results underline an opinion which is held by many Gestalt therapists and put into words by Yontef very clearly:

... because the patient's present is related to his past experience, it does not mean that in the past he was victim of his environment. Rather, the patient and environment are and were in constant interaction, and the patient brought something into the interaction ... (1993, p. 337)

A different branch of research also provides some evidence that the symptoms which in the past have been primarily related to the so-called "early disturbances" can be evoked during the *complete* life span of the person (see Staemmler 2000). This research deals in part with the psychological aftermath of severe trauma following the experience of war, rape, and other forms of massive abuse of power (see Herman 1992). These empirical data very much call into question the phase-specific theories of psychopathology which have been proposed by Kernberg (see above) and other analysts. They rather add substance to positions like this one:

It may also be that in certain instances severe trauma after the age of three can be causative in the development of borderline conditions. This might very well be the case in the borderline condition known as multiple personality disorder, where 98 percent of patients so diagnosed have undergone physical and/or sexual abuse, abuse which not infrequently occurs later in childhood rather than in the earliest years. (Willick 1990, pp. 1077f.)

All these recent findings contribute to the uncertainty of the existence of linear links from certain phases of development in children relating to specific psychopathological phenomena in adults. Of course, this is *not* to say that there are no such links. It is to say that they appear to be less direct and much more variable than has been previously assumed. Therefore, in individual cases they have to be seen not as *re*-constructions of quasi-objective facts but rather as subjective *con*structions or contexts of meaning which are synthesized by the client on the basis of memory, reports by parents and other significant persons, gap-filling assumptions, summarization and other kinds of mental processing.

Certainly, within the frame of their dialogue with their clients, therapists exercise some influence on the construction of context and meaning also. That is why from a *Gestalt therapy* point of view I find it important for the therapist to take a stance of "cultivated uncertainty" (see Staemmler 1997) and to "bracket" (see Husserl 1980, pp. 53ff.) preexisting assumptions about the genesis of disturbance. Saying this, on the one hand I think of assumptions like those of Kernberg (see above). On the other hand, I refer to the grotesque generalizations by Perls:

> All the so-called *traumata*, which are supposed to be the root of the neurosis, are an invention of the patient to save his self-esteem. None of these traumata has ever been proved to exist. I haven't seen a single case of infantile trauma that wasn't a falsification. They are all lies to be hung onto in order to justify one's unwillingness to grow. (1969, p. 43 — italics in original)

To people who have already experienced severe trauma, it compounds the trauma to have another significant person not believe their report of the trauma or its effects on them. For me it follows that, when in doubt, I prefer to assume I know little or nothing about the backgrounds and motivations of my clients. This means to take a hermeneutical stance, since "we must be hermeneutical where we do not understand what is happening but are honest enough to admit it . . ." (Rorty 1980, p. 321). In practice this means that the therapist

> Seeks to reveal or even give meaning to the material brought by the patient, rather than discover in it a meaning that has in some way been established in advance.

Considers that this "assignment" of meaning takes place through the joint effort and close collaboration of the therapist and the patient.

Is little concerned with empirical, historical, or objective truth, except where it serves to situate a meaning that one seeks to develop: the narrative truth. (Bouchard & Guérette 1991, p. 387 – italics added)

In my view, the meanings that are attributed to the past life events of the client during the course of therapy *emerge* from the dialogue between client and therapist. They are *common* meanings which develop firstly from the subjective meanings the client brings into the session, and secondly from the influence of the therapist who, under the phenomenological condition of suspending former assumptions, in cooperation with the client works on an increasingly more detailed and precise comprehension of the more or less roughly intuited meanings the client has presented to him in the first place (see Staemmler 1993, pp. 75ff.).

Approaching a Gestalt Therapy View of "Regression"

On the previous pages I have critically dealt with mainly the temporal aspect of the psychoanalytic term of regression. Firstly, I have drawn upon the results of several branches of research and, secondly, I have taken a *Gestalt* therapy point of view. I intend to intensify the second approach now. For this purpose I will take a closer look at the temporal aspect of regression by relating it to the *Gestalt therapy* notion of the "Here and Now."

As all Gestalt therapists are familiar with, Frederick Perls frequently underlined the following:

Nothing exists except the here and now. The now is the present, is the phenomenon, is what you are aware of, is that moment in which you carry your so-called memories and your so-called anticipations with you. Whether you remember or anticipate, you do it now. The past is no more. The future is not yet.... Nothing can possibly exist except the now. (1969, p. 41 — italics in original)

The "Here and Now" in *Gestalt* therapy is one of the catch-words which much too often has been used as a somewhat primitive cliché. Historically the "Here and Now" is a rudimentary and shortened version of a term coined by Frank (1939) and introduced into psychology by Lewin (1952), the "time perspective." Frank stated: "... the dimensions of the past are shaped by the present which imposes upon previous events a perspective that is governed by the necessities and the values of the *present*" (ibid., p. 301 — italics added).

Lewin relied on Frank's view and built his "field-theory principle of contemporaneity in psychology" upon it, which "... means that the behavior b at the time t is a function of the situation S at the time t only (S is meant to include both the person and his psychological environment), $b^t = F(S^t)$" (Lewin 1952, p. 48).

Using the term of the „time perspective," Lewin specifies this statement as such:

It is important to realize that the psychological past and the psychological future are simultaneous parts of the psychological field existing at a give time t. *The time perspective is continually changing.* According to field theory, any type of behavior depends upon the total field, including the time perspective at that time, but not, in addition, upon any past or future field and its time perspectives. (ibid., p. 54 — italics added)

In other words, at a certain point in time past and future indeed do play an important part for the individual, though always depending on how they appear from the current perspective from which s/he, at this moment, looks at them.

The past manifests itself in the form of memories, attitudes, and images of the self and the world as they are experienced by each person at the given time. Further experience in the life of a person provides additional impressions and experiences, which again are represented and integrated into the hitherto existing stock, thereby enlarging and modifying it. Therefore past and future of a person are always *changing* from moment to moment: ". . . man has realized that human nature can be changed because it is constituted of the ever-changing past, and the ever-changing future time perspectives that he himself imposes upon what has happened and what will happen" (Frank 1939, p. 310).

If one shares the views of Frank and Lewin, which I do, one will have difficulties with the temporal aspect of the concept of regression. A "reversion to past phases of . . . development," as this aspect was defined by *The Language of Psychoanalysis*, seems hardly possible, since it would mean to assume an earlier time perspective. But this has already been overtaken and modified by the events that happened later and therefore is irreversibly altered. One must have already reached a higher level in order to be able to fall back again. (When this is not the case, we should talk of *retardation*, not of regression.) Time cannot be turned back, not even by mechanisms such as repression or denial, for the application of such mechanisms would be an element of the later field and its time perspective; it would differ from the earlier field and its time perspective, because then the intervening events would not have taken place and could not have been represented (they may have been fantasized as *future* events, though) and repressed or denied: "The time perspective is continually changing."

If you look at it this way, you will have to conclude that, strictly speaking, there cannot be such thing as regression in the *temporal* sense of the word ("retrogression"); only some forms of brain damage may in some regard be seen as exceptions. An earlier time perspective may be contained within a later field as a memory of some sort, but this memory will be governed by the later time perspective. Even if a person would to a high degree succeed in identifying with the earlier time perspective, this identification would be a later activity, a so-called "mental simulation," by which the person would behave *as if* the later time perspective did not exist. The identification, the mental simulation, the behavior "as if," would be a later activity that takes place under the current time perspective. "We can't return, we can only look behind from where we came..." Petzold hit the bull's eye when he said that even a very

> ..."deep regression" must not be understood as a factual, temporal return. What you can observe in babies and what shows in the treatment of adult patients in the course of "extensive regressions," *in spite of many similarities of certain phenomena is never the same* ... An adult may feel *like* a baby, but s/he will never again feel *the same as* a baby ... (1993, p. 863 — italics in original)

In his definition of regression Petzold tries to take into account these facts. He sees regression as

> ...an activation of cognitive-emotional-sensorymotor recollections as they are saved within the life chronicle of the body-memory and which because of their emotional components inundate the ego and the self of the individual.[3] His perception, thinking and behavior are temporarily influenced in a way which is not experienced to be age-adequate by observers (as well as by the relics of the

---

[3] According to my experience this does not always have to be the case. Some situational regressive behaviors rather take on the character of stereotyped role clichés, which people sometimes can reproduce easily just because they do *not* imply emotional involvement.

self-monitoring ego). *Phenomenologically speaking, regression in this process is not temporal, since it takes place in a given here and now;* rather it must be seen as a general or partial inactivation or break-down of the current cognitive, emotional and behavioral levels of differentiation in competence and performance for a shorter or longer period of time ... This happens in such a way that earlier, respectively more archaic forms of cognitive, affective and behavioral functioning become effective in the present; thereby an experientially intense memorative approximation to past biographical events and the ways of experience which are linked with them become possible. (ibid., p. 864 — italics added)

If you read this definition thoroughly, you will find some kind of a swinging movement between the temporal and the formal aspects of regression: after regression first is presented under the temporal aspect ("activation of recollections from the life chronicle"), the following reference to the phenomenological approach leads to a challenging of the temporal aspect and to a fostering of the formal aspect which is characterized "as an inactivation of the current levels of differentiation." Then the swing goes back again to the temporal aspect in that the inactivation of the levels of differentiation is defined by the effect of "earlier, respectively more archaic forms of functioning." In the final sentence, the temporal aspect is put in question once more by the use of the word "*approximation* to past biographical events." In all, Petzold's definition leaves me with the impression that he, who seems to be fully aware of the given time perspectives, on one hand tries to free himself from the temporal aspect in his definition, but on the other hand does not succeed in doing so and is caught by the temporal aspect again and again.

Probably the time dilemma can only be overcome, if the development of a Gestalt therapy understanding of regressive phenomena is not only grounded in the phenomenological approach but also in a decided dismissal of the traditional time-based paradigm, which I have illustrated in *Figure 1*. Therefore I now want to introduce a different paradigm as it has been proposed by Stern (1985). In addition to the many important insights into *The Interpersonal World of the Infant*, I regard Stern's new developmental paradigm to be one of his most important contributions. He has illustrated it himself:

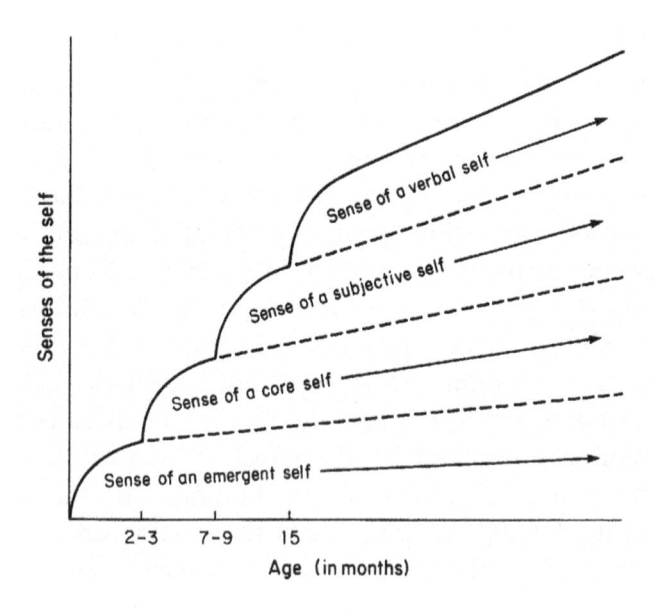

Figure 2: New Developmental Model (Stern 1985, p. 32)

Obviously this picture differs from *Figure 1* essentially. The various "senses of self"[4] described by Stern follow each

---

[4] It does not come as a surprise that Stern's use of the term "self" differs in many respects from the "self" Perls, Hefferline and Goodman

other successively in regard to the time of their first emergence, *but they do not take their predecessor's place*! One sense of self *remains* after the following one has emerged, and it keeps on developing *parallel* to the others for the whole lifetime of the person.

> All domains ... remain active during development. ... none of them atrophy, none become developmentally obsolete or get left behind. And once all domains are available, there is no assurance that any one domain will necessarily claim preponderance during any particular age period.... Once formed, the domains remain forever as distinct forms of experiencing social life and self. None are lost to adult experience. Each simply gets more elaborated. It is for this reason that the term *domains* ... has been chosen, rather than *phases* or *stages*. (ibid., p. 31f. — italics in original)

This point of view bears an important consequence for the understanding of regression: *the temporal aspect becomes irrelevant!* To make a certain domain of the senses of self accessible for himself or herself a person does not have to regress in the temporal meaning of the word, for all domains, once they have been formed, still exist in the here and now and will keep on existing in the future. Therefore "... no extraordinary conditions or processes need be present to permit the movement back and forth between experiences in different domains, that is, between different senses of self" (ibid., p. 30).

It follows that no extraordinary (logically and phenomenologically impossible) event as regression in the temporal sense has to be assumed to make such a movement explicable.

(1951) talk about. In spite of these differences, I think that Stern's term "*sense* of self" can also be applied in a gestalt therapy context.

Proposal for a Gestalt Understanding of Regressive Processes

Summing up his ideas about the psychological development Stern writes: "Development is not a succession of events left behind in history. It is a continuing process, constantly updated" (1985, p. 260).

This "update" is, in other words, what Frank and Lewin called the "time perspective." With his view Stern also is in accordance with one of the most famous "fragments" by Heraclitus with which many Gestalt therapists including myself agree:[5] "One cannot step twice into the same river, nor can one grasp any mortal substance in a stable condition, but it scatters and again gathers; it forms and dissolves, and approaches and departs" (1979, p. 53).

If we accept the philosophy of Heraclitus, the phenomenological approach (see Petzold's remark), the hermeneutical procedure, the "principle of contemporaneity" of Lewin's field theory, and, last but not least, the results of Stern's research, and if we use them as our basis for an understanding of the regressive processes in our clients, then we will derive a notion which discards the temporal aspect of the psychoanalytic term of regression; instead, its formal aspect will have to be in the focus of our thinking.

At first sight it may appear as contradictory evidence that as therapists we frequently observe behaviors in our clients that seem childlike to us, or, as is sometimes said in a more denigrating way, "infantile" or even "primitive." In fact, many descriptions our clients report of their experience contain similar expressions, such as "I feel very small,

---

[5] Interestingly, there is also a number of gestalt therapists who use static diagnostic categories (such as "schizoid," "borderline" etc.). Many of them quote Heraclitus's fragment, too, but only its first eight words.

just like a baby" or "I would like to sit on your lap like a little child."

These impressions of therapists and expressions of clients seem to hint at regressive processes in general. Moreover, they also seem to underline specifically the temporal aspect of regression which I have discarded in the previous chapter. If this would be true, it would seriously challenge my line of thought, since a Gestalt therapy theory of regressive processes cannot and must not ignore the phenomenology of the experience of the people it aims to describe and understand.

But I am convinced that the impressions and expressions mentioned above do not really form a contradiction to my theoretical considerations. The strong influence our culture exerts on the way people represent their experience verbally needs to be taken into account. In this context I want to remind you of Whorf's "linguistic relativity principle,"

> ... which means, in informal terms, that users of markedly different grammars are pointed by their grammars toward different types of observations and different evaluations of externally similar acts of observation, and hence are not equivalent as observers but must arrive at somewhat different views of the world.
>
> It is not so much in ... special uses of language as in its constant ways of arranging data and its most ordinary everyday analysis of phenomena that we need to recognize the influence it has on other activities, cultural and personal. (1956, pp. 221, 134f.)

What in our culture is taken for "childlike" or "infantile," what is labeled with these words and what is judged that way, is not like that *per se* but because of our ideas of how children and — to mention the other pole, too: — adults are and are supposed to be. These ideas have a strong impact on our verbal descriptions, and again our language has an influence on our ideas. The psychoanalytic way of thinking is also an offspring of our culture and language and as such has had a remarkable impact on our culture and language for about one hundred years. It has coined many aspects of popular psychology; for instance in respect to how the connection between past and present is seen or in respect to the relative neglect of the body and the greater value that is attributed to verbal ways of expression and contact — to mention only two examples which are relevant to the discussion of regressive processes.

> In fact, much of what is meant by "socializing" is directed at focusing awareness on a single domain, usually the verbal, and declaring it to be the official version of what is being experienced, while denying the experience in the other domains ("unofficial" versions of what is happening). (Stern 1985, p. 31)

In concrete terms, in many situations we regard it as "adult" behavior to have smart conversations with other people, and we find it "infantile" to touch each other. Accordingly, in psychotherapy we find it more "grown-up" when the client conveys to the therapist *verbally* what s/he feels, whereas we tend to find it "childlike" when s/he tries to make *physical* contact. It is almost as if being adult would consist of a more or less exclusive turning-into-language of one's being and of one's contact with other people by leaving behind the "low points" of one's physical life — aside from the exceptions of sexual contact within private relationships.[6] Within the frame of *Gestalt* therapy theory

---

[6] In this context it is interesting to note that the proponents of deviant points of view who slowly gain some acceptance among today's psychoanalysts (see Moser 1989; 1994a; Heisterkamp 1993) are confronted with *two* kinds of accusations by their orthodox critics: as soon as they demand the integration of the client's body into the therapeutic endeavor they are either blamed for the *sexualization* of the therapeutic situation or, with equal vehemence, of the *infantilization* of their clients (see Bittner 1988).

which operates from a phenomenological basis such presumptions and prejudices need to be put into "brackets."

It is not by chance that I have come to mention the body/language polarity, since it relates to the domains of Stern's "senses of self," especially to the domains of the "core self" and the "verbal self." In what follows I shall use these domains as examples to elaborate on my Gestalt therapy understanding of regressive processes. Let us assume the case of a client who for many sessions has articulated herself in a primarily *verbal* manner; until now she has reflected upon and worked on her difficulties mainly by *talking* to her therapist. Then, during the next session, she "loses" her language: instead of *saying* "I'm afraid" she *jerks* back, instead of *saying* "I would like to come closer to you" she hesitantly *gropes* her way to her therapist, instead of *saying* "I feel you understand me" she comfortably *snuggles* up to her therapist. It is very likely that most therapists would call this behavior "regressive." They would be ruled by the cultural stereotype, I have described above, which determines that non-verbal, physical communication is more "infantile" than verbal communication, just because small children use it to express themselves until they learn to speak. What follows is the assumption that the client must have regressed to an infantile phase of development.

It can easily be seen that this line of thought corresponds to the paradigm which I have illustrated in *Figure 1* and which conceives of regression primarily in the temporal aspect. I want to contrast it now with a different view which follows Stern's paradigm as illustrated in *Figure 2*. From this view one would have to see the client like this: during the first sessions she was mainly identified with the domain of her "verbal self." In the following session this domain recedes into the background, and she experiences herself predominantly in the domain of her "core self."[7] Since the domain of her "core self" has not been replaced in the course of her development by the domains which emerged later but has kept on existing and therefore still exists under the time perspective given, the client is *not* regressed in the *temporal* sense.

If she, as I have put it, "lost" her language, i. e. if for a certain time she *is not able* — not only does not *want* — to make use of her verbal capabilities, then her situation can be understood as a regression in the *formal* sense of the word. I would like to repeat the definition of the formal aspect of regression here: "In the *formal* sense, regression means the transition to modes of expression that are on a lower level as regards complexity, structure and differentiation" (Laplanche & Pontalis 1988, p. 386 — italics in original).

If the client can *only* actualize one domain, her "core self," and is *not able* to also access the domain of her "verbal self," then her behavior is clearly less complex compared to a situation in which *both* or *all* of her senses of self are available to her. In this case she is regressed in the formal sense.

For all the reasons I have mentioned before, I hold — in congruence with Goldstein (see above) — that a Gestalt therapy definition of regressive processes should not be based on the temporal but *only* on the *formal* aspect of the psychoanalytic definition. Then, *a regressive process is a (transitional or lasting) restriction of a person's current possibility to realize all of her formerly acquired competencies according to her needs in the given situation.* Such a restriction can relate to competencies which have been acquired both in early and in later periods of psychological development.

---

[7] The domain of the "core self" is *non*-verbal, it is not automatically *pre*-verbal. Even if it has emerged earlier than the verbal, it still exists parallel to the verbal. — I say this to suggest that the words "non-verbal" and "pre-verbal" should not be used as synonyms.

This definition differs not only from the psychoanalytic point of view, it also differs from what Frederick Perls termed "regression" when he said, "regression means a withdrawal to a position where you can provide your own support, where you feel secure" (1969, p. 61). An *equation* of regression with withdrawal of the person to a self-sufficient and pleasant position does not make sense to me, because I cannot see a practical benefit for the therapist dealing with the therapeutic processes in question. However, there is an aspect to Perls's definition which I think is important. I shall return to it later.

My definition of regressive processes has some implications which I want to make explicit now, because they may not yet be evident. One is that in my definition all competencies of the person are dealt with *equally*. To use Stern's terms as an example again: the domain of the "verbal self" is not of greater value than the one of the "core self," the former is not more "adult" than the latter. Generally speaking, no competence is "childlike" or "adult," just be-cause it was aquired sooner or later. Once a person is grown up *all* domains and *all* competencies are "adult" — of course, this is not to say they are necessarily "healthy" or "mature." This view is compatible with the holistic notion in Gestalt therapy (see Staemmler & Bock 1991, pp. 94ff.) and does not depend on disturbances in certain domains; disturbances grow up in the course of time, too.

> To the extent that the sense of self remains fragile (and we are all fragile to some extent), the need for the affirmation of the other continues throughout life. That this phenomenon makes its appearance at an early stage of life and persists through development does not imply that a regression has taken place. (Modell 1984, pp. 112f.)

Therefore, in a *theoretical* discussion[8], I don't find it adequate to use the words "infantile" or "adult." It also displaces the talk about the "inner child" which has become some kind of cult both in the United States of America and in Europe in recent years. Much too often this talk supports the self-victimization of clients in a shocking way. It is not long ago that Helm Stierlin, one of Germany's most famous psychoanalytic family therapists, warned us of the fact that the focus on the "inner child" — quite like fixed diagnoses (e. g., "borderline," "schizophrenic," etc.) — ". . . turns one's look back to the past which cannot be changed" (1995, p. 40). Yontef, from a field theory perspective, has given some supplemental reasons against the talk of the strange homunculus called the "inner child"; he pointed out, that this "makes a thing out of a process," and:

> Sometimes when I hear "My inner child did it," it sounds like a bad joke, as if saying: "I am not responsible, my inner child did it." When someone even leaves out the word "inner" and says "my child" felt such and such, and for a moment I think the patient is talking about one of his or her actual children, it seems like a bad joke indeed. The attitude is sometimes that "It is not I who has this feeling — and I am not responsible for and have no choice about the inner child, it was created in the past by my abusive parents." (Yontef 1993, p. 294)

For me, it follows that the question, how to deal with regressive processes in my clients, must *not* be put in the way Philippson puts it: "Clinically, the question for therapists is whether to work with the client in that regressed state directly or whether to 'call back' some more *adult* functioning" (1993, p. 121 — italics added).

---

[8] Of course, in my everyday therapeutic work with clients, I leave it up to them to describe their subjective experience in their own words.

According to my definition I will have to speak of a regressive process also in cases, in which a person for a certain time loses the availability of a domain or a competence, which s/he had acquired in *earlier* times, and has only access to those, which had been acquired in *later* times. (By the way, this view is supported by Lewin's assertion that "retrogression" is not equal to "regression.") Remember the client who has related to her therapist for many sessions mainly in a verbal manner. Under a certain condition we would have to call this behavior "regressive," too, although it was regressive in a very different way than the behavior she displayed after the shift in her experience. The condition, under which it would be justified to call her behavior (exclusively talking) "regressive," is that she was *not able* to also activate her "core self" — even though she *wanted* to do so. Let me say it more dramatically by using one of Frederick Perls's well-known catch-words: according to my definition, even very intelligent "mind-fucking" is regressive, if a person cannot let go of it though s/he wants to, for instance when it is time to put the "mind" into the background and let the experience of the body come to the foreground.

Of course, there are infinite situations in which human beings do not make use of all their capabilities, because they are not necessary in order to meet the personal needs and the demands of the situation. In such situations certain capabilities are not activated, which is consistent with the intentions of the respective person. (While I am dancing I normally refrain from activating my capability to think about regression theoretically.) Therefore in these cases I do *not* talk of regressive processes. One can think of these situations as of examples of adequate *figure formation*, through which a certain domain of the person gets into the foreground whereas others recede into the background so that the conditions of the field are responded to adequately. This view takes into account what McDougall meant when he said that "... not every instance of functioning of the lower levels should be called regression" (1926, pp. 297f.), this term is only justified "... *when circumstances call for the higher modes of functioning*" (ibid.).[9]

In my theorizing I make a distinction between such processes of figure formation, which are adequate to the given needs and situations of the person, on one hand and regressive processes as defined above on the other hand. This distinction is closely related to the differentiation between forms of psychological functioning we call "self-support" and other ways of functioning that indicate a lack of self-support. I have defined "self-support"

> ... as the sum of the capabilities a person can activate in a given situation in order to fulfill a given need. Respectively, a lack of self-support consists of the capabilities a person must activate in pursuit of a given need, but either has not acquired and/or does not use, though acquired. (Staemmler 1993, p. 249)[10]

It follows that regressive processes can be understood as instances of a *lack* of self-support in the person. Therefore my basic attitude towards regressive processes as I have defined

---

[9] This view also resembles an understanding of regression which stands in the tradition of Vygotski's developmental theory and which is characterized by Kozulin as such: "... an important indicator of the advanced psychological form is not so much its conceptual form as such, but rather the ability of the individual *to control his behavior* on different developmental levels, to *integrate* them, and to activate an *appropriate* level depending on required type of activity. Regressive processes express themselves not only in a deficiency of conceptual reasoning, but also in a person's inability to *switch, when appropriate*, from the conceptual to the 'complex' level" (1990, p. 233 — italics added).

[10] To avoid misinterpretation I want to point out that "self-support" for me is not synonymous with "self-sufficiency," as Perls sometime implied. The capability to turn to other people and ask for help, if necessary, in my view is a way of supporting oneself.

them is this: since regressive processes represent a lack of self-support in the person, it is almost superfluous to say that I do not see a reason to either *support* them or even *induce* them by the use of any methods. On the contrary, it is part of the therapist's task to support the processes of figure formation mentioned above and to work with the client in a way that helps her or him to develop the necessary self-support, which makes it possible for the client to feel, think and behave in accordance with his or her needs and the conditions of the given situation.

My attitude is reinforced by the experience that for some clients it can have detrimental psychological consequences to be exposed to their own regressive processes. Sometimes during the course of a regressive process and sometimes only in retrospect they become aware of the tremendous impoverishment of their behavior and experience which takes place or has taken place before. The awareness of having experienced themselves not up to their own standards and, even worse, having shown themselves to others in that condition may induce pain, shame and a severe injury to their feeling of dignity. This can easily contribute to an impairment of their general well-being and especially of their self-esteem.

Therefore it is also an ethical matter for me not to induce or support regressive processes in my clients. My therapeutic attitude towards these processes is a consequence from what Scharfetter calls an *"eros therapeutikos"*: "Therapeutic love can be supportively demanding, since it takes a stance against malignant regression, against degradation, against interdiction, and against dependency of the patient" (1993, p. 259).

At the end of this section I now want to comment on the terminology problem which may arise from the fact that now we are dealing with two quite different definitions, on one hand with the traditional psychoanalytic definition of regression which includes the temporal aspect, and on the other hand with my definition of regressive processes which excludes it. In one sense my definition is narrower and in another sense it is wider than the analytic one. It is narrower in that I do not regard the phenomena as regressive processes which in psychoanalysis would clearly be seen as regression; as an example I think of the above mentioned capability of an adult to immerse in a game, a creative activity or into making love. In another sense my definition is wider, because it includes fixed behaviors such as "mind-fucking" which traditionally are taken for "adult" (= not regressive).

This difference in the meanings and the scopes of application may lead to misunderstandings when it is not clear which definition one uses. Therefore in the preceding text I have spoken of "regression" when relating to the *psychoanalytic* definition, and I have spoken of "regressive processes" when thinking in a *Gestalt therapy* framework. I shall continue in that manner. Besides I shall not, in accordance to my ideas of the therapeutic relationship and of dialogical diagnosis (see Staemmler 1993), label *people* as being "regressed"; I shall only say that certain psychological processes are regressive in kind. (In the preceding text I have only left this policy when I was quoting analytic thinking.) I find it useful to qualify temporary processes that are subject to change. In the context of psychotherapy that is devoted to change, I do not find it useful to attribute more or less permanent characteristics to people (see Staemmler 1989).

Balint's Theory of Regression and Its Yield for a Gestalt Understanding of Regressive Processes

The stage has been set to approach the Gestalt therapy context of some important differentiations made by Michael Balint. First of all I am thinking of his terms "benign" and "malignant" regression, respectively of the two "types of regression" which he termed "regression aimed at gratification" and "regression aimed at recognition" (1968). Similar differentiations have been made by Kris (1977) who spoke of "regression in the service of the ego" on one hand, and of the ego that has been "overwhelmed by regression" on the other hand (see Haynal 1989, p. 90). All of these terms become important as soon as we deal with the question, which practical procedures may be useful in the therapeutic situations, in which therapists find the psychological processes of their clients to be regressive in kind. I shall discuss these issues in what follows.

At first I want to point out that Balint's thoughts must be comprehended within a theoretical frame which was characterized by his theory of the "basic fault." This is to say, he did not have in mind quickly transient or minor forms of regression; instead, he related to processes, during which his clients for several sessions or weeks regressed from an "oedipal," conflictual level to the level he called the "level of the basic fault." In the following I shall also deal with such generalized regressive processes, since firstly they are therapeutically more important and therefore, secondly, better apt to develop a theoretical position.

The "level of the basic fault" differs from the oedipal level in that ". . . the nature of the dynamic force operating at this level is not that of conflict, and adult language is often useless or misleading in describing events at this level, because words have not always an agreed conventional meaning" (Balint 1968, pp. 16f.).

> The patient says that he feels there is a fault within him, a fault that must be put right. And it is felt to be a fault, not a complex, not a conflict, not a situation. Second, there is a feeling that the cause of this fault is that someone has either failed the patient or defaulted on him; and third, a great anxiety invariably surrounds this area, usually

expressed as a desperate demand that this time the analyst should not — in fact must not — fail him. (ibid., p. 21)

This mode of experience in most cases has a strong impact on the therapeutic relationship: at the time such a failure takes place — which unavoidably must happen sooner or later —,

> ...the fact remains that at any frustration these patients feel that it was intentionally inflicted upon them. They cannot accept that there exists any other cause for a frustration of their desires than malice, evil intention, or at least, criminal negligence. Good things may happen by chance, but frustrations are unchallengeable proofs of evil and hostile sentiments in their environment.
>
> It is definitely a two-person relationship in which, however, only one of the partners matters; his wishes and needs are the only ones that count and must be attended to; the other partner, though felt to be immensely powerful, matters only in so far as he is willing to gratify the first partner's needs and desires or decides to frustrate them; beyond this his personal interests, needs, desires, wishes, etc. simply do not exist.
>
> I must be loved and looked after in every respect by everyone and everything important to me, without anyone demanding any effort or claiming any return for this. It is only my own wishes, interests, and needs that matter; none of the people who are important to me must have any interests, wishes, needs different from mine, and if they have any at all, they must subordinate theirs to mine without any resentment or strain; in fact, it must be their pleasure and their enjoyment to fit in with my wishes. If this happens I shall be good, pleased, and happy, but that is all. If this does not happen, it will be horrifying both for the world and for me. (ibid., pp. 19, 23, 70f.)

Presumably, this client does not always feel this way; in different situations and in different relationships s/he may definitely be able to realize and accept the intersubjective fact that other people have their own rights and needs and feelings. However, as therapy progresses this ability may get lost towards the therapist for a certain time — *or* recede into the background. If it *gets lost* and for a certain time is not available for the client or if it only *gets into the background* and, therefore, remains available at least latently, is a decisive criterion of my definition of regressive processes. This criterion makes it possible to distinguish, whether in a certain case the therapist is confronted with a regressive process or with a process of figure formation, which is adequate to the needs of the client and to the current situation.

It follows that I do *not automatically* regard the described process as a regressive one. This is because one can easily think of the case that the client in the course of this process behaves in accordance with an important need. This need may be the wish to put into the foreground a domain of his or her experience and/or relatedness to other people, in which s/he has problems and therefore intends to *show* it to the therapist.[11] If language, as Balint underlines, in the context of the "basic fault" for the client does not have its usual meaning, then such a *non-verbal enactment* could definitely be an adequate way of communication, which could fulfill the need of the client to convey her or his problems more appropriately than is possible with verbal utterances. Moreover, her or his behavior would also have to be seen as adequate to the situation: where else, if not in therapy, could s/he be in a better place to present his or her problems?

However, not to regard this as a regressive process but as one of figure formation would only be correct with the

---

[11] The parallels to Freud's concept of the "repetition compulsion" (1920/1957) are evident.

precondition that it is still *possible* for the client to bring into the foreground other domains, for instance the verbal one, whenever internal and external demands let it appear useful. With this precondition given, *both* ways of behavior, the non-verbal enactment as well as the verbal communication, must be understood as elements of a process, during which the client, in accordance with the given need and the given situation, puts into the foreground different domains of himself or herself. Balint has called attention to the basic need, which could be relevant here: "*Once and for all we have to recognize the fact that the first wish of a patient is to be understood*" (ibid., p. 93 — italics added).

In the case discussed above Balint would probably have talked of "benign regression" or of "regression aimed at recognition." In Kris's terminology it is a case of "regression in the service of the ego." All of these wordings signal some understanding of the client's intention, but at the same time they seem to *pathologize* respectively *infantilize* his or her behavior unnecessarily by terming it "regression" in the first place. (I guess that this is rather a consequence of the traditional paradigm than Balint's or Kris's design.) I would not call this process regressive; I would prefer to look at it as a manifestation of the fact that the client makes use of the capability to support herself or himself and of *all* of his or her possibilities to make herself or himself be understood. If s/he will in fact feel understood by the therapist does not only depend on the client but also on whether or not the answer s/he will receive is *adequate*.

Of immediate notice is that I have now proceeded to the field of the interaction between client and therapist, which must not be left out, if practical considerations are to be of any value. Therapeutic reality always takes place between two people. Therefore reflections on therapeutic practice cannot remain within the frame of a one-person psychology;

they have to include the dimension of the relationship, too. I do not only want to mention this in general, but to underline it in regard to regressive processes. Again, Balint was one of those who pointed to this dimension repeatedly: "... all events which lead ultimately to therapeutic changes in the patient's mind are initiated by events happening in a two-person relationship, i. e. happening essentially *between* two people and not inside only one of them" (ibid., p. 9).

This also means "... that regression is not only an intrapsychic phenomenon, but also an interpersonal one; for its therapeutic usefulness, its interpersonal aspects are decisive" (ibid., p. 147). For this reason I find it necessary at this point to explicitly introduce another important element of Stern's developmental theory which until now has only played an implicit role in my considerations: Stern's theory does *not* confine itself to the domains of the several senses of *self*, it adds "domains of *relatedness*" to them, which evolve in connection with and parallel to the senses of self, since for Stern "... the infant from the moment of birth is deeply social — being designed to engage in and find uniquely salient interactions with other humans" (1985, p. 235).

This disposition lasts for the whole life and keeps on developing continually; it obeys the same paradigm as the domains of self. Stern himself has illustrated this in Figure 3. shown on the next page.

I want to use this element of Stern's theory now in relation to the client's wish to be understood and as a means to determine more specifically, what an "adequate" answer to it would be: for the client to feel understood the therapist must answer within the domain(s) of relatedness, in which the client has addressed herself or himself to the therapist in the first place.

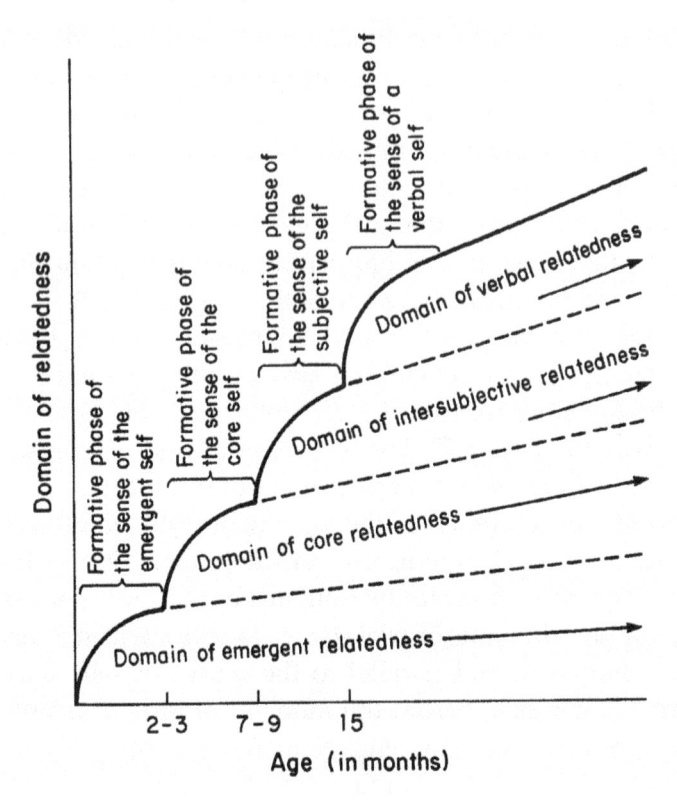

Figure 3: Domains of Relatedness (Stern 1985, p. 33)

To be able to do so the therapist in the course of therapy again and again has to oscillate between the different domains; Moser (1994a; 1994b) has demonstrated this in his impressive case studies very clearly (without using my terminology, of course). It is self-evident that the therapist can carry out this oscillation only, if he has access to these domains within himself and if he is flexible enough to put any of them into the foreground on demand.[12]

---

[12] Some writers have represented this requirement differently; Petzold, e. g., who draws on Balint in this respect, expects "... the

To give an example, while a message given within the verbal domain is likely to be experienced as understood, if it is answered predominantly within the verbal domain, the same does not hold true for messages given within the domain of "core relatedness." If the therapist wants to communicate to the client that s/he has understood this kind of message, s/he needs to give an answer within this domain primarily. Here the words "communication," "understanding," "answering" etc. do not mainly refer to verbal content. If the therapist does not realize this and responds predominantly or even exclusively with words, the client will either feel misunderstood or s/he will be likely to find herself or himself in another kind of desperate situation, which Moser (1989, pp. 107ff.) in his critique of Kohut has characterized as such: "It is my basic hypothesis . . ., that purely verbal ways of understanding, even if communicated in a non-interpretative and empathic way, can become traumatic, if in certain phases the patient is deprived of tangible, physical support" (ibid., p. 109; see also Polenz 1994).

For instance, this may be the case in a situation, in which the client is exposed to intense feelings of pain or despair primarily experienced within the domain of her or his "core self;" from her or his perspective this experience very often calls for direct physical support and containment. If in this situation s/he is given a very sympathetic but only verbal

---

therapist to accompany the regression of the patient with his own regression" (1993, p. 865). Under the preconditions, which I have set up by my definition of regressive processes and by the use of Stern's developmental model, I cannot agree with this representation. However, this disagreement rests, at least in part, upon the different terms of regression respectively regressive processes. If you look at how Petzold, in his *own* words, reformulates the above quoted statement, obviously the agreement with my view is much greater. He demands ". . . the ability and preparedness of the therapist . . . to answer the client's 'affective inquiries' in an emotional and physically-direct way, to immerse in co-affectivity, to allow being touched and moved . . ." (ibid.).

answer and if physical distance is maintained, this may appear cynical and cruel to her or him, just like a cold-hearted and deliberate kind of exposure. In spite of the positive intentions of the therapist the intervention may be experienced by the client as a ". . . sadistic infliction or repetition of an extreme lack of support, presence and security." "Instead of sophisticated verbal empathy to such a patient being touched by a calm hand can convey in a much more tangible way that the therapist empathizes and feels with her or him" (Moser 1989, pp. 137, 124; see also Moser 1994a).

I have been so lucky to grow up in a family, in which physical contact and holding were natural aspects of human communication. Therefore for me — at first in a very naive way — it was more or less a matter of course to practice this aspect of communication in my therapeutic work, too. Later, this attitude was strongly reinforced by the holistic approach of Gestalt therapy. However, the decisive step towards my *conscious* appreciation of physical support took place when, many years ago, a client confronted me with vehement accusations.

> One day this client blamed me for being emotionally frigid and heartless. At first I could only see this reproach as an expression of his distorted perception, because I experienced myself as being empathetic, attentive and benevolent. However, he persisted with his accusations, even when I told him how I felt for him and that I did not recognize myself in his description. Finally he yelled at me: "That can't be true, even now you don't take me into your arms!" Obviously, through my lack of understanding I had contributed to an intensification of his emotional emergency. Now he made it very clear that my attempts to comprehend his situation cognitively-verbally would not bring about resolution for him, because I did not communicate my response on the same level. Then, because we had engaged in a severe conflict it was not

easy for me to give up my self-righteousness or to give in to the wish that I could now see hidden in his reproaches. But when I finally did so, the situation relaxed immediately, and both he and I, who had not felt understood by each other, had tears of relief coming up in our eyes. Then it became very easy to discuss what had happened. With the physical contact sustained, the words now had a healing and clearing effect, too.

I report this event extensively, because for me it led to my understanding of what the above mentioned conditions for an adequate answer of the therapist to the client have to be. Further, the vignette shows that, if the therapist does not give an adequate answer, both s/he and the client are not sufficiently related to each other. In Gestalt therapy terms, there is no personal contact, and there is a great risk for the dialogue to collapse.

This collapse may take place in one of two ways which both follow from the fact that the client had been frustrated in her or his desire to be understood, though s/he contributed all that was in her or his control. The first way is described by Balint as such: the patient is forced "... either to remain at the Oedipal level during the whole of the treatment, or to return there speedily after very brief regressions into the other areas of the mind" (1968, p. 99).

> ... the patient, prompted by his overwhelming need to be understood, ... learns ... to accept tacitly that analysis can deal properly only with such experiences as can be verbalized without great difficulty, the intensity of which does not rise beyond a certain, critical, level. (ibid., p. 106)

Of course, this means that the issue which the client, aiming at recognition, tries to convey, remains without understanding and unworked. As a consequence, the potential successes of the therapy are diminished — if the frustrated and hurt client does not withdraw and quit therapy completely.

The second possibility is this: the client repeats her or his attempt to be understood. In case s/he receives an adequate answer within an appropriate time, this will certainly have a positive effect on the further course of the therapy. In case s/he does not get this answer and decides not to withdraw but to *insist* on her or his need to be understood, serious problems may occur. Here Balint talks of "... the patient's imperative need to regress..." (1959, p. 107) and of "... vehement and noisy reactions, caused by very painful, almost unbearable tensions in the patients" (1965, p. 232). Within the frame of my example, these behaviors in the first place are the results of the therapist not understanding the client's message. In the second place, they also follow from the client's persistence: both the repeated frustration and the increasingly desperate fight for understanding are very likely to put her or him into a hardened position, stuck in the attempt to enforce by means of various forms of psychological pressure what has been withheld from her or him. There is a great danger for this fight to become an end in itself — the fight of Kleist's Michael Kohlhaas, who, as his hostility increases, gets more and more out of touch with his original needs.

What had started as a process of figure formation, by which the client tried to pursue his therapeutic needs, has now turned into a *regressive* process of an obsessional quality. Even worse, the therapist may look at it like Nicoll:

> Patients frequently seem unable to give up their symptoms — at times they even seem to cling to them doggedly, although consciously they declare they long to be well. Something very powerful drags them down and holds them fast in the grip of the neurosis. (quoted in McDougall 1926, p. 284)

The path into the vicious circle of "negative diagnostics" is very short now, and very easily the therapist forgets, "... that the clinical appearance of a regression will depend also on the way the regression is recognized, is accepted, and is responded to by the analyst" (Balint 1968, p. 162).

With the description of this fictitious interaction I certainly do *not* want to say, that *all* regressive processes are induced by a lack of understanding on the part of the *therapists*. To mention a different example, one can imagine a client, who due to negative transferences does not expect to be understood and therefore, out of an ancient resignation, ignores all the positive signs the therapist communicates. In this context I recall an event that recently took place in one of my therapy groups:

> One of the women participants observed with obviously strong empathy the emotionally intense work of another group member. Before this work had come to an end, she burst out saying how much she was moved by what she had seen and that she felt reminded of some of her own experiences, but could not exactly figure out which ones. She did not know how to cope with all the feelings that had been triggered, nor could she say what they were connected to; she just felt completely helpless and upset. The urgency she conveyed by the sound of her voice and the accompanying gestures appeared exaggerated to most of the group members and to myself. Her internal turmoil was obvious; yet, she seemed to radiate some sort of incongruence which elicited hesitation and uncertainty in the group. As soon as she realized that she did not get the expected reaction, she started panicking, burst out crying, appealed with dramatic words and gestures to the group to immediately give her the help she urgently needed, and asked with helplessly looking eyes if there was nobody to understand her.

All of this only took a few minutes. But this had been long enough for the situation of the client on one side and the rest of the group on the other side to come to a critical point. The client had moved into an obvious state of emergency, in which only panic and dramatic appeals were available to her. Both of these evoked the impression of an incongruence to the group members and triggered some sort of paralysis, from which they did not seem to be able to free themselves. This again reinforced the emergency of the client ... I went over to her, sat down at her side, and touched her shoulder with my hand. I told her in a friendly voice that I saw her emergency and that I would like to understand it, while at the same time I felt being pressured by the way she expressed it. Her expression had made it hard for me to come to her spontaneously.

Her first reaction was twofold: On one hand she seemed to relax a little, and on the other hand the look in her eyes appeared one of suspicion. Then, with a mixture of skepticism and confidence, she asked me if I only meant to quiet her. I only needed to repeat the word "... quiet?," and she began a process which illuminated the background of her behavior. Her experience had been that her feelings, especially when they were important to her, had been calmed and placated; as a consequence, she had decided to exaggerate them in cases of emergency and express them as strongly as possible. Thereby she hoped to finally be heard. In case this strategy was not immediately successful, she thought her only chance was to exaggerate her expressions even more.

With this example I want to show that the experience which stimulates a regressive process does not necessarily or exclusively have to take place in the therapeutic situation initially. This example and the previous one indicate two complementary aspects, and in most real situations probably *both*, the client *and* the therapist, will contribute more or less to the misunderstanding. However the responsibility may be distributed in a specific case, my experience as a therapist over the years has lead me to the following hypothesis: *in most cases the regressive processes of the clients are preceded by the desire to be understood, which – for whatever reasons – has been frustrated.*

In this context it is interesting to recall what academic psychology has known about the processing of frustrations for a long time.

First, there is the "frustration-*aggression*-theory" which assumes that frustration often leads to aggression or, in a modified version, that frustration may stimulate various reactions, one of which is aggression.

Second, there is the "frustration-*regression*-theory" according to which after a few frustrations a previously well coordinated pattern of behavior breaks down and gives way to a less differentiated, more "primitive" pattern.

Third, there is the "frustration-*fixation*-theory." It suggests that under frustrating conditions human behavior tends to become rigid, compulsive or aimlessly blind.

Last but not least, there is the possibility for people to withdraw or flee from the frustrating situation. Lewin has called this reaction "leaving the field" (for all four frustration theories see Graumann 1969).

All of the behavioral patterns described by these four theories can be found in the characteristics of regressive processes which I have mentioned above. Though it does not logically follow that frustrations always result in regressive processes, the frustration theories and the psychological research behind them may be seen as indicators which support my hypothesis.

In any case, in my work as a therapist I have taken on the habit of asking my clients, if they feel understood by me, whenever I get the impression that their behavior may be a manifestation of regressive processes. Sometimes I may also ask them, if they might need some other form of support from me than the one they have yet received. From their *nonverbal* reactions to these questions I frequently perceive clues which help me to understand them better or to recognize that they are in need of a clearer *signal* of my understanding. (In most cases my personal contribution to the misunderstanding is not a lack of understanding as such, but a relative unclarity of my nonverbal signals with which I try to communicate my understanding.)

My view on regressive processes and my strategy to deal with them is very much in tune with the basic strategy and relational structure Balint recommends for the work with regressed patients. The far reaching analogies to my view of the therapeutic relationship (see Staemmler 1993) cannot be ignored:

> ... I tried to establish a relationship in which neither of us would be all-powerful, in which both of us admitted our limitations in the hope that in this way a fruitful collaboration could be established between two people who were not fundamentally different in importance, weight, and power.... It was done by the analyst avoiding even a resemblance of being omniscient and overpowerful; on the other hand he demonstrated the willingness to accept the role of a primary object whose chief function is recognizing, and being with, the patient. (Balint 1968, pp. 171f.)

Very often the question, if s/he feels understood, has a positive effect on the client just because it implicitly conveys that the therapist *tries* to understand her or him. Of course, this is rarely sufficient for the client to be able to say *in words*, how s/he did not feel understood. But it frequently helps her or him to stop the regressive process and again to activate her or his verbal capabilities. In the dialogue that ensues it can be clarified how the misunderstanding began, and a joint reconciliation to the message which the therapist had not understood at first, can take place. This facilitates the therapist's deeper understanding of the client's next attempt to enact and thus communicate his or her problem.

It may be superfluous to point out that during this dialogue the therapist has to attend to not remaining within the verbal realm for longer than is absolutely necessary. The verbal level must only *transitionally* come into the foreground to serve as a means to establish a new frame of mutual understanding. Within this frame, the client can again return to the figure formation process, which brings into the foreground the important other domain of her or his sense of self and relatedness — now with a greater chance to receive an adequate response from the therapist. Without sharing the structural formulations, I agree with Petzold's following opinion:

> An exclusively verbal approach to therapy, which focuses only on cognitive insight and which, by means of verbal interpretations, tries to find an access to the atmospheres of the preverbal realm, to the sensations and feelings of the *primary structure* of the personality, i. e. to the *archaic self of the body* — such approach will only, or at least predominantly, find access to the *secondary structure* of the personality ... (1989, 63 — italics in original)

I now want to summarize the thoughts I have tried to put forth in this section: in my Gestalt therapy point of view, the nonverbal enactment of the client, which from a psychoanalytic standpoint may appear as a form of regression, is not in every case a regressive process. It frequently is rather an act of self-support of the client, a nonverbal *signal* to the therapist meaning that the client hopes for an understanding *act* instead of a primarily verbal reaction. It can be regarded as a *scenic message*, with which the client tries to convey that s/he needs a handhold — not only the one that can be given with empathic words, but also and especially the security, safety and existential reassurance that sometimes only *physical* contact and support can provide (see Winnicott 1965, pp. 240ff.; Staemmler 1981; Kepner 1988).[13] Sometimes the enactment of the client is also some kind of test, where s/he tests "the quality of the analyst's holding capacities" (Stewart 1989, p. 226). As soon as s/he can be sure that her or his desire for understanding and holding will be fulfilled, s/he is likely to immerse into the realm of herself or himself which s/he wants to show to the therapist.

As Balint said,

> ...the regression for the sake of recognition presupposes an environment that accepts and consents to sustain and carry the patient like the earth or the water sustains and carries a man who entrusts his weight to them.... The analyst must not resist, must consent, must not give rise to too much friction, must accept and carry the patient for a while, must prove more or less indestructible, must not insist on maintaining harsh boundaries ... All this means consent, participation, and involvement, but *not* necessarily action, only understanding and tolerance ... The symbolic expression of this ... relationship in the analytic situation is often some sort of physical contact with the analyst ... This contact is ... vitally important for the progress of the treatment; with it the patient can get on, without it he may feel abandoned, lost, despoiled of his possible changes, incapable of moving. (1968, p. 145 — italics in original)

The latter situation is very likely to be experienced by the client as a repetition and reinforcement of the original

---

[13] I presuppose the ethical standards that are generally accepted (see for instance Kertay & Reviere 1993).

trauma, "... since reliving trauma without appropriate interpersonal support is simply to be overwhelmed again by the experience and to be retraumatized" (Chu 1991, p. 329).

Regressive processes in the sense of my definition are, according to my hypothesis, very likely to happen, if the longing of the client to be understood is repeatedly frustrated; both client and therapist may contribute to that frustration. In the interest of the client and of a fertile progress of the therapy, such processes need to be interrupted as soon as possible, because they are counterproductive and threaten the basis of the therapeutic relationship. The therapist can do this by negotiating with the client the possibility of a misunderstanding and her or his own contribution to it in order to prepare a frame for an improved understanding during the further course of the work. He should invite the client to enact his problem again, as soon as the intermediate verbal clarification has sufficiently taken place. From this point the therapist can support the process of the client best "... by sincerely giving up, for the time being, any attempt at forcing the patient back to the verbal level" (Balint 1968, p. 177).

Under these conditions, a figure formation process can take its course, by which the client can put forth the domain of his sense of self that he needs to make the therapist understand. Such a process is not regressive in kind, it is a desirable act of self-support of the client. The more such processes of figure formation are recognized, welcomed and adequately answered by the therapist, the less there is a need for the client to embark in regressive processes.

Final Considerations

In this final section I want to turn to some questions which now have a more complete base. The first question addresses the criteria which make it possible in practice to discern, whether the therapist is confronted with a regressive process of the client or with a process of figure formation. This will lead to the question, how the first one can be transformed into the second one.

A figure formation process of the kind I have described above can be differentiated from a regressive process essentially by the fact, that during the former the client also has the other domains of his or her senses of self at hand, if they are needed. S/he is not imprisoned in the domain, which s/he first chose to bring into the foreground of her or his experience and with which s/he first related to the therapist. In contrast to this, during a regressive process the flexibility in the change between figure and ground is seriously restricted; the client is not able to activate and use another (as an example: the verbal) than the momentarily dominating domain of her or his senses of self (as an example: the "core self"). I now want to deepen the example I have just indicated in brackets, but before I do I would like to mention that, according to my definition of regressive processes, the reverse case could also be discussed — the case in which the client is restricted to the verbal domain and cannot activate her or his "core self." (For Gestalt therapists this is probably the more familiar case, though it is usually not discussed in terms of a regressive process.)

In practice, my example manifests itself in the inability of the client, to report her or his experience to the therapist verbally *during* the regressive process. If in such a situation the therapist insists on a *verbal* description of the client's internal experience, the client has only two choices: either s/he fails or s/he complies by interrupting the ongoing (regressive) process. From the perspective of the therapist, this very likely means that the therapist either gets the impression not to reach the client with her or his verbal message or feels that s/he is disturbing the client. In other words, in her or his personal resonance (which I do *not* like to call "countertransference" — see Staemmler 1993, pp. 158ff.) the therapist feels being restricted to a certain domain of relatedness by the behavior of the client; s/he does not feel free to choose any domain, within which s/he wants to communicate with the client.

Therefore, in order to be able to intervene appropriately, the therapist has to free herself or himself from the seeming restriction of her or his behavioral margin. In my example s/he may do this with a forcible request to the client to *talk* about her or his experience; in many situations this may be an effective method to disturb or interrupt a regressive process.[14] A lengthy verbal message of the therapist may have a similar effect, if it is expressed in an emphatic way which is apt to attract the attention of the client. Very often it is helpful to so to speak "by the way" make some sort of physical contact with the client at the same time; this insures that the client does not only feel interrupted but also feels accepted. In cases in which the client is very heavily involved in a regressive process, the attempt to interrupt her or him without any concomitant physical contact remains futile.

I have already explained why, as a rule of thumb, I find such an interruption desirable. I cannot see the therapeutic sense in not using all possible kinds of self-support of the client. To do so would passively condone or even encourage a state of the client, in which s/he does not have important resources available to her or him; for example, to work successfully with intrapsychic difficulties and to maintain contact with the therapist.

---

[14] In the reverse case, the one more familiar to gestalt therapists, the regressive process can be interrupted by the request to the client to express herself or himself with gestures, sounds, movements etc. instead of words. "The mode of dialogue can be dancing, song, words, or any modality that expresses and moves the energy between or among the participants" (Yontef & Simkin 1989, p. 326).

Therefore the interruption of a regressive process serves the necessary *clarification of the relationship* (especially the "working alliance") and the *renewal of the understanding* between therapist and client. It also reestablishes the *flexibility* of figure and ground in the experience of the client and thereby opens up the *access to additional domains of relatedness* between therapist and client. The interruption does *not* serve to *prevent* the foreground experience of the sense of self, to which the client had been restricted during the regressive process. To the contrary, the clarification that takes place during the interruption forms a precondition for the client to be able to bring the respective domain into the foreground again without having to isolate it from the other domains, i. e. *without* engaging in a regressive process.[15]

If a process of figure formation takes place in the client — either primarily (within the frame of a successful communication with the therapist) or secondarily (after a successful interruption of a regressive process and a clarification of the kind described above) —, in which, as an example, her or his "core-self" comes into the foreground, the therapist's request for a verbal report normally does *not* lead to an interruption of the ongoing process but to an *additional* dialogue on the verbal level. Even if the verbal level should force the other domains into the background for a while, their return into the foreground, for example: the revival of the "core-self," is quite easily possible. The general flow of the therapeutic process as a whole, i. e. the work on the actual theme, continues. And, last but not least, the therapeutic contact is not disturbed.

---

[15] If it proves to be impossible to reestablish the flexibility of figure and ground by the means mentioned above, this could be a hint to the use of splitting mechanisms, by which the client tries to isolate the different domains from each other (see Staemmler 1995, pp. 61ff.).

Now I want to relate an example from one of my clients:

The client (and frequently me, too) found this work quite difficult. She often complained that she did not adequately convey to me how profoundly desperate and hopeless she felt. Most of her attempts to share her feelings failed; when she started to talk, she immediately interrupted herself again and collapsed into a silence of deep resignation, because she thought that words could never express her feelings anyway. When in rare moments she managed to describe her internal experience in fluent speech, she also was later frustrated, since as she had talked she had felt completely disconnected from the feelings she had talked about.

This discrepancy was easily observable. Yet, I was fairly certain to reflect my client's reality accurately. The words, with which I fed back to her what I had understood, were usually reconfirmed by her, but they did not affect her sense of failure to communicate how disastrous she felt. All of her troublesome efforts did not result in the satisfaction to feel understood by me.

As time went by, it became increasingly clear that neither her efforts to make herself understood nor my attempts to convey my understanding would lead to the desired aim. Finally I decided to look for another access. I asked her, if she could imagine what I would do, if I really understood her. Her nonverbal reaction looked like a mixture of alarm, amazement, and hope to me; so I continued this thread. However, it took many sessions of detailed work before her inhibitions and barriers of shame were overcome to a degree that allowed her to dare to tell me what her spontaneous fantasy in response to my question had been: she would curl up while I held her in my arms, and then she would suck my thumb.

The next four or five sessions she dealt with the question, if she should ask me to do with her what she had fantasized. Many more inhibitions and sentiments of shame and fear had to be worked through, before she risked the first step to lean on my shoulder carefully with our chairs side by side. Many more hours went by as she slowly approached in reality what in her mind's eye she had kept seeing ever since I had first asked my question. As she did so, it occurred to me that the closer she got physically, the better she was able to maintain eye contact with me, and the easier it seemed to be for her to describe her experience in words from time to time. To my surprise she even changed perspectives at a certain moment and asked me if I was comfortable while I held her in my arms — she had never showed any interest in my experience before.

Parallel to the process of her coming closer to me, the difficulties of the client became more and more evident to confess to herself (and to me) her desires for holding, closeness and shelter; these desires appeared so monstrous to her, that the idea of giving way to them made her extremely afraid of destroying her relationship with me. When she finally found the courage to take my thumb into her mouth, she started — surprisingly even to herself — to suck it quickly and very greedily. As soon as she realized what she did, she interrupted herself again, looked at me with eyes full of fear, and said she was afraid I would withdraw from her once and for all. It seemed as if the physical contact had made it possilie for some of her problems to become clearer and hence amenable to therapeutic processing. Neither her troublesome verbal efforts to behave adjustedly (as an "adult") nor her taciturnity had in former sessions opened up an access to these problems.

In Balint's terms, one could describe this process as a "regression aimed at recognition," which made it possible for the client "... to give up the security gained by relying on the 'caretaker' services of (her) false ego..." (1968, p. 111). In Gestalt therapy terms, we are dealing with an experiment, in which the client tried out a desired behavior (sucking my thumb) she at first had only fantasized, and by doing so became aware of the *theme* (see Staemmler 1993, pp. 232ff.; 1994, p. 16) he was working on. This theme on one hand consisted of her intense longing for closeness, her desire to confidently turn with all her unfulfilled needs to another person and let herself fall into her or his arms. On the other hand, there was her fear to be abandoned exactly in that moment, when she would surrender to her immense neediness in the face of a significant other. Her fear had a very high *rank* (probably of the fifth degree – see Staemmler 1993, pp. 275ff.), since she was afraid to be annihilated by the expected abandonment.[16]

What at first sight may seem as the fulfillment of a need (the sucking of my thumb), at a closer look reveals itself as a (for the time being) *failing* attempt to fulfill the desire for closeness. A need fulfillment does not take place, because it is prevented by the tremendous fear. The experiment – the client's really sucking my thumb, not just fantasizing about it – at first only opens up the way for her becoming aware of both her need *and* her fear (i. e. of the theme) and thereby forms the necessary precondition for her to be recognized (as well as understand herself).

In other words one could say, the physical holding made it possible for the client to transform her problem into a gestalt, which made it easier to be worked on therapeutically. Thereby her problem, of course, had not been solved; a first stage had been reached, in that the client had taken one step further into the relationship with me.

---

[16] The terms "theme" and "rank of a theme" form the cornerstones of the dialogic approach to diagnosis, which I have proposed in one of my books (1993).

Now her problem became more evident within this relationship (some may prefer to say: within the transference) and promoted the client to participate more actively and responsibly in the therapeutic process. The intention of the client to make her problem visible and to engage into its change on one side, and my intention to provide sufficient support for that on the other side, started to develop a cooperative, synergetic effect, after communication led to a joint level of understanding. For this to happen, two conditions had to be met: the interruption of her regressive process (the troublesome and unsuccessful effort to express herself only with words) and the offer to bring into the foreground a domain of relatedness she had not used before.

*

Let me briefly repeat the difference I see between regressive processes and processes of figure formation of the kind I have described above: in a regressive process a certain domain of the senses of self and/or relatedness *forces* itself upon the experience of a person and annuls the other domains for a certain period of time; in a figure formation process the person still has a *choice* to *decide*, if s/he puts a certain domain into the foreground of her or his experience, which s/he feels is useful in a given situation and/or for a given task.

In what I have said in this article, I have presupposed that both kinds of processes, at least when taking place in a therapeutic setting, rest upon a certain motivation: in my view it is the client's intent to focus the therapist's and her or his own awareness on the domain, within which s/he — at first in most cases more or less vaguely — senses the source of some of her or his sufferings. If the therapist provides sufficient understanding, this suffering can be explored, the theme can come into awareness and worked with.

Just as any other form of behavior and experience both of the processes in discussion here may not only spring from the client's need for change. They may as well be put in the service of avoidances. To this distinction I shall turn now.

In psychoanalytic literature I have found a similar distinction: Alexander talks of "two forms of regression." The first one is described as a "return to ... unsettled traumatic experiences of the past" (1956, p. 179). Ferenczi characterizes this phenomenon as such: "... the patient, in the attempt to uncover the origin of his illness suddenly lapses into a childish or childlike attitude" (1931/1955, p. 131). I think, I do not need to again mention the theoretical and practical difficulties that arise from the use of the words "return," "childish," and "childlike." At this point I use the quotations only to allude to the positive intent of the wished for therapeutic process which the clients pursue by both their regressive and their figure formation processes. These intentions are in accordance with the *need for change*, even if the external shape they sometimes take on may evoke a contrary impression.

The second "form of regression," to which I want to refer only briefly, obviously springs from a different motive. It is "... a return to a previously successful form of adaptation. ... the mental apparatus is seeking gratification according to an old pattern" (Alexander 1956, p. 179). This description resembles both Balint's "regression aimed at gratification" and Perls's definition of regression, which I have already quoted above: "Regression means a withdrawal to a position where you can provide your own support, where you feel secure" (1969, p. 61).

If you regard a regressive process as a restriction in the capacity of a person to realize earlier acquired competencies according to her or his needs and the conditions of the situation, you do not assume at first sight that Alexander's second form of regression as well as the behavior described by Perls, were the results of regressive processes. Alexander and Perls both suggest that, in those respective instances, the person tries to fulfill a need for pleasant feelings of security, safety, and gratification. What should be regressive about that?

The question can only be answered, if one takes into account the circumstances, under which the respective behaviors take place. According to my definition, they would only have to be called regressive, if the person was bound to them in spite of a given need and a situation, which call for different, or at least additional, competencies. As a matter of fact, in the therapeutic situation the aim of the client is to pursue her or his wish for growth and for the resolution of her or his personal problems; security, safety, and the gratification of needs may to a certain degree be supportive for this pursuit, but they are not the actual aim of therapy. They do not even take up the majority of time. To the contrary, the confrontation with fears, deficiencies and frustrations as well as the demand for the therapist's support are frequent and necessary steps on the therapeutic path of the client.

In *such* moments an exclusive withdrawal to a secure and self-sufficient position would have to be called regressive. One sometimes encounters regressive processes of this kind in people, who have a hard time standing intra- and/or interpersonal tensions. Instead of experiencing these tensions and trying and learning to deal with them, which would be the best thing to do in the interest of health, growth and satisfactory human relationships, they do not seem to be engaged in doing anything other than having a "good" time (for instance, through the use of addictive substancies). In therapy some of these clients exhibit manipulative behaviors which are designed to make the therapist satisfy their need to feel "good." Under such circumstances a regressive process takes on the function of an avoidance in respect to the clients' wish to cope with their problems.

For most Gestalt therapists it is a matter of course, that any behavior and experience does not have a meaning *per se*, but acquires its meaning by context and background. This also holds true for regressive processes; they can be congruent with the client's need for change, and they can function as a means of an avoidance of this need. Again, a Gestalt therapists' view converges with one of Balint's assertions: "Evidently, the two functions that an analyst can observe most frequently during treatment are regression as a form of resistance, and regression as a therapeutic ally" (1986, p. 127).

*

At the end of this article I want to deal with a question, which is closely related to the therapeutic handling of regressive processes and is often controversial. The polarized positions are reflected in the two following quotations: "... we are a long way away from an approach based on 'regress the client to the traumatic situation and then reparent them'" (Philippson 1993, p. 122). The contrary is held by Petzold:

> In the transference the therapist "becomes" the mother, father etc. and, in regression, "embodies," what the patient has missed on the different levels of development. He anchors deficient relatives (for instance, the absent father) by "becoming father" for the patient, by emotionally adopting him, so to speak ... Within the frame of the patient's regression in age the therapist *renourishes* the patient within the "prevalent pathogenic milieu," i. e. where the privations have taken place. (1989, p. 61 — italics in original)

"Reparenting" and "re-nourishing" are the key words of this controversy. These words refer to a therapeutic strategy, which sometimes is called "regressive work" and is characterized as follows:

> Regressive work ... is a therapeutic technique in which the client contracts to function as if younger than his or her chronological age and to allow the therapist to provide healthy parenting.... In regressive work, the client focuses, primarily through role play, on an earlier developmental period in order to reexperience the feelings and conflicts of that age and ultimately to resolve treatment issues through a corrective emotional experience. The therapist usually acts as a beneficient caretaker, providing support, discipline, insight, wisdom, and guidance. (Smith 1990, p. 253)

For me the first question which arises is this: is it possible at all, as Philippson says, to have the clients "regress to the traumatic situation and then reparent them" or, as Petzold puts it, to "re-nourish the patient *within* the prevalent pathogenic milieu?" After all I have said about the temporal aspect of the term regression, I have to negate this question. Petzold contradicts his own insight; he himself has clearly underlined the phenomenological fact, that "regression ... is not temporal, since it takes place in a given here and now." In his sentences about "re-nourishing" the traces of this insight can only be found in the inverted commas in front and behind the words "becomes," "embodies" and "becoming father." If one takes Petzold's hint to phenomenology seriously the client can never again — not even during a regressive process — find himself "*within* the prevalent pathogenic milieu." Even if a time machine would make it possible, I would not wish for the client to return exactly to that milieu, which happens to be just the one, "where the privations have taken place."

Where the client goes to in her or his mind is the domain of her or his senses of self and/or relatedness, within which s/he, *within the given time perspective*, experiences her or his psychological problems. These problems may have started in earlier traumatic situations and milieus, but since then they have been subjected to various influences and trans-formations. They do not exist in their original condition anymore; therefore it is impossible to regress to them. Today, as an adult, the client can immerse into subjective conditions, which may *resemble* the past ones, and thus s/he may relatively well *remember* early events (see Bower's "state-dependent memory," 1981). But s/he will never be in the exact condition as before; the recollections here and now may be as exact as can be, but they will always differ from the immediate experience there and then.

No therapist can turn back time. We can never undo our clients' past sufferings; we cannot, by means of a quasi-magical act, put our clients back into their pretraumatic condition in order to then "reparent" them in a better way than they were actually parented. A "new beginning" (Balint) is possible today only in today's time perspective; the famous somersault of Balint's client (see 1968, p. 128) exemplifies this clearly. The chances for change are to be found in the present situation, i. e. in the *new* milieu of the present therapeutic relationship: in this relationship the client can discover that today there are different realities and possibilities than in former times, and s/he can learn to attribute new meanings to what has happened in the past.

Psychic deficits, which originally have been the outcome of deficient relationships, cannot be deleted by simple "re-nourishing." They, too, require a process of change within the *client* (see Staemmler 1993, pp. 251ff.); a friendly substitution from the outside is not enough. Balint explicitly warns the therapist of the temptation to think he could

> ... compensate for the patient's early privations and give more care, love, affection than the patient's parents have given originally (and even if he tried, he would almost certainly fail).... The aim is that the patient should be able to find himself, to accept himself, and to get on with himself, knowing all the time that there is a scar in himself, his basic fault, which cannot be "analysed" out of existence ... (1968, pp. 179f.)

Of course I do not speak against care, love and affection. But I do object to any competition with the client's past significant relationships and to the futile effort to try and prove to her or him that the therapist is the *superior* person, who can therapize the wounds of the past away. Human beings are not machines, whose broken parts can simply be substituted by new ones; a repair paradigm is not a paradigm of *human* or even *humane* change. In other words: "The patient is not simply a vessel which has been filled up with bad experiences, and consequently, can be emptied out and refilled with remedial messages" (Haaken & Schlaps 1991, p. 44).

The therapeutic relationship can be helpful in that it provides the client with the chance to form new representations of herself or himself as well as of significant others. But this cannot simply be induced by a compensatory abundance of love and care used as a forcible means to delete old representations and to implement new ones. There is no way around the necessity for the client to deal with the difficulties which have for her or him followed from the unchangeable *historical facts* of her or his life. There is no way around the necessity to thoroughly work on the psychic mechanisms with which the client stands in her or his own way, for instance by resisting the assimilation of new, positive experiences.

The therapist's love and care for the client are important aspects of her or his part of the therapeutic relationship, but they neither free the therapist from the concrete therapeutic work nor do they free the client from her or his responsibility for how s/he *today* creates her or his life. The therapist must accept this; if s/he does not, s/he is in danger of a severe fallacy, which

> ... may be described as being seduced by the unending suffering of the regressed patient into accepting responsibility for creating conditions in which, at long last, no more unnecessary suffering will be inflicted on him. Although this appears to be a highly commendable rational, experience shows that in pratice it rarely works. (Balint 1968, p. 111)

By the way, even Ferenczi had to face this when he reflected upon the results of his experiments at the end of his life (see Haynal 1989). I do not mention this to depreciate the great courage with which he opposed the abstinent and hence sometimes traumatic attitude of Freud's psychoanalysis; nor do I mention this to support the errant conclusion that the attitude of orthodox analysis would have been proved right by the results of his experiments. I do mention this, because with Balint I hold that

> this sort of response to the regression inevitably impresses the patient as an acceptance that his basic fault was caused by a "bad" environment and that his analyst is willing and able to structure the world so that the effect of malicious and harmful influences may be greatly reduced. As we have here to deal with experiences belonging to the area of the basic fault, it does not make any difference whether the analyst has stated this in so many words or has only tacitly allowed the patient to interpret his behaviour as implying it, the resulting expectations will be the same. (1968, p. 111)

They are the expectations of a person, who feels powerlessly and helplessly exposed to both bad and good circumstances, who sees herself or himself as a suffering victim of an evil past or, as long as everything goes well, as a happy victim of a superior therapeutic present, but still rather as a *victim* than as a person, who takes the lead in her or his life herself or himself. Balint has strongly advised against this constellation:

> If the analyst's response, e. g. satisfying the patient's expectations, creates an impression in the patient that his analyst is knowledgeable and capable, bordering on being omniscient and omnipotent, this response should be considered as risky and inadvisable; it is likely to increase the *inequality* between patient and analyst, which may lead to the creation of addiction-like states by exacerbating the patient's basic fault. (ibid., p. 168 — italics added)

In many cases the result will be perpetual regressive processes, because one cannot cure one evil with another evil: the aftermath of past relational patterns of inequality cannot be cured with a therapeutic relational pattern of inequality.

Therefore I don't find it desirable for me as a therapist to try to "become" a better mother or father of my clients. I prefer to express and use the motherly and fatherly aspects of my personality *as a therapist*. Maybe for a certain time the client sees me through the glasses of transferences or idealizations as a positive motherly or fatherly person; s/he certainly has the right to do so. Sometimes I find it makes sense not to challenge this form of experience. Sometimes I find it necessary to question it carefully or strongly; I have elaborated on this question elsewhere (see Staemmler 1993, pp. 120ff.). In any case, for me it never means to identify with the client's perspective and to try myself to "become father" for her or him. That is why in a therapeutic context for me the term "adoption" has quite a different meaning as it does for Petzold. When I talk of "adopting" a client, I certainly do not mean to put the client into an infantile position and myself into the position of a parent. For me it means

> ... an unconditional offer to engage in a relationship, an offer which is valid from a certain point in time on, even if at this point in time it is not fully clear to me, who the person is, whom I am "adopting." (This kind of "adoption") is of extreme one-sidedness, some sort of advance concession, a generous gift to the other person, for which I do not expect to get back anything. (ibid., p. 115)

It is only on the basis of this kind of decision for a certain person that I feel able to engage in a long term therapeutic relationship with clients, who to me appear to suffer from severe psychological disturbances and frequently use regressive processes. Only on this basis is it possible for me to respond adequately to the messages of these clients, with which they relate to me both within the verbal and the nonverbal domain. And only on this basis do I have the strength again and again to protect them from the degrading wake of their regressive tendencies and offer my help to turn them into fertile processes of figure formation.

References

Abend, S. M., Porder, M. S., & Willick, M. S. (1983). *Borderline patients: Psychoanalytic perspectives.* Madison, CT: International Universities Press.

Alexander, F. (1956). Two forms of regression and their therapeutic implications. *Psychoanalytic Quarterly 25*, 178-196.

Balint, M. (1959). *Thrills and regression.* London: Hogarth Press.

Balint, M. (1965). *Primary love and psychoanalytic technique.* London: Tavistock Publications.

Balint, M. (1968). *The basic fault: Therapeutic aspects of regression*. London: Tavistock Publications.
Bittner, G. (1988). Heilende Körpererfahrung? In H.-V. Werthmann (Ed.), *Unbewußte Phantasien – Neue Aspekte der psychoanalytischen Theorie und Praxis* (pp. 285-300). München: Pfeiffer.
Bouchard, M.-A., & Guérette, L. (1991). Psychotherapy as a hermeneutical experience. *Psychotherapy 28/3*, 385-394.
Bower, G.H. (1981). Mood and memory. *American Psychologist 36*, 129-148.
Chu, J. A. (1991). The repetition compulsion revisited: Reliving dissociated trauma. *Psychotherapy 28/2*, 327-332.
Dornes, M. (1993). *Der kompetente Säugling – Die präverbale Entwicklung des Menschen*. Frankfurt/M.: Fischer.
Ferenczi, S. (1928/1955). The elasticity of psychoanalytic technique. In S. Ferenczi, *Final contributions to the problems and methods of psycho-analysis* (M. Balint, Ed.). London: Hogarth Press.
Ferenczi, S. (1931/1955). Child-analysis in the analysis of adults. In S. Ferenczi, *Final contributions to the problems and methods of psycho-analysis* (M. Balint, Ed.), London: Hogarth Press.
Frank, L. K. (1939). Time perspectives. *Journal of Social Philosophy 4*, 293-312.
Freud, A. (1963). Regression as a principle in mental development. *Bulletin of the Menninger Clinic 27*, 126-139.
Freud, S. (1900/1958). The intepretation of dreams. In The standard edition of the complete psychological works of Sigmund Freud, Vol. 24. London: Hogarth Press.
Freud, S. (1914/1957). On the history of the psycho-analytic movement. In S. Freud, *Standard edition, Vol. 14* (J. Strachey, Ed.). London: Hogarth Press.
Freud, S. (l920/1957). Beyond the pleasure principle. In S. Freud, *Standard edition, Vol. 18* (J. Strachey, Ed.). London: Hogarth Press.
Freud, S. (1953/1964). An outline of psychoanalysis In S. Freud, *Standard edition, Vol. 23* (J. Strachey, Ed.). London: Hogarth Press.
Goldstein, K. (1939). *The organism: A holistic approach to biology derived from pathological data in man*. New York: American Book Company.
Graumann, C. F. (1969). *Motivation*. Frankfurt/M.: Akademische Verlagsgesellschaft & Huber.

Haaken, J., & Schlaps, A. (1991). Incest resolution therapy and the objectification of sexual abuse. *Psychotherapy 28/1*, 39-47.
Haynal, A. (1989). *Die Technik-Debatte in der Psychoanalyse – Freud, Ferenczi, Balint*. Frankfurt/M.: Fischer.
Heisterkamp, G. (1993). *Heilsame Berührungen – Praxis leibfundierter analytischer Psychotherapie*. München: Pfeiffer.
Heraclitus (1979). *The art and thought of Heraclitus: An edition of the fragments with translation and commentary* (C. H. Kahn, Ed.). Cambridge: Cambridge University Press.
Herman, J. L. (1992). *Trauma and recovery*. New York: Basic Books.
Husserl, E. (1980). *Ideen zu einer reinen Phänomenologie und phänomenologischen Psychologie – Erstes Buch: Allgemeine Einführung in die reine Phänomenologie*. Tübingen Niemeyer.
Kepner, J. I. (1987). *Body process: A Gestalt approach to working with the body in psychotherapy*. New York: Gardner Press.
Kernberg, O. F. (1985). *Internal world and external reality: Object relations theory applied*. New York: Jason Aronson.
Kertay, L., & Reviere, S. L. (1993). The use of touch in psychotherapy: Theoretical and ethical considerations. *Psychotherapy 30/1*, 32-40.
Kozulin, A. (1990). The concept of regression and Vygotskian developmental theory. *Developmental Review 10/2*, 218-238.
Kris, E. (1977). *Die ästethische Illusion – Phänomene der Kunst in der Sicht der Psychoanalyse*. Frankfurt/M.: Suhrkamp.
Laplanche, J., & Pontalis, J.-B. (1988). *The language of psycho-analysis*. London: Karnac.
Lewin, K. (1952). *Field theory in social science: Selected theoretical papers*. London: Tavistock Publications.
Lichtenberg, J. D. (1983). *Psychoanalysis and infant research*. Hillsdale, NJ: Erlbaum.
Mahler, S. M., Pine, F., & Bergman, A. (1975). *The psychological birth of the human infant: Symbiosis and individuation*. London: Hutchinson.
Mc Dougall, W. (1926). *An outline of abnormal psychology*. London: Methnen.
Modell, A. H. (1984). *Psychoanalysis in a new context*. New York: International Universities Press.
Moser, T. (1989). *Körpertherapeutische Phantasien – Psychoanalytische Fallgeschichten neu betrachtet*. Frankfurt/M.: Suhrkamp.
Moser, T. (1994a). *Stundenbuch – Protokolle aus der Körperpsychotherapie*. Frankfurt/M.: Suhrkamp.

Moser, T. (1994b). *Ödipus in Panik und Triumph – Eine Körpesychotherapie*. Frankfurt/M.: Suhrkamp.
Perls, F. S. (1969). *Gestalt therapy verbatim*. Moab, UT: Real People Press.
Perls, F. S., Hefferline, R., & Goodman, P. (1951). *Gestalt therapy: Excitement and growth in the human personality*. New York: The Julian Press.
Peterfreund, E. (1978). Some critical comments on psychoanalytic conceptualizations of infancy. *International Journal of Psycho-Analysis 59*, 427-441.
Petzold, H. G. (1989). Die "vier Wege der Heilung" in der Integrativen Therapie – Teil II, Praxeologische Grundkonzepte, dargestellt an Beispielen aus der Integrativen Bewegungstherapie. *Integrative Therapie 15/1*, 42-96.
Petzold, H. G. (1993a). *Integrative Therapie – Modelle, Theorien und Methoden für eine schulenübergreifende Psychotherapie, Bd. 2: Klinische Theorie*. Paderborn: Junfermann.
Petzold, H. G., Goffin, J. J. M., & Oudhof, J. (1993). Protektive Faktoren und Prozesse – Die "positive" Perspektive in der longitudinalen, "klinischen Entwicklungspsychologie" und ihre Umsetzung in die Praxis der Integrativen Therapie. In H. G. Petzold (Ed.), *Psychotherapie und Babyforschung, Bd. 1: Frühe Schädigungen, späte Folgen? – Die Herausforderung der Längsschnittforschung* (pp. 345-497). Paderborn: Junfermann.
Philippson, P. (1993). Gestalt and regression. *British Gestalt Journal 2/2*, 121-124.
Polenz, S. v. (1994). *Und er bewegt sich doch – Ketzerisches zur Körperabstinenz der Psychoanalyse*. Frankfurt/M.: Suhrkamp.
Rorty, R. (1980). *Philosophy and the mirror of nature*. Princeton, NJ: Princeton University Press.
Rutter, M. (l989). Pathways from childhood to adult life. *Journal of Child Psychology and Psychiatry 30/1*, 23-51.
Scharfetter, C. (1993). Eros therapeutikos – Liebe und Ethik in der Therapie. *Psychotherapie, Psychosomatik und medizinische Psychologie 43*, 254-261.
Smith, S. (1990). Regressive work as a therapeutic treatment. *Transactional Analysis Journal 20/4*, 253-262.
Staemmler, F.-M. (1981). Bitte berühren! *Psychologie heute 6*, 34-37.

Staemmler, F.-M. (1989). Etiketten sind für Flaschen, nicht für Menschen — Anmerkungen zur Diagnostik-Diskussion. *Gestalttherapie 3/1*, 71-77.

Staemmler, F.-M. (1993). *Therapeutische Beziehung und Diagnose — Gestalttherapeutische Antworten*. München: Pfeiffer.

Staemmler, F.-M. (1994). On Layers and Phases - A Message from Overseas, in. The Gestalt Journal 17/1, 5-31.

Staemmler, F.-M. (1995). *Der "leere Stuhl" — Ein Beitrag zur Technik der Gestalttherapie*. München: Pfeiffer.

Staemmler, F.-M. (1997). Cultivated uncertainty: An attitude for Gestalt therapists. *British Gestalt Journal 6/1*, 40-48.

Staemmler, F.-M. (2000). Der schiefe Turm von Pisa — oder: Das unstimmige Konzept der "frühen Störung." *Integrative Therapie 26/1*, 64-95.

Staemmler, F.-M., & Bock, W. (1991). *Ganzheitliche Veränderung in der Gestalttherapie*. München: Pfeiffer.

Stern, D. N. (1985). *The interpersonal world of the infant: A view from psychoanalysis and developmental psychology*. New York: Basic Books.

Steward, H. (1989). Technique at the basic fault/regression. *International Journal of Psycho-Analysis 70/2*, 221-230.

Stierlin, H. (1995). Wir müssen lernen, innere Konflikte auszuhalten — Interview. *Psychologie heute 22/4*, 35-41.

Whorf, B. J. (1956). *Language, thought and reality*. Cambridge, MA: MIT Press.

Willick, M. (1990). Psychoanalytic concepts of the etiology of severe mental illness. *Journal of the American Psychoanalytic Association 38/4*, 1059-1081.

Winnicott, D. W. (1965). *The maturational process and the facilitating environment: Studies in the theory of emotional development*. London: Hogarth Press.

Yontef, G. (1993). *Awareness, dialogue and process: Essays on Gestalt therapy*. Highland, NY: The Gestalt Journal Press.

Yontef, G. M., & Simkin, J. S. (1989). Gestalt therapy. In R. J. Corsini & D. Wedding (Eds.), *Current psychotherapies* (pp. 323-361). Itasca, IL: Peacock.

Section 3

Understanding

4

Dialogue and Interpretation in Gestalt Therapy –

Making Sense Together

Frank-M. Staemmler

> At the heart of any dialogue is the conviction that what is exchanged has meaning.
>
> (Holquist, 1990, p. 38)

Human beings are no stimulus-response-machines. They attribute meanings to the stimuli and respond to these meanings. Human beings do not respond to some kind of "objective" world: they *interpret* the stimuli to which they respond. This is the case in general as well as in therapeutic dialogue.

In this paper I will formulate some thoughts about dialogue and interpretation in Gestalt therapy. I have come to believe that one cannot exist meaningfully without the other. In what follows I will try and underpin this assertion. It is my hope that this will lead to a rehabilitation of interpretation in Gestalt therapy.

I will approach this aim from different angles, which at first glance may seem a little fragmented. However, if my strategy is successful the reader will be able to construe a coherent picture of my thoughts in the end.

With this strategy I want to illustrate what the so-called "hermeneutic circle" is all about: the construction and creation of meaning unfolds in a pendulous movement between partial aspects of the picture and the (sometimes only anticipated) picture as a whole.

I invite you, the reader, to follow me in this movement.

Part 1

In which I try to reconstruct how interpretation acquired a bad reputation in Gestalt therapy and a grand delusion was born

In Gestalt therapy interpretation has a bad reputation. To understand this, you need to take a brief look at its history. In one of his early papers (first given as a lecture in 1946 or '47) Perls wrote:

> ... I rely upon the patient's detailed descriptions of his experiences and my own observation, and try to use as little construction and guesswork — for instance interpretation — as possible and endeavor to stick to the reality of the analytical situation. (Perls, 1979, p. 13)[1]

If you try to make sense of this statement (a part of the whole), you need to take the context (the whole) within which it was made into account: at that time the term "Gestalt

---

[1] In a paper written ten years later, Laura Perls assisted: "The patient learns to work with material that is immediately available to him in the actual situation, without speculation or interpretation... description prevails over explanation, experience and experiment over interpretation" (L. Perls, 1992, p. 95).

therapy" had not yet been coined. Perls was still regarding himself as an *analyst* and hence spoke of "the reality[2] of the *analytical* situation" in which he would "use as little interpretation as possible." Moreover, he was giving his lecture to a *psychoanalytic* audience. Therefore we have to assume that what he intended to say with the term "interpretation" here was the *psychoanalytic technique* of interpreting a patient's conduct and words within the framework of Freudian theory and metatheory.

However, this framework lost its relevance as time went on. *Gestalt Therapy* (Perls et al., 1951) was published and introduced a largely new way of thinking about psychotherapy, in which psychoanalytic theory and metatheory did not play a decisive role (although its traces can be found in many places). Still later, in the 1960's when Perls became famous and ran his workshops at Esalen and other places, he did not think of himself as an analyst anymore, and his audiences were mixtures of people with various backgrounds.

Within *this* context the critical remarks about interpretation Perls would drop every now and then inevitably acquired a *new* meaning — a meaning that was enhanced by the radical and simplified style of speaking he liked to entertain now. When in *this* context he simply stated, "... *never, never interpret*" (Perls, 1969, p. 121 — original italics), his advice was most likely to be understood as meaning that *any* kind of interpretation, not only psychoanalytic interpretation, was to be avoided.

---

[2] Perls's use of the term "reality" can be a fallacy: it may nourish the illusion that anybody — for instance a therapist — has access to ("objective") reality. Nobody does. All that is accessible to both client and therapist is their respective *actuality*. Perls did not differentiate these terms: "To me reality *is* actuality" (Perls, 1979, p. 13 — my italics). — For a thorough discussion of the terms "reality" and "actuality" see Staemmler (in press).

The *zeitgeist* that was the wider contextual background for Perls's catch phrases was the (counter-)culture of the 1960's and early "70"s in California and other places in the world — a *zeitgeist* that emphasized spontaneity, liveliness, ("free") love, anti-intellectualism etc., and that did not only affect psychotherapy but also other social realms such as art and literary criticism.

In 1964 a proponent of the latter realm, Susan Sontag, wrote an influential essay with the title *Against Interpretation* in which she maintained:

> To interpret is to impoverish, to deplete the world — in order to set up a shadow world of "meanings." It is to turn *the* world into *this* world. . . . the world, our world, is depleted, impoverished enough. Away with all duplicates of it, until we again experience more immediately what we have! (Sontag, 1967, p. 7 — original italics).

This was the climate in which Gestalt therapy became known in greater circles. As a result you can still hear or read several Gestalt therapists claim that they do not interpret at all. And they appear to believe it. Some of them swear that they stay with the so-called "obvious" — as if calling something "obvious" was not already an interpretation! But even Perls warned us: "We take the obvious for granted. But when we examine the obvious a bit closer, then we see that behind what we call obvious, is a lot of prejudice, distorted faith, beliefs and so on" (Perls, 1973, p. 177) — in other words: a lot of interpretation. Unfortunately he used to frequently forget his own insights.

Some others profess to work "phenomenologically" and appear to believe that the noble vaccine of phenomenology can immunize them against the dangerous interpretive infection. They are equally wrong. Most of them are no phenomenologists at all; they should be called "naïve realists" who in many cases are unaware of their arrogant assumption of a god-like "view from nowhere" (Nagel, 1986).

They all hold on to a grand delusion — just like Perls himself who did not hesitate to advocate that any element in a dream was a representation of some disowned aspect of the dreamer's personality. If that is no interpretation I do not know what is. And if you read the transcripts of Perls's workshops you frequently come across other bold and generalized interpretations. For instance, on one and the same page you can read: "If you avoid looking at another person, it means that you're not open. ... By the way, this low voice is *always* a symptom of hidden cruelty" (Perls, 1973, p. 135 — my italics).

One of the first Gestalt therapeutic writers who clearly and explicitly broke away from that grand delusion was Gary Yontef when he underlined that

> ... any claim that Gestalt therapists make no analysis or interpretation at all is nonsense. Any observation adds to the data in many ways. The choice of what to observe, what to emphasize, what meanings come out of the interaction between the observer and the observed, all add to the data. Our suggested experiments, observations, homework assignments, our emotional response, all arise in part out of the meanings that arise in the phenomenological interaction, including inferences. (Yontef, 1993, p. 405)

Part 2

In which old friends meet surprisingly, start to communicate, and a lot of interpretation unavoidably takes place

"You haven't changed a bit!", she exclaimed when I met her again after ten years. I was puzzled: what did she mean to tell me? Was she cajoling me or even trying to seduce me just as ten years before? Or was she offending me? (After all, this was not the most flattering thing to say to a Gestalt therapist.) Or was she simply happy to recognize me at all?

Of course there are many more ways *to make sense* of a statement like that. Put differently: there are many ways *to understand* a statement like that. And, again differently: there are many ways *to interpret* a statement like that. — Interpretation can be defined as the process of attributing meaning; it is the means to the end of understanding.

However, the questions that came up as a first reaction to that statement pointed only in *one* direction: what did *she* mean to tell me? They largely neglected *my* part in the communication:

> In case she meant to cajole and seduce me, which meaning would *I* ascribe to this? Was I to be happy to still be an attractive man to her at the age of 53 years? Was I to take it as an offense that she saw me as an object of her desires in the first place? And in case she was meaning to offend me, which meaning would I ascribe to that? Did I agree that my growth had been stagnating for the past ten years and feel ashamed about it? Or did I feel proud of myself to obviously have been true to myself, reliable and recognizable?

Of course there are many more ways in which I could have given *my* meaning to *my* interpretation of what *she* had meant to say. Generally speaking, this little everyday example illustrates how people are creating meaning — or better: — multiple meanings all the time. We "... cannot not communicate," Watzlawick (1967) once wrote. He was certainly right. But his sentence does not mention the fact that communication does not take place without meaning-making. So we can also say: *we cannot not make sense; we cannot not understand; we cannot not interpret.*

Having made this most basic observation, I would like to return to my example of the two friends meeting after many years in order to demonstrate to the reader, to whom I apologize, that things are even a little more complicated than they may appear at first:

> "You haven't changed a bit!" my friend exclaimed. Seeing the puzzlement in my face she understood it as a question such as, "What do you mean?", and realized that her statement had been ambiguous and might lead to a misunderstanding.[3] She suddenly became aware that in fact she had not been clear about what she wanted to say. Trying to avoid a negative turn in our conversation she decided to counterbalance my puzzlement with a clearly positive message. She added, "You look great!", thereby indirectly and retroactively ascribing a meaning to her first statement that it did not have for her, at least not as clearly, in the first place.
>
> From my point of view things looked like this: I realized that she had become aware of my puzzlement. I understood her next utterance ("You look great!") as an attempt to confine the range of my interpretations about her first statement to a number of possibilities that she thought might most likely *elicit positive feelings in me. How was I to make sense of that? Was her second sentence a clarification of the first? Was it a correction? Or maybe a polite camouflage of a negative attitude?*

Obviously there is neither a causal nor a one-way connection from the meaning a speaker intends to convey and the understanding of the speaker's message by a listener. To the contrary, to a certain degree we realize what

---

[3] For simplicity's sake at this point the term "*mis*-understanding" might be defined as an interpretation by the listener that does not accord with the aware intention of the speaker.

we meant to say only after the fact, when we respond to implicit or explicit questions and other messages by the partners in our dialogues. Together we cocreate and elaborate on the interpretations of both our own and the other's utterances until we reach an agreement about their meanings or, respectively, conclude that we failed to do so.

This means that to a great extent the meaning of what we say emerges from the dialogue in which we engage. The sense of our utterances is partly a result of our attempt to understand them. And the success of a communication depends both on the speaker and the listener, who in many instances are one and the same: I listen to myself as I speak, you listen to me and at the same time your face "speaks" to me; what I hear of myself influences what I will say the next moment, and the expressions in your face also have an impact on what I am going to say next. And vice versa. "Every word is directed toward an answer and is profoundly shaped and influenced by the answering word it anticipates" (Penn & Frankfurt, 1994, p. 226).

Meaning is being produced by the two persons involved in the conversation, it is not merely expressed by one person and received by the other. "Understanding, after all, is not a simple act of decoding, as in that well-known telegraphic model of communication... Understanding is a much more complex process..." (Morson, 1986, p. 3). In Gendlin's words,

> My sense of you, the listener, affects my experiencing as I speak, and your response partly determines my experiencing a moment later. What occurs to me, and how I live as we speak and interact, is vitally affected by every word and motion you make, and by every facial expression and attitude you show. (Gendlin, 1962, p. 38)

Part 3

In which I compile a few quotations, for instance from phenomenological and hermeneutic writings, and make a distinction between the micro- and macrolevels of interpretation

If as Gestalt therapists we want to take our phenomenlogical background seriously, we must not deny that both in everyday life and in therapy interpretations are ubiquitous. Phenomenological, and, even more so, hermeneutic philosophy have made it very clear that interpretation is an essential aspect of our human condition. Accordingly, already on the first pages of his book with the telling title, *The Interpreted World: An Introduction to Phenomenological Psychology*, Ernesto Spinelli points out:

> ... that which we term reality, that is, that which is *experienced* by us as being reality, is inextricably linked to our mental processes in general, and, in particular, to our in-built, innate capacity to construct meaning. (Spinelli, 1989, p. 2 — my italics)[4]

And he continues:

> Phenomenologists argue that this interpretational process must be acknowledged in our statements about reality. Indeed, phenomenologists suggest that, in our everyday experience of reality, this process is to all intents and purposes indivisible from the reality being perceived. Reality, as far as each of us experiences it, *is* this process. (*ibid.*, p. 4 — original italics)

The interpretational process Spinelli talks about is already intrinsic in what we call "perception." In an earlier paper (Staemmler, 2002) I have described in more detail that

---

[4] That which is *"experienced as reality"* I call *actuality* (see footnote 2).

there is no such thing as "immaculate perception," as Nietzsche ironically called it. Neuroscientist Gerhard Roth calculated that

> ... for every neuron which processes primary sensory data, about one hundred thousand neurons process this "information" further, compare it with past experience and use it to construct cognitive reality. We can say without exaggerating that the *memory is our most important sense organ*. (Roth, 1987, p. 280 – my emphasis; see also Roth, 1995, p. 111)

That is to say: we draw heavily on our memory and on our other mental capacities in order to make sense of even the most simple sensory information, for instance when we look at a thing like a stone or some other physical object. I think of this as the "*microlevel*" of interpretation of which we cannot be conscious in principle. Both in the neurosciences and in modern philosophy there is no doubt that

> ... we never have direct access to, or knowledge of, the real world as it is. Since ours is an object world, it can be stated that, even at the most basic level of consciousness, an interpretative act has occurred. ... the sensory data at our disposal, which respond to the unknown stimuli emanating from the physical world, undergo a basic, unavoidable "translation" or interpretation that leads us to respond to the stimuli as if they were objects. (Spinelli, 1989, p. 12)

This means that we are in principle unable to escape from

> ... a basic *invariant* relationship that exists between the real world and our conscious experience of it. Unable to bracket this relationship, we are forced to acknowledge ... the undeniable role of interpretation, which lies at the

heart of all our mental experience.[5] (*ibid.*, p. 12 — original italics)

So if Susan Sontag claimed that "to interpret is to impoverish, to deplete the world ..." (Sontag, 1967, p. 7), one has to respond that on a microlevel a world without interpretation would be extremely much poorer: it would not be a "world" at all, it would only be a meaningless agglomeration of neuronal spikes that would not make any sense. It would be tantamount to "los[ing] your mind and com[ing] to your senses" (Perls, 1969, p. 69) — a condition I would wish for my worst enemy only if I was also prepared to kill him. And if applied to the macro-level Sontag's position "against interpretation" is just another way of looking at (= interpreting) things.

Gadamer, a prominent German hermeneutic philosopher, put it briefly: "The so-called 'given' cannot be detached from the interpretation" (1989, p. 33). But when he said this he did not only think of the interpretative microlevel. In principle, it does not make a difference if we see a set of sensory stimuli *as* a stone (microlevel) or if we regard an element in a dream *as* a projection of the dreamer (macrolevel). On both micro- and macrolevels we make sense of a phenomenon by interpreting it *as* something.

That is what Heidegger called the "as-structure" (1962, p. 189) of all understanding. And his famous student Gadamer echoed: "It is interpretation that performs the never fully complete mediation between man and world, and to this extent the fact that *we understand something as*

---

[5] In his later years even the philosopher Edmund Husserl, who spent many years of his life in search of a "transcendental ego" — an ego that would be free of this alleged handicap and find access to the "things themselves" — had to admit that this would not be "a human ego" (1962, p. 275).

something is the sole actual immediacy and givenness" (1989, p. 30 — my italics).

In other words, it is the universal presence of interpretation that *connects* us to the world on the one hand and that also stands *between* the world and us on the other hand. — Do these words have a familiar ring in your ears? If yes, you have most likely heard of the Gestalt therapeutic concept of the "contact-boundary" before: Perls et al. wrote that "... the contact-boundary, where experience occurs, does not *separate* the organism and its environment, rather it limits the organism, contains and protects it, and *at the same time* it touches the environment" (1951, p. 229 — original italics).

Interestingly, the headline of the section under which this quote can be found is: "What is the Subject-Matter of Psychology?" (*ibid.*) This context reminds me of another quote which I will use to point out "... that the central concept of a human psychology is *meaning* and the process and transactions involved in the construction of meanings" (Bruner, 1990, p. 33 — original italics).

Part 4

In which two people (one of them called the "client," the other one called the "therapist") engage in an interpretative dialogue (called "therapy") trying to make some more sense of the client's experience

The client is thirty-six years old and works as a masseur and physiotherapist in a cancer rehabilitation clinic where she works with patients who have undergone major surgery.

This is the nineteenth session. The numbers indicate the time: "00:50" means that it is fifty seconds after the beginning of the session; this information is meant to enable you, the reader, to get an impression of the pace at which the session proceeds. I have added some comments to the first six minutes (in brackets, italicized); they point to a few interpretations that are taking place; of course they are my (retrospective) interpretations. If you want, you may continue making comments about the interpretations happening in the rest of the transcript. But please don't be compulsive! You may never get finished. (To be honest, that's why I stopped after the first six minutes and only resumed commenting in the very end of the transcript.)

Therapist: Last time we finished our session when we had just discovered that a certain kind of closeness is lacking between the two of us. (*The therapist speaks about his understanding of the previous session's end.*)

Client: That's right. I also realized at home that I am either too compliant, for instance with my son [who is twelve years old], or too stern, for instance with my patients in the hospital . . . It seems like two poles: I am either too soft and too sloppy or I almost freak out when things don't go well. And somehow it is just like that with closeness and distance too. (*The client interprets some of her behaviors as representing two poles.*)

Th. (00:50): Yes, we have also found out between us that although you enter into contact with me some closeness is missing. — How do you experience that? Do you have a wish for that? (*The therapist says some more about his take on the last session and then asks the client for her interpretation of it.*)

Cl.: I am not sure if that has something to do with my wishes, certainly not only . . . It also has to do with getting involved with somebody else. I experience that with my patients too. Always a certain distance remains even with those I get on with well and with whom I feel a certain connection from the very beginning. (*The client tries to find contexts that can help her to make sense of her experience.*)

Th. (02:15): Yes, that matches my impression: I find that we are getting on well with each other, I like you, and I also have a sense that you like me too. You talk to me in a trusting manner and speak openly about the things that occupy or even oppress you. And yet I feel as if a sense of nearness or some sort of a warm reverberation does not come about — or maybe some cordiality. (*The therapist conveys his understanding of an aspect of their relationship.*)

Cl.: That's true. To a certain degree it feels well rounded, but then there is a limit.

Th. (03:00): Maybe you can describe this limit in more detail?

Cl.: Yes, but it's strange... There is something... (Pause) Even with my son I draw this limit, although I frequently wish it were different. Sometimes I make it, but I easily fuse and am affected too much when he finds himself in situations that aren't pleasant for him. I don't want that... But I am not sure if that's a different problem again. If I think of you and me... There is something... (*The client is still looking for relevant contexts in order to make sense of herself.*)

Th. (04:30): I don't know, if that would already be too close for you, but I would find it easier to look at what it is like between you and me. That's probably the most tangible, and we both have impressions, which we can share. (*The therapist suggests one context, which he thinks might be most useful for the creation of meaning.*)

Cl.: OK, fine.

Th. (05:00): Well, try and focus your attention on your awareness of the closeness between us: how do you experience that with me now?

Cl.: I don't feel completely good about it, not really flowing... A few minutes ago I was a little surprised when you said that I appeared trustful to you. I do not really feel that myself fully. I'm not really aware of that. (*The client refers to the therapist's previous interpretation of their relationship and points out that she has a different take on it.*)

Th. (06:00): You don't clearly *feel* trustful, although you *behave* that way... (*The therapist expresses his interpretation of her interpretation.*)

Cl.: Yes, right... But something is missing, something that would make me feel completely good so I could let go... Sometimes I have felt that more clearly, for instance when I have cried here. Then I have felt you more and differently, your attention, your favor...

Th. (07:00): Are you saying that when you are more involved emotionally you also have a clearer sense of me?

Cl.: Yes, then it is OK, then there is something well-rounded that does me good, that makes me feel wrapped up.

Th. (07:15): I am just thinking if we could try an experiment, which would require you to entrust yourself a little more...

Cl.: Oh!

Th. (07:30): ... and that would make it easier for us to find out, what's possible for you and what isn't. — What is your reaction to this idea?

Cl.: Well, it is like I don't really dare to... Although I would like to try it out...

Th. (08:00): OK, let me make a suggestion. You do not have to accept it; we can also consider if there is another possibility that's better for you. — The idea I have is this: I could sit down on the floor cross-legged, then you could lie down in front of me on your back and place your head on my lap. Then I would place my hands underneath your head and move it gently to and fro. So you could get a sense of the degree to which you can give your head into my hands.

Cl.: (pauses, laughs, then:) Oh! ... Trust! — I started feeling dizzy for a moment when you said that... But I'm going to do it anyway!

Th. (09:30): I find it important that you do not take the bull by the horns if that means for you to pass over something that's difficult for you rather than to attend to it and do it carefully so that you become exactly aware of what is going on in you. — This is not a feat to be performed, it is rather a discovery to be made.

Cl.: Yes. (pauses, remains motionless)

Th. (10:15): I know you're courageous. You don't have to prove that to me.

Cl.: (remains silent for a while, then slowly begins to cry softly)

Th. (11:30): What are you experiencing?

Cl.: I am touched by what you said, that you mentioned that intermediate step. I tend to forget that. It was important for me that you mentioned it... I felt seen by you. I was ready to jump over it and to do quickly what you had suggested.

Th. (12:30): I guess you would have come to me outwardly, but not inwardly; inwardly you would have stayed in your chair.

Cl.: (laughs) Right! — And for a moment I thought: "I don't want to."

Th. (13:00): You don't want to come closer? — Can you hear your voice as you say, "I don't want to."?

Cl.: (begins to sob) I do not want to be forced! — I do not want to be forced to be close.

Th. (13:45): Of course...

Cl.: (blows her nose, then cries again)

Th. (14:20): This seems to move you a lot...

Cl.: But I'm not sure what it is... I don't know...

Th. (15:15): To me you look as if you are at a very delicate point right now. (Pause) I get the impression I need to be very careful with you now.

Cl.: (Pause) I don't know what's going on... My head is pulsating.

Th. (16:15): You look very vulnerable to me, very sensitive.

Cl.: (Pause) I feel blank. I have no idea, no thought...

Th. (18:00): It seems almost as if you were not there — no idea, no thought... nothing...

Cl.: (Pause)

Th. (18:45): Maybe a little lost too. As if you were in nowhere land now...

Cl.: Hm... (pauses, blows her nose) Yes, I have the feeling... I feel empty. As if I was going out of my head here... (points to a place at the back of her head)

Th. (20:00): Can you try to follow that? Where are you going?

Cl.: Away, backward, but there is still a connection, I only go that far (points to a place about two yards behind herself).

Th. (20:30): And in front there remains your empty body?

Cl.: Yes, I can see it.

Th. (20:45): And everything that I would get to feel, if I came closer to you, was this empty body. You wouldn't be there in your body. — I can understand that pretty well, if I recall that you said you did not want to be forced to be close. That seems like an efficient way to elude that force. If you cannot evade it outwardly, you can still evade it inwardly.

Cl.: Yes! (pauses, then begins to cry again)

Th. (22:30): Give way to that feeling.

Cl.: I'm thinking of the experiment you suggested... I imagined you sitting there with my head in your hands...

Th. (23:20): And then you start to cry?

Cl.: Hm.

Th. (23:30): Stay with that image for a while. You see me sitting there with your head in my hands.

Cl.: I really would like to be there...

Th. (24:00): Do you long for it?

Cl.: Yes, but only briefly. And then I am going away again.

Th. (24:20): With the longing you were in your body briefly, and then you emptied yourself again?

Cl.: Yes, exactly. It's not possible with an empty body.

Th. (24:30): And you don't get anything out of it.

Cl.: Strange... (pauses), to be this way, so empty... (pauses). Now it occurs to me that in everyday life I'm also frequently leaving myself, daydreaming, not really being there...

Th. (25:30): Yet there was also the longing...

Cl.: But only very briefly! (laughs loudly) In the end I don't dare...

Th. (26:20): Yes, if you do not pass over it you feel how shy you are and how hard it is to come close. Of course you would be able to pass over it and do it with your body emptied...

Cl.: ...just functioning. — Now I realize what it is that I experience with my patients. I have to function no matter how they smell, how they look with their scars, I have to touch them, I have to do my work...

Th. (27:20): Isn't that like being *forced* to be close in your work?

Cl.: Yes, it is. (begins to cry again) That's exactly what it is. (sobs vehemently) Oh, gee! Every time it is like being raped... I have to do it, and I know I can do it...

Th. (28:30): ...if you empty yourself. If you don't, it's like being raped, if you stay in your body and feel it...

Cl.: Yeah, I couldn't bear it, if I would stay there... Many of my patients are mutilated. They have been raped by the operations and radiations. I couldn't bear it, if I would be there... I can only do it, if I don't feel it.

Th. (30:00): If you would let their bodies come close, these raped bodies, it would feel like you being raped yourself. (Pause). Then you would fuse and also feel what it means to be in a physical state like that?

Cl.: Yes. Sometimes I do it (sighs deeply)... A few weeks ago, for instance, I worked with a patient who had had an operation in her womb area. There was a huge edema at her pubic bone. It looks terrible and feels terrible. Then I thought to myself: of course I, I can do it, I can cope with it, I can help her, I can do it all. — But it also made me angry: I *have* to do it. I cannot say, "I can't get it done." Then I thought, I wouldn't want to know what had been destroyed in her body, burnt by the radiation... She can forget her sex life, it is lost forever... (cries). There is also a part in me that likes to help and give some relief, but I hate to *have* to do it on orders. Then I function: I can do it... (*At this time the client's avoidance of closeness as observed by the therapist in the beginning of the session is understood in a new way, i.e. her attempt to resist to being forced to be close, her attempt to escape from her tendencies to become confluent with the suffering of her patients etc. The reader may have noted that this new interpretation emerged from a pendulous movement between the details of the client's experience and reflection on the one hand and a more overall look at the context and at the connections between the details. Therapy proceeds in a kind of hermeneutic circle.)*

The session continues for about fifteen more minutes.

Part 5

In which his majesty, the German Jewish theologian and philosopher Martin Buber, is invited to share his throne with the Russian linguist and literary theorist Mikhail Mikhailovich Bakhtin[6], and in which the meaning of "dialogue" is enlarged

When Gestalt therapists talk or write about dialogue, as a rule of thumb one can say that they are thinking within the context of Martin Buber's anthropology. This is the merit of Lynne Jacobs (1989), Richard Hycner (1991), Hycner and Jacobs (1995), Frank-M. Staemmler (1993), Gary Yontef (1993), and others. In this context, the focus is on the meeting, the relationship, the "relational attitude" (Yontef, 2002) etc., all of which are of basic importance to Gestalt therapy.

However, one aspect of dialogue has pretty much been ignored in Gestalt therapeutic literature so far — an aspect to which the Greek word "λογοσ" that is a major building block of "dia–*logue*" also alludes: the word, the meaning. In the same vein, when Buber's terms such as "inclusion" or "imagining the real" have been adopted, the *relational* and *attitudinal* components of these terms were discussed almost

---

[6] For reasons, which are beyond the scope of this paper, the French philosopher Emmanuel Lévinas should take his seat there too.

exclusively. This is justifiable in so far as it was Buber's focus too.[7] But Buber, and with him his Gestalt therapeutic followers, have neglected the *semantic* aspect of the dialogue, which is also essential.

As Balint observed, "once and for all we have to recognize the fact that the first wish of a patient is to be understood" (1968, p. 113). In many life situations — both as a client and as a "private" person — I do not feel understood only by seeing a friendly and compassionate face looking at me. Affect attunement is great, but in addition I wish to convey my thoughts, fantasies, memories and feelings to the attuning person; moreover, I need to know that this person understands me also in terms of *content*. Most people I know feel the same.

However, it is noteworthy that my need to feel understood on a content level springs not only from the urge to find my preexisting meanings reflected in another person's mind, although this urge is very strong in itself.

> The *I* hides in the other and in others, it wants to be only an other for others, to enter completely into the world of others as an other, and to cast from itself the burden of being the only *I* (*I-for-myself*) in the world. (Bakhtin, 1986, p. 147 — original italics)

There is still another urge that plays an important role here: it has to do with the fact that my own preexisting meanings always feel more or less *incomplete*. And as far as I know I am in good company: who has not had the experience that only after *sharing* one's preexisting meanings with another person one feels satisfied and is left with the impresssion that one has understood oneself fully? As Taylor observes,

---

[7] This is even true of his essay *The Word That is Spoken* (Buber, 1962), the title of which might elicit different expectations.

even as the most independent adult, there are moments when I cannot clarify what I feel until I talk about it with certain special partner(s), who know me, or have wisdom, or with whom I have an affinity.... This is the sense in which one cannot be a self on one's own. I am a self only in relation to certain interlocutors ... (Taylor, 1992, p. 36).

This is so because as human beings we are fundamentally dialogical in our nature. Individual meanings are derivatives or distillates from previous dialogues; like powdered milk they need to be watered in dialogue again to become complete. The Thou can actually be said to be both developmentally and ontologically *prior* to the I: the Thou is the I's necessary precursor and precondition.[8]

Therefore an interpretation of one's experience is only fully satisfactory if it is cocreated through an empathic exchange that takes place between persons who treat each other as subjects (see Weingarten, 1991). "... I become myself only by revealing myself to another, through another and with another's help.... Cutting oneself off, isolating oneself, closing oneself off, those are the basic reasons for loss of self," Bakhtin (quoted in Todorov, 1984, p. 96) underscored.[9] To a great extent this takes place through the use of language (see Mercer, 2000). Cocreative understanding of content (as described by Bakhtin) and treating each other as subjects (as described by Buber) are inseparable and equally essential aspects of a therapeutic dialogue.

---

[8] "I realize myself initially through others: from them I receive words, forms, and tonalities for the formation of my initial idea of myself" (Bakhtin, 1986, p. 138). This is why Buber's "I and Thou" can be criticized for giving a false sequence (see Petzold, 1996, who drawing on Lévinas and Bakhtin suggests that the correct title should have been "Thou, I, We").

[9] Bakhtin's claim will be no news to readers who are familiar with Perls's et al. (1951) theory of the self.

Being a linguist and literary theorist, the Russian Mikhail Bakhtin had a personal background that explains his sensitivity to what one could call the "third dimension" of the dialogue: the "content," "subject matter," or, in his words, the "object" about which the dialogue takes place.

> The relationship to others' utterances cannot be separated from the relationship to the object (for it is argued about, agreed upon, views converge within it), nor can it be separated from the relationship to the speaker himself. This is a living tripartite unity. (Bakhtin, 1986, p. 122)

Actually it should go without saying that there is not only an "I" (say: the therapist) and a "Thou" (say: the client), there is also an "It" (in therapy: the actual topic).[10] (See Illustration 1 on the adjacent page.)

Maybe I should clarify this a little more: the fact that the subject-matter ("It"[11]) of therapeutic dialogues to a great extent refers to aspects of the client's experience may make it seem somewhat artificial to distinguish between the Thou (the client) and the It (the topic). Nevertheless, I think that the distinction does make sense.

---

[10] In the theory of Ruth Cohn's "theme-centered interaction" (TCI) this triangle is central: "TCI is based on the hypothesis, that each person ('I'), the interaction of the group ('We'), and the work on a certain task ('It') must be regarded equally important.... The acknowledgement and support of the equal importance of the factors I-We-It ... is the basis of leading and working in an TCI group" (Farau & Cohn, 1984, p. 353 – original italics). For the purpose of the paper at hand please replace "interaction of the group ('We')" with "the other person ('Thou')." — Why this has been overlooked in gestalt therapy I do not know, but maybe the reason is that the reputation of content is as bad as that of interpretation.

[11] Note that this "It" is used in the sense of "subject-matter," not as an element of Buber's "I-It."

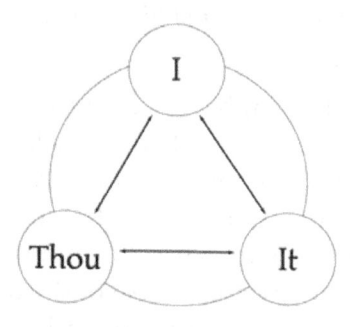

Illustration 1

There are at least three reasons for that: first, per definition the *aspect* of the client's experience that is the actual subject-matter of the dialogue is never identical with the client herself or himself as a *whole* person.

Second and more importantly, if therapy goes well the client again and again assumes a stance of "eccentricity" (*sensu* Plessner, 1983, pp. 191ff.) in respect to what s/he works on; the transcript in part four provides many examples. (If the therapist is not confluent s/he takes a look from a perspective, which is different from the client's, anyway.)

Third and most importantly, in a relational approach to therapy aspects of the therapist's experience as well as aspects of the contact between client and therapist always have a good chance to become subject matters too.

Certainly this does not mean to throw the baby out with the bathwater. In full accordance with the traditional Gestalt therapeutic position Bakhtin was aware that

> the expression of an utterance can never be fully understood or explained if its thematic content is all that is taken into account. The expression of an utterance always *responds* to a *greater or lesser degree, that is, it expresses the speaker's attitude toward others' utterances and not just his*

attitude toward *the object of his utterance*.[12] (1986, p. 92 — original italics)

However, I emphatically insist that Perls was fundamentally mistaken when he said in *Gestalt Therapy Verbatim*, "a good therapist *doesn't listen to the content* of the bullshit[13] the patient produces, but to the sound, to the music, to the hesitations. Verbal communication is usually a lie. The real communication is beyond words" (1969, p. 53 — my italics). When in one of his other books he said in more moderate words that "we ... will look at the *process* rather than the substance" (Perls, 1973, p. 58 — original italics), he was equally wrong. He simply ignored the fact that he himself would always *also* listen to the substance, even when his primary attention and his therapeutic responses were focused on the process. For instance, without listening to the content it would be impossible for him (and any other therapist) to confront a client with any inconsistencies: "I'm aware that you're doing a lot of smiling. And *even when you talk about unpleasantness* ... you are still smiling, and to me this is inconsistent" (*ibid.*, p. 127 — my italics).

In *Gestalt therapy* a much more sophisticated viewpoint is proposed. In this book one finds an entire chapter with the title "Verbalizing and Poetry," in which "contactful speech" is advocated, a speech that "... is good contact when it draws energy from and makes a structure of the three grammatical persons, I, Thou, and It; the speaker, the one spoken to, and the matter spoken about ..." (Perls et al., 1951, p. 322).

---

[12] There is a footnote to this statement: "Intonation is especially sensitive and always points beyond the content" (*ibid.*).

[13] His dismissive choice of words must of course be criticized too.

Part 6

In which the contents of the previous parts are integrated and brought to a conclusion

As well as in any other human conversation (see part two, in which old friends meet) interpretation plays a central role in therapeutic dialogues too (see part four with its transcript). Interpretation is what creates meaning and what makes understanding possible. Interpretation can be seen as a "boundary-" phenomenon that links people with their worlds and, if I say it more fundamentally, allows for the common creation of worlds (see part three, in which the word "world" occurs frequently).

Interpreting and understanding take place both on a micro- and a macrolevel (see part 3). They are ubiquitous. To deny their existence or to demand their abolition (in therapy or elsewhere) is to ignore the human condition or to believe in a grand delusion (see part 1) or to abandon the subject-matter of psychology (see section 3) or in short: to impoverish the world (to use Susan Sontag's word against her). According to Heidegger, understanding and interpreting are not only a human *activity*, which one might as well not exercise; more than that they are central traits of *being human*: "From the very beginning our essence is to understand and to create comprehensibility" (Heidegger, 1983, p. 444).

We cannot not interpret, but we can choose *how* to interpret. In Gestalt therapy we prefer not to interpret analytically, i.e. "... to go behind or beneath the presented (or 'manifest') material contained in a statement so that its hidden (or 'latent') meaning may be ascertained" (Spinelli, 1996, p. 198). We rather interpret *descriptively*, i.e. in a way that

> ... retains its focus on the manifest material and seeks to extract the meaning of that material to the client by engaging the client in a descriptively focused process of clarification wherein the manifest material may be "opened up" to mutual investigation. This might be done, for example, by focusing on various elements contained in the manifest material and considering what they express to the client about his or her currently lived experience, what they reveal or imply about his or her self-construct, relations with others, and so forth. (*ibid.*, pp. 199f.)

In a therapeutic conversation, which deserves to be called "dialogue" in a profound sense, a triangular relationship exists between the person of the client, the person of the therapist, and the topic or content (see Spinelli's "manifest material") they are dealing with (see part five). The third corner of this triangle must not be neglected or devalued, it must be *understood*, and under-standing does not take place without interpretation. If I may paraphrase a formulation by Lynne Jacobs ("Task as Thou" — 1989, pp. 53ff.), I would like to say that the third dimension of the dialogue, its content or the "It," has to be treated just as seriously and respectfully as the "Thou."

Since Gestalt therapy is a dialogical process, in general Gestalt therapeutic interpretations are not provided to the client as insights of a therapist who assumes to know better what the client's experience "really" means than the client herself or himself. Importantly, our approach to interpretation is based on awareness work:

> Since it is the very nature of the perceiving organism to interpret — i.e., to synthesize the parts, resolve the parts of the field into an organized whole — the supplying of ready made interpretations to the subject by the therapist (or other change agent) may not be necessary, may even be counterproductive, depending on the nature of the

particular change being sought. Mere concentration of attention, by or with the subject, especially on some parts of the field that are characteristically out of awareness, will by definition produce some reorganization of the field — and the potential, at least, for a corresponding behavioral change, of one kind or another. (Wheeler, 1998, p. 39)

"Organizing the field" is a synonymous formulation to what I have called "interpretation"; "figure formation" is another synonymous term. "*Reorganizing* the field" is tantamount to a "*new* interpretation." If I remember correctly, it was Dilthey (1910/2002) who pointed out almost one hundred years ago that the human capacity to interpret the world in new ways again and again is an important contribution to its continuous vitality. In my view, Gestalt therapy's commitment to life as well as its roots in field theory, Gestalt psychology, phenomenology, and existential dialogism all call for a positive valuation of interpretation in Gestalt therapy.

If we could take a "view from nowhere" at some "objective" world, there would be only *one* world for all of us — forever. Life would be boring: "The world about us would be desolate except for the world within us" (Stevens, 1990, p. 188). But since you can look at the world only from your own (and, of course, your culture's) point of view, there is interpretation and the creation of meaning. As a result, your world can be different from mine and my view of the world today can be different from that of tomorrow. There are as many worlds as there are interpretations. Interpretation makes life both colorful and creative.

References

Bakhtin, M. M. (1986). *Speech genres and other late essays* (C. Emerson & M. Holquist, Eds.). Austin: University of Texas Press.

Balint, M. (1968). *The basic fault: Therapeutic aspects of regression.* London: Tavistock.
Buber, M. (1962). Das Wort, das gesprochen wird. [The word that is spoken] In M. Buber, *Werke, Erster Band – Schriften zur Philosophie* (pp. 442-453). München: Kösel.
Bruner, J. (1990). *Acts of meaning.* Cambridge, MA & London: Harvard University Press.
Dilthey, W. (1910/2002). *Selected Works, Volume III: The formation of the historical world in the human sciences* (R. A. Makkreel & F. Rodi, Eds.). Princeton, NJ: Princeton University Press.
Farau, A., & Cohn, R. C. (1984). *Gelebte Geschichte der Psychotherapie – Zwei Perspektiven* [A lived history of psychotherapy: Two perspectives]. Stuttgart: Klett-Cotta.
Gadamer, H.-G. (1989). Text and interpretation. In D. P. Michelfelder & R. E. Palmer (Eds.), *Dialogue and deconstruction: The Gadamer-Derrida encounter* (pp. 21-51). Albany, NY: State University of New York Press.
Gendlin, E. T. (1962). *Experiencing and the creation of meaning: A philosophical and psychological approach to the subjective.* New York: Free Press of Glencoe.
Heidegger, M. (1962). *Being and time.* San Francisco: Harper.
Heidegger, M. (1983). *Die Grundbegriffe der Metaphysik* [Basic terms of metaphysics] – *Gesamtausgabe 29/30.* Frankfurt/M.: Klostermann.
Holquist, M. (1990). *Dialogism: Bakhtin and his world.* London & New York: Routledge.
Husserl, E. (1962). *Phänomenologische Psychologie – Gesammelte Werke, Bd. IX.* Den Haag: Nijhoff.
Hycner, R. (1991). *Between person and person: Toward a dialogical psychotherapy.* Highland, NY: Gestalt Journal Press.
Hycner, R., & Jacobs, L. (Eds.) (1995). *The healing relationship in Gestalt therapy: A dialogic/self psychology approach.* Highland, NY: Gestalt Journal Press.
Jacobs, L. (1989). Dialogue in Gestalt theory and therapy. *The Gestalt Journal 12/1,* 25-67.
Mercer, N. (2000). *Words and minds: How we use language to think together.* London & New York: Routledge.
Morson, G. S. (Ed.) (1986). *Bakhtin: Essays and dialogues on his work.* Chicago & London: University of Chicago Press.

Nagel, T. (1986). *The view from nowhere*. New York: Oxford University Press.
Penn, P., & Frankfurt, M. (1994). Creating a participant text: Writing, multiple voices, narrative multiplicity. *Family Process* 33/3, 217-231
Perls, F. S. (1969). *Gestalt therapy verbatim*. Moab, UT: Real People Press.
Perls, F. S. (1973). *The Gestalt approach & Eye witness to therapy*. Palo Alto, CA: Science & Behavior Books.
Perls, F. S. (1979). Planned psychotherapy (edited and with footnote commentary by Laura Perls). *The Gestalt Journal 2/2*, 5-23.
Perls, F. S., Hefferline, R. F., & Goodman, P. (1951): *Gestalt therapy: Excitement and growth in the human personality*. New York: Julian Press.
Perls, L. (1992). *Living at the boundary: Collected works of Laura Perls* (J. Wysong, Ed.). Highland, NY: Gestalt Journal Press.
Petzold, H. G. (1996). Der "Andere" — der Fremde und das Selbst — Tentative, grundsätzliche und persönliche Überlegungen für die Psychotherapie anlässlich des Todes von Emmanuel Lévinas (1906-1995) [The "other" — The stranger and the self: Tentative, basic, and personal considerations in regard to psychotherapy on the occasion of the death of Emmanuel Lévinas (1906-1995)]. *Integrative Therapie 22/2-3*, 319-349.
Plessner, H. (1983). Die Frage nach der Conditio humana [The question of the human condition]. In H. Plessner, *Gesammelte Schriften VIII — Conditio humana* (pp. 126-217). Frankfurt/M.: Suhrkamp.
Roth, G. (1987). Autopoiese und Kognition: Die Theorie H. R. Maturanas und die Notwendigkeit ihrer Weiterentwicklung [Autopoiesis and cognition: H. R. Maturana's theory and the necessity of its further development]. In S. J. Schmidt (Ed.), *Der Diskurs des Radikalen Konstruktivismus* [The discourse of radical constructivsm] (pp. 256-286). Frankfurt/M.: Suhrkamp.
Roth, G. (1995). *Das Gehirn und seine Wirklichkeit: Kognitive Neurobiologie und ihre philosophischen Konsequenzen* [The brain and its actuality]. Frankfurt/M.: Suhrkamp.
Sontag, S. (1967). *Against interpretation and other essays*. New York: Farrar, Straus, & Giroux.

Spinelli, E. (1989). *The interpreted world: An introduction to phenomenological psychology*. London: Sage.
Spinelli, E. (1996). *Demystifying therapy*. London: Constable.
Staemmler, F.-M. (1993). *Therapeutische Beziehung und Diagnose* [Therapeutic relationship and diagnosis: Answers in Gestalt therapy]: *Gestalttherapeutische Antworten*. München: Pfeiffer.
Staemmler, F.-M. (2002). The here and now: A critical analysis. *British Gestalt Journal 11/1*, 21-32.
Staemmler, F.-M. (in press). On metaphors, myths, and minds: Boundary disturbances in Gestalt therapy theory. In G. Wheeler (Ed.), *Reading Paul Goodman*. Cambridge, MA: GestaltPress.
Stevens, W. (1990). *Opus posthumous* — Revised, enlarged and corrected Edition (M. J. Bates, Ed.). London: Faber & Faber.
Taylor, C. (1992). *Sources of the self: The making of the modern identity*. Cambridge: Cambridge University Press.
Todorov, T. (1984). *Mikhail Bakhtin: The dialogical principle*. Manchester: Manchester University Press.
Watzlawick, P. (1967). *Pragmatics of human communication: A study of interactional patterns, pathologies, and paradoxes*. New York: Norton.
Weingarten, K. (1991). The discourse of intimacy: Adding a social constructionist and feminist view. *Family Process 30*, 285-305.
Wheeler, G. (1998). *Gestalt reconsidered: A new approach to contact and resistance* (2nd edition). Cambridge, MA: GIC Press.
Yontef, G. M. (1993). *Awareness, dialogue, and process: Essays on Gestalt therapy*. Highland, NY: Gestalt Journal Press.
Yontef, G. M. (2002). The relational attitude in Gestalt therapy theory and practice. *International Gestalt Journal 25/1*, 15-35.

5

Cultivated Uncertainty –

An Attitude of Gestalt Therapists[1]

Frank-M. Staemmler

Introduction

The stereotyping of one group of people by another is an act of power and control. Stereotyping occurs when a group, for their own purposes, tries to define other people, and in so doing, sets boundaries and limitations for them.

(Introduction to "Fluffs and Feathers," an exhibition on the identity of the American Indians as it has been defined by Europeans ever since the European colonization of North America, presented by the National Museum in Montreal, Canada, April 1993.)

---

[1] This article was first published in the German journal *Integrative Therapy* (1994, 20/3, 272-288) and later translated by the author and corrected by Bruno Just. The English version first appeared in the *British Gestalt Journal* (1997, 6/1, 40-48).

The exertion of power by therapists on their clients takes place on various levels and can occur in many different forms. Without the possibility of influencing another person in one way or the other, therapeutic effectiveness cannot be conceived of; therefore this possibility always and necessarily also implies the risk of effects detrimental to the clients. To prevent them is in my view not only an obligation of the therapists, who again and again ought to think over their ways of using their power and to implement adequate methods of control, like supervision, but is also the task of those who are most likely to suffer from the abuse of power, i.e. the clients, for what is *done* to them is also what they *allow* to be done.

That is why in this article I don't only want to stimulate my colleagues to reflect on certain ways of exerting their power on their clients. Although I am writing from the point of view of a therapist and address myself primarily to therapists, I also have in mind both the people who currently undergo psychotherapy and those who are planning to do so in the future. I would be glad if the following text could hand some criteria to them, which may help them to find out whether the attitudes and behaviors of the therapist are in tune with their own interests.

"I Only Came to Use the Phone"

I want to start with the summary of a short story that I recommend to anybody to read in full length because of its mental clarity and its literary quality. Nobel prize-winning Gabriel Garcia Márquez (1994) describes what happens to a young woman, whose car breaks down on a country road in the pouring rain and who tries to get a lift to the next telephone. After a long time she is picked up by the driver of a van in which a group of passengers covered with blankets is sleeping. As she is cold and wet, the woman sitting next to the driver gives a blanket to her too.

After a while the van stops. Together with the other passengers she gets out and enters a building. She meets a woman in uniform and tells her she wants to make a phone call. She is ordered to join the other women in the communal dormitory. Suddenly awake to the fact that she is in a psychiatric hospital, she tries to escape — to no avail. Her explanations, protests and attempts to leave the building are answered with force and sedation and remain without success. The next day, she is introduced to the medical director of the hospital. He deals with her in a very friendly and patient manner. She tries to convince him that she has only come to make a phone call and repeatedly demands to be permitted to call her husband and inform him of her whereabouts. The doctor speaks to her in a fatherly voice saying "Everything in due course" — and finishes the conversation.

A few weeks later, she manages to send a message to her husband. The price is high; she has to give in to the sexual advances of a night nurse. The visit of her husband to the hospital from which she expects her liberation begins with a conversation between him and the medical director. The latter explains to the former the mental disease of his wife. He talks of states of excitation, vehement outbursts of aggression and fixed ideas (especially the one to make phone calls); further treatment as well as the sympathetic cooperation of the husband for the sake of a positive course of the disease are strictly indicated.

After having been informed in this way, the husband sees his wife. He soothes her, encourages her that she will soon feel better and promises to come to visit with her on a regular basis. First she is perplexed; then she starts to rave and to scream like a maniac. On her husband's next visit, she refuses to see him. The doctor says to him calmly: "That is a typical reaction. It will pass."

The Need for Certainty

At this point I don't want to comment on Márquez' story, it speaks for itself. I'd rather like to put some sort of "antithesis" against it: I contend that all psychotherapists feel a legitimate need for certainty when at work with their clients. This is a basic need of human beings in general as we know from Maslow's hierarchy of needs (see Maslow 1954/1970). But it is a special need, too, which arises from the condition of our daily work as therapists. If we were to feel uncertain all day long, we would be burnt out soon.

However, we don't have this need for certainty only for the sake of our own mental hygiene. Moreover, it is important for the quality of our work: in the work with our clients we are permanently in need of certain criteria and orientations. In every session we are confronted with an abundance of verbal and non-verbal "material." We would be overwhelmed by the multitude of stimuli if we had no criteria to decide at a given moment what we regard as important and what as irrelevant. Though there are divergent criteria among different therapeutic "schools" and also among different therapists of one school, they all serve the same purpose. They are to provide us with some certainty so that we do not get paralyzed by the mass of information, not knowing what to relate to. These criteria serve our clients, too. If we, for instance, say to a client a sentence like, "This seems to be an important point," we assort (and sort out) and lend weight to the information we get. Thus we provide her or him with the opportunity to quarrel and come to terms with our view and, by doing this, to find her or his own stance.

I want to add one more reason why the need of therapists for certainty is useful for the clients as well: if we meet them with a fair amount of certainty, we are likely to be convincing as persons. From the comparative research on the outcome of psychotherapy we have learnt that the so-called "persuasive potency" of therapists contributes strongly to the success of any therapy. A therapist who conveys a *congruent* impression to the client, because he is convinced of what he does, is much more likely to have a healing effect on the client — no matter which therapeutic methods s/he employs (Frank 1961).

Diagnoses and Certainty

To say that the certainty of therapists to a large extent derives from the fact that they sort the information they get is almost identical with the following assertion: the certainty of therapists stems, at least partially, from a diagnostic process. We sort by assorting, attributing, finding similarities and differences, looking for contexts and relevances. We form terms and categories that enable us to organize and reduce the amount of information, which would be impossible for us to survey without evaluation.

The subjective feeling of certainty arises from the impression that one knows with what one deals, what is what, to what group of phenomena a thing belongs. If I would not be able to identify the chair I sit on as a "chair," just because it looks different from the one I have at home, it would become rather troublesome and laborious to make it through life. But fortunately I can assort things and events to certain categories, and that helps me to master life with relative efficiency and security.

Any kind of psychological diagnosis is based on the same principle — no matter which theoretical approach it may follow. Any diagnostic system tries to provide us with criteria for the answers to questions like, "What is the problem?" and, in consequence, "What is there to be done in this case?"

The Significance of Meanings

This may seem quite simple at first, but if you look at it a little closer, it appears more difficult. For in psychotherapy we in most cases don't only have to deal with simple facts and external events but with the *meanings* our clients attribute to facts and events. I'd like to explain this with a "classical" example: if a client remembers his mother, it can mean to him to still feel controlled, dominated or tortured by her today. Or it may have the meaning of a memory of a cute old lady to whom he loves to talk from time to time. It is not the fact that he had a mother nor the fact that perhaps she used to control and torture him during his childhood. In case the former events don't *mean* a problem to him today, he does not have to work on them. So in therapy, not the facts but the meanings somebody attributes to the facts are essential.

I already mentioned that any diagnosis is a categorization from which follow criteria for the actions to be pursued. In addition, we now have to take into account that these categorizations relate to *meanings of behaviors and experiences, not to behaviors or experiences "per se" (if there is such a thing at all). The meaning, which is attributed to a behavior or experience, is decisive for the diagnostic categorization. The roughest categorization I can think of in this context is the "healthy/sick" polarity, which is nevertheless applied frequently.*

Let us remember the woman in the short story by Márquez. She wants to make a phone call. To her this wish means a healthy, responsible attitude towards her husband, whom she wants to inform of her delay. For the staff in the hospital it means a sick, obsessive idea, and this meaning determines the diagnosis and the "treatment" that follows. It is not the wish of the woman to make a phone call which is decisive for the diagnoses of psychosis, it is the pathological meaning that is attributed to it.

The Power of Interpretation and Its Distribution

Since meanings are essential, the question of power in psychotherapy is the question of who possesses the power to confer meanings. In other words, who is able to push through his own interpretation, even against the resistance of the other person? Let me quote Max Weber's famous definition of power: "Power is any chance within a social relationship to succeed with one's own will, if necessary against opposition, no matter what this chance is based upon" (1985, 28).

If we specify this definition and apply it to psychotherapy and the attribution of meanings, we can say: somebody possesses the power of interpretation if he has the chance within the therapeutic relationship to push through the meaning he ascribes to a behavior even against the resistance of the other person.

Now let us take a brief look at how the power of interpretation is distributed in conventional forms of psychological diagnosis. Here you find the therapists collecting information from their clients (sometimes from relatives or previous therapists of their clients too), taking the anamnesis, observing behaviors etc. Then they filter the information through the cognitive patterns of their theory, sort and weigh data, relate them to each other and in the end set up their diagnoses. It is obvious: the power of interpretation is distributed very one-sidedly; the therapists claim it more or less for themselves.

Remember my initial quotes from the exhibition on the colonization of the Canadian Indians: by an act of power and by the use of stereotypes, someone's identity is defined for certain purposes. Amundson et al. underline that "as the selection/diagnostic/categorizing process proceeds, a colonial discourse can be created..." (1993, 113) in the therapy room.

Pseudo-certainty

I do not want to regard those facts from an ethical perspective only, though it may be important enough. I also want to look at them from a scientific point of view. From this, it occurs to me, that anybody exerting one-sided power of interpretation puts herself or himself into a position of certainty, which proves to be a pseudo-certainty at closer examination. For, within this system, there is no way of verification of the certainty that has been gained. There is no authority to challenge (or confirm) the meanings, which have been put down by this one person, because nobody else is regarded to be competent to do the job. The clients, who possibly could constitute another position, in most cases do not understand the terminology of the diagnostic theory. They know even less about the theoretical implications that are part of the diagnostic labels. And, very often, they do not have a chance to supply themselves with the theoretical information, because they are not told which diagnosis has been ascribed to them. The result of the one-sided power of interpretation, the diagnosis, is kept as a secret of the ones in power. (This has been a well-known strategy for ages; you can preserve your power by hiding it.)

From this, I draw the following conclusion: if the power of interpretation is distributed one-sidedly, it can induce a feeling of certainty on the part of the therapist which — from a superior point of view — can easily be unmasked as an illusion, a mere pseudo-certainty. Márquez' story illustrates it very clearly. To the reader who takes a superior stance, it is easy to see that the staff of the clinic feels fully certain about how to interpret the behavior of the woman "patient." And there is no position, which could challenge their interpretation, because the only position, which would be able to do, so is the "patient" herself, and her view is not taken seriously. To her no power of interpretation is distributed. Thus, it becomes possible that the staff executes what to the reader is obviously based on false assumptions. The subjective certainty of the staff remains unquestioned. Even in the case of a positive diagnosis, which would have led to the discharge of the "patient" from the hospital, this would be true — without the negative consequences for the woman, of course.

At this point I would like to sum up what I have said till now: the certainty of therapists that results from a *one-sided* distribution of the power of interpretation in principle cannot be challenged and therefore *always* must be a pseudo-certainty — even if from a superior stance the meanings that are attributed to the behavior of the client may turn out to be "right."

This statement is not only relevant to the realm of psychiatric hospitals, from which Márquez' example is taken, it is — with less severe consequences — also relevant to the realm of private practices, including those of Gestalt therapists, if they follow the conventional paradigm of diagnosis. Some do (see e. g. Delisle, 1991, and, to lesser degrees, Melnick & Nevis, 1992, or Yontef, 1993). Since I know some of them personally, I am convinced that these authors would never proceed in a manner similar to the psychiatrists in Márquez' story. Yet they vote for the same paradigm. Very often, they start their argument as follows: "... one cannot not diagnose.... One constantly derives meaning after first making patterns out of unorganized experience" (Melnick & Nevis 1992, 57f.).

With this, I completely agree (see Staemmler 1997). Without forming patterns ("Gestalten") and generating meanings nobody could get very far in this multi-dimensional and complicated world. The important question is (maybe for Gestalt therapists more than for others), *how* do we do these things? Do we do them in a way, which is consistent with the basic tenets of our theory, or do we prefer to do them in a way, which may be consistent with the demands of insurance companies or diagnostic manuals of a very different theoretical orientation?

The authors mentioned above wind up saying that "... diagnosing prevents the Gestalt therapist from becoming isolated from others with different theoretical orientations.... Thus, although the use of diagnostic categories may not be totally congruent with our theory, we still employ them in communicating with others" (Melnick & Nevis 1992, 60).

Of course, being isolated from other therapists would not be good for both ourselves and our clients; I agree again. But for me this cannot be a reason to howl with the pack of conventional diagnosticians. I am convinced that we are able and ought to do *two* things, i. e. on one hand remain true to our principles and use *Gestalt* forms of diagnosis when we work with our clients — I have elaborated on one in my book on *Therapeutic Relationship and Diagnosis* (Staemmler 1993) —, and on the other hand communicate with therapists of other orientations like we communicate with people of other countries by learning their language. In order to do this, we need not and must not give up our own identity and language. Instead, we can stay aware of the fact that, for communication's sake, we sometimes decide to speak a *foreign* language.

Howling with the pack very easily leads to falling among thieves. Only recently I had an experience that was alarming to me, because the power of interpretation was claimed by a Gestalt colleague for himself in an absolutely one-sided manner. In this case it was not a matter of diagnosis in the strict sense of the word, but a similar phenomenon that appears useful to me to be mentioned here.

At a Gestalt conference the co-director of our center, my friend Werner Bock, and I conducted a supervisory seminar, which offered to the participants the opportunity to work with one of their clients under our supervision. One of them who took the chance asked a client of hers if she would be prepared and interested in coming to the seminar and working with her under supervisory conditions. The client, who was in Gestalt training herself, agreed gladly, because both as a client and as a trainee she expected to benefit from the experience. (Indeed, the session that took place with her was very satisfying for her and to a large extent confirmed her expectations.)

Another Gestalt colleague who had not been a participant in our seminar was told of our procedure. In the evening she approached us and criticized us for what she called an "abuse" of the client. As any client, the colleague continued, she was in a dependent relationship with her therapist and thus was not free to refuse the invitation to our seminar. We told her that our clients are used to negotiating or even negating our proposals and ideas from time to time and that in this case, too, we had had the impression of a client who had made up her mind in the spirit of freedom and of choice. We at least had made it very clear that we would accept *any* decision of hers. (After this conversation we asked the client one more time, whether she had felt free to do what she wanted, and she again said she did.)

However, the colleague would not accept our comment. She contended, "It doesn't make any difference what the client says." To her the client was a prisoner of transference and in principle not free to make up her own mind. Thus, she would have to be saved from abuse — "even if she doesn't want it!"

Rosenhan's Research

I want to report a study now which, when it was first published in 1973, evoked vehement reactions. Today, its results are widely accepted. It underlines that the negative consequences of one-sided distribution of the power of interpretation are not only fiction as in the story by Márquez, but can also be hard-core reality within our social system.

Rosenhan's research illustrates in a dramatic way the failures that can take place when working within the frame of conventional diagnosis. Within a period of three years he sent eight volunteer pseudo-patients to the admissions offices of varied psychiatric hospitals. Each pseudo-patient was instructed to complain that he had been hearing voices.

> Asked what the voices said, he replied that they were often unclear, but as far as he could tell they said "empty," "hollow," and "thud".... The choice of these symptoms was occasioned by their apparent similarity to existential symptoms.... The choice of these symptoms was also determined by the *absence* of a single report of existential psychoses in the literature. Beyond alleging the symptoms and falsifying name, vocations, and employment, no further alterations of person, history, or circumstances were made.... Immediately upon admission to the psychiatric ward, the pseudo-patient ceased simulating *any* symptoms of abnormality.... Despite their public "show" of sanity, the pseudo-patients were never detected. Admitted, except in one case, with a diagnosis of schizophrenia, each was discharged with a diagnosis of schizophrenia "in remission".... The uniform failure to recognize sanity cannot be attributed to the quality of the hospitals, for, although there were considerable variations among them, several are considered excellent. Nor can it be alleged that there was simply not enough time to

observe the pseudo-patients. Length of hospitalization ranged from 7 to 52 days, with an average of 19 days. (Rosenhan 1973, 251f. – italics in original)

Rosenhan's conclusion was this: "... psychiatric diagnosis betrays little about the patient but much about the environment in which an observer finds him" (*ibid.*). – I will say something about field theory later.

Context and Meaning

Rosenhan's research shows how the context in which meanings are attributed directly flows into the content of these meanings. In the setting of a psychiatric ward it is a priori defined who is "crazy" and who is not, just as in prison it is clear who holds the keys and who does not. The reason the patient is meant to be "crazy" in the first place is only that he can be found in this situation, into which he has come because of the diagnosis. So it can happen that doctors and psychotherapists with good intentions – I don't want to impute bad will to them at all, because they themselves are also parts of this field – are in danger of viewing things only from the angle their context suggests to them.

As Gestalt therapists who work in different institutions we are in a similar social field and in a similar danger. We need to be aware that as soon as we meet our clients in our offices we tend to attribute meanings to behaviors we would not attribute under different circumstances. Just the fact that I as the "therapist" in the "therapeutic situation" watch the "client" may make some behaviors of her or his seem strange or even pathological to me. Were I to observe the same behaviors in everyday life, say in a café, it would probably appear incidental to me, and I would regard it as a crotchet or would not take notice of it at all.

These factors can lead to an absurd extreme. Therapists who occupy the power of interpretation for themselves to

100 per cent may without any doubt insist on their interpretation of a situation in spite of many contradicting facts. They are the "therapists," and this to them is reason enough to understand their certainty as an expression of their professional competence. The clients with whom they are confronted may also, without the least doubt, insist on their view of things in spite of many contradicting facts. Both parties hold onto their belief systems, though there is contradictory evidence; neither party investigates its interpretation by taking into account the context and/or the opposite's point of view. Both of them basically do the same. But guess who is more likely to be regarded as healthy and who is more likely to be seen as ill? In this extreme case the application of a delusory system defines what is taken as a delusory system.

One-Sided Power of Interpretation and Necessary Uncertainty

From the thoughts I have presented above, I draw the following conclusion: as long as I, as the therapist, do not share the power of interpretation with my clients, as long as I think I can one-sidedly attribute meanings to their behaviors, I can actually only be uncertain *– or* pseudo-certain*. Should I under these conditions feel* certain*, I have denied that I know which errors can result from the one-sided exertion of the power of interpretation, and that in fact I can only be pseudo-certain. Or, I take my knowledge seriously. Then I will remember that, under the conditions given, I do not have a choice and* must *be uncertain. This uncertainty is* adequate *to the present interpersonal reality and therefore is to be welcomed!*

But at this point in my line of thought I get into trouble with my legitimate human and therapeutically important need for certainty which I have mentioned above. How can I welcome my uncertainty, when at the same time I feel a wish for certainty?

Cultivated Uncertainty

My idea of how to overcome this dilemma is this: instead of leaving the uncertainty in its naive and unproductive state that may give rise to a lack of orientation and take away any persuasive potency, I try to *cultivate* my uncertainty. What I cannot avoid, and in this case do not want to avoid, I have to cultivate.

Cultivating my uncertainty to me means two things: first, I have to stay aware that all the time I am uncertain in regard to *my attribution of meanings, I deal with a positive, desirable feeling that reminds me of the interpersonal reality I am a part of. On another level, this can provide me with a feeling of security, for it tells me that I am in touch with reality. My uncertainty becomes an aspect of my internal support system. It warns me not to attribute meanings one-sidedly and reinforces me to regard my client as a partner in the therapeutic process.*

Secondly, cultivating my uncertainty means to use it to the advantage of my clients, i. e. to have attitudes and procedures at hand that make it possible both to find an orientation for myself and to give support to the process of change in my clients. I then can remain uncertain without becoming helpless and losing my direction. And I can stand by my uncertainty in a convincing way so that I radiate the persuasive potency my clients need from me.

From my point of view there is a long list of attitudes and procedures in Gestalt therapy, which support a therapist's uncertainty and contribute to its cultivation. In what follows I want to mention some examples. My aim is to illustrate the versatility of our theoretical and methodological background in Gestalt therapy, which I think is suitable to help us to abandon the pseudo-certainty of conventional diagnoses and other forms of pigeon-holing, and to use our uncertainty in a therapeutic way instead. Cultivated uncertainty to me is a Gestalt therapist's attitude (see also Miller 1990).

I-Thou-Relationship

In his philosophical anthropology, Martin Buber (1958) indicates that in one regard all human beings are equal: they are *unique*. With this word he does not talk of being special as you do when you attribute a superior or minor value to a person. He only wants to say that in the essence of her or his being every person is different from every other person in the world. So in every person you meet you can discover something you have not encountered before. This person, at least in some respect, will differ from anybody you have already gotten to know. Therefore, it would be strange to assume that after a short time one could be able to certainly know the person one meets. The uncertainty that has to remain can be cultivated and transformed: one can become *curious* to find out in which way each person one meets is different from any other person one has met before.

Of course this is only possible under the condition that one is prepared to look for the uniqueness of that person instead of searching for another incarnation of a given diagnostic category. You have to *refuse* (or at least "bracket," if possible) *the pre-shaped categories* in order to practice what Buber calls "inclusion." To stay open to novelty may cause uncertainty, but if you cultivate it, it may transform into a remedy against professional boredom and routine and may help you to sustain your *aliveness* at work.

Being open to new encounters is giving up the stance of a seemingly objective observer, who from the distance of his conventional diagnostic perspective, classifies and estimates the other person. It means coming down to the level of direct personal contact on which the *subjectivity both of the client and the therapist is the essential dimension. It means to avoid the security of a subject-to-object-relationship. For any attempt to negate subjectivity would mean to negate one's own subjective humaneness and thereby to withhold exactly the human counterpart from the client who s/he urgently needs for her or his personal development. If you look at it this way, the subjectivity that goes along with uncertainty can end up in a gain of humanity.*

Phenomenology

One of the most important methods in my therapeutic work is the phenomenological method of "bracketing" my presuppositions. It can be traced back to Husserl (1913/1980) and is described by Hycner as follows: "... the therapist attempts, at least momentarily, to suspend all her/his *general* knowledge about people, *general* knowledge about psychopathology and diagnostic categories in order to be as *completely open to the uniqueness of the other person as possible*" (1985, 37 — italics in original).

Thus, the perspective of the therapist can change and widen. Of course this may take place only to a certain extent, since many presuppositions do not enter awareness (see Staemmler 2006, 15ff.). But it still is very useful, as you can see from the research about which Spinelli (1989, 56) reports. This research suggests that uncertainty in its cultivated form can lead to *creativity*.

A second phenomenological method follows almost by itself from the method of bracketing. If you suspend your theoretical assumptions and interpretations, you have to rely on what you can *perceive* and *describe*. Of course, our perception already contains various interpretations and is always subjective, because it is influenced by social conditioning as well as by biochemical, physiological and some genetically determined psychological factors of our organism. Nevertheless we can try to put in brackets as many of these factors as possible and confine ourselves to the description of perceptual data. On the visual channel we can name colors and shapes, on the acoustic channel we can talk of rhythms and modulations, etc. Sometimes the agreement upon the obvious is the only basis a client and a therapist have in common, if their judgments differ very much.

Another means of a phenomenological procedure is the willingness to lend the *same weight to any information at first*. If one is too quick in regarding some information as important or unimportant, this may easily block one's view on constellations one has not seen before. Under this aspect, cultivated uncertainty gives way to new discoveries.

Constructivism

The basic tenet of constructivism is the assumption that — within certain constraints — people, communities, and cultures *create* their realities; reality is not already "there" and all that is to be done is to discover it. This tenet is especially applied to social and psychological realities, which we have to deal with in psychotherapy. You do not see your client as he *is* in an absolute sense of the word, instead you construct him for yourself, and your construction has an influence on the way he constructs his reality for himself.

My constructions are always subjective and relative. They can never convey the certainty of a worldview that assumes one could know *the* reality. The uncertainty that results from this may in its cultivated form become a *modesty*, which helps me not to put myself above other people and not to ascribe more validity to my view of things than to that of others.

If I acknowledge my responsibility for my constructions, I can also cultivate my uncertainty into an awareness of *freedom*. Since the more I am aware of constructing my reality myself, the more I have the choice to construct it in a different manner. This allows more *flexibility* for myself as a therapist and in return creates more chances for my clients to construct themselves differently.

The constructivist tenet in my view is useful to the largest extent in regard to the meanings people attribute to events and in regard to the hunches they develop about "causes." How often do we behave in a certain way, "*because*" we have had an experience that had a certain consequence. We *construct* these causal links, "because" we tend to draw generalized conclusions from single events in order to make sure that successes will be repeated and failures avoided. Less differentiated organisms do that, too. I think, for example, of Skinner's "superstitious" pigeons in their boxes: at regular moments like, say, every two minutes an automatic feeding device made a grain of seed drop into the box. Very soon the pigeons displayed some peculiar and stereotyped behavior. One of them walked around in the same manner all the time, the other one permanently turned its head as if it was looking around, the third one did not stop cleaning itself...

It may hurt our human pride, but I think my guess is right that many "causal" links people construct in the course of their lives are not much more rational than those of the pigeons. For me this guess is an *encouragement to challenge the "causal" links my clients construct for themselves ("I am such and such and behave such and such, because..."). It is also some support to question my own constructions of myself and my clients again and again ("S/he is such and such and behaves such and such, because..."). Doing so makes me uncertain every now and then, but I hope it lends some more cultivation to my procedure than that of the pigeons* — and then my pride is soothed again.

Field Theory

The psychological field theory as put forward by Kurt Lewin forms one of the most important historical backgrounds of Gestalt therapy. In my view it represents another source from which one can cultivate one's uncertainty as a therapist. Lewin has pointed out that the behavior of a person "... depends not on the presence or absence of one fact or of a number of facts as viewed in isolation, but upon the constellation (the structure and forces) of the specific field as a whole" (1952, 150).

A person who observes another person becomes a part of her field and must not be isolated from it — neither in practice nor in theory. Imagine somebody's face on a photograph: very often it exhibits the pinched reaction to the situation of a photograph being taken. It does not necessarily show a person who in general wears a pinched face.

For the field of clients in therapy this means that you can only understand their particular behavior, if you take into account the influence of the therapists. Our clients in our presence and in the therapeutic situation behave differently than under other circumstances. Therefore, a diagnosis a therapist sets up is only complete if it implies the influences under which it is set up, i. e. the fact that there is somebody diagnosing, how s/he relates to the person getting the diagnosis, how they see each other, etc. We have to realize: there are limits to the generalizability of the diagnosis. It cannot be transferred to different situations easily in which the person exists in a different field. To each field there is its "singularity" (see Parlett 1991, 72) and its particular "time perspective" (Frank 1939) — to mention only two more terms that are important in this context.

Every impression I get from my clients I get at a unique point in time, in a situation that cannot be repeated, and under my particular influence. There are so many factors inherent in this complex interaction that any uncertainty I feel in regard to the generalizability of my impressions can only be understood as an adequate reaction to the versatility, complexity and — last but not least — variability of the situation.

And this takes me to my last point:

Process

In Gestalt therapy we have always found it important to think of human beings and even things as being in constant flux, instead of seeing them as fixed, solid, immobile and unchangeable entities. Many of us have appealed to Heraclitus in this context who 2,500 years ago held the opinion that "everything flows." There is another famous fragment by Heraclitus; it begins with the following words, which all of you may know: "One cannot step twice into the same river..." But it goes on: "...nor can one grasp any mortal substance in a stable condition, but it scatters and again gathers; it forms and dissolves, and approaches and departs" (in Kahn 1979, 53).

Heraclitus wanted to underline that human beings live in a constant process of change. Sometimes this change happens quickly, sometimes it takes place very slowly and can hardly be discerned. Therefore we sometimes have to look at a long span of time if we are to discover change (see Yontef 1988). One can compare it to a movie: if you watch a brief section only, you see a fixed picture, but if you watch it for a little longer, it becomes alive and you see the movement. People who appear unchanging appear so as a result of the shortened way you look at them, not as a result of their way of being. A static diagnosis reveals more of the person who sets it up than of the person to which it is ascribed.

The conclusion I want to draw from that and from all I have said before is this: changeability goes along with uncertainty; you do not know what will happen the next moment, the next day, the next year. To cultivate uncertainty means to become *optimistic* and to expect change to be possible, even if you (yet) cannot discern it. It also means to be ready to throw any impression of our clients out of the window again, if necessary right after you have had it, so that you are *open* to form new pictures again and again.

References

Amundson, J., Stewart, K., & LaNae, V. (1993): Temptations of power and certainty. *Journal of Marital and Family Therapy* 19/2, 111-123.
Buber, M. (1958). *I and Thou.* New York: Scribner's Sons.
Delisle, G. (1991). A Gestalt perspective of personality disorders. *British Gestalt Journal* 1/1, 41-50.
Frank, J. (1961). *Persuasion and healing: A comparative study of psychotherapy.* Baltimore & London: John Hopkins University Press.
Frank, L. K. (1939). Time perspectives. Journal of Social Philosophy 4, 293-312.
Husserl, E. (1913/1980). Ideen zu einer reinen Phänomenologie und phänome-nologischen Psychologie. Tübingen: Niemeyer.
Hycner, R. (1985). Dialogical Gestalt therapy: An initial proposal. *The Gestalt Journal* 8/1, 23-49.
Kahn, C. H. (Ed.) (1979). The art and thought of Heraclitus: An edition of the fragments with translation and commentary. Cambridge: Cambridge University Press.
Lewin, K. (1952). *Field theory in social science.* London: Tavistock.
Márquez, G. M. (1994). *Strange pilgrims.* London & New York: Penguin.
Maslow, A. (1954/1970). *Motivation and personality.* New York: Harper & Row.
Melnick, J., & Nevis, S. M. (1992): Diagnosis: The struggle for a meaningful paradigm. In E. C. Nevis (Ed.), *Gestalt therapy: Perspectives and applications* (pp. 57-78). New York: Gardner Press.

Miller, M. V. (1990). Toward a psychology of the unknown. *The Gestalt Journal 13/2*, 23-41.
Parlett, M. (1991). Reflections on field theory. *British Gestalt Journal 1/2*, 69-81
Rosenhan, D. L. (1973). On being sane in insane places. *Science 179*, 250-258.
Spinelli, E. (1989). The interpreted world: An introduction to phenomenological psychology. London: Sage.
Staemmler, F.-M. (1993). Therapeutische Beziehung und Diagnose [Therapeutic Relationship and Diagnosis] – Gestalttherapeutische Antworten. München: Pfeiffer.
Staemmler, F.-M. (1997). Prozeß und Diagnose – Einführende Gedanken zur Eröffnung der 10. Münchner Gestalttage, 1996. In M. Billich, H. Koch, & R. Merten (Eds.), *Dokumentation der 10. Münchner Gestalttage 1996 – Prozeß und Diagnose – Gestalttherapie und Gestaltpädagogik in Praxis, Theorie und Wissenschaft* (pp. 9-23). Eurasburg: GFE.
Staemmler, F.-M. (2006). The willingness to be uncertain: Preliminary thoughts about interpretation and understanding in Gestalt therapy. *International Gestalt Journal 29/2*, 11-42.
Weber, M. (1985): Wirtschaft und Gesellschaft – Grundriß der verstehenden Soziologie, Bd. 2. Tübingen: Mohr:
Yontef, G. (1988). Comments on 'Boundary Processes and Boundary States'. *The Gestalt Journal 11/2*, 25-35.
Yontef, G. (1993). Awareness, dialogue, and process: Essays on Gestalt therapy. Highland, NY: Gestalt Journal Press.

Selected Titles from GestaltPress

Organizational Consulting: A Gestalt Approach
    Edwin C. Nevis

Gestalt Reconsidered: A New Approach to Contact and Resistance
    Gordon Wheeler

Gestalt Therapy: Perspectives and Applications
    Edwin C. Nevis, editor

The Collective Silence: German Identity and the Legacy of Shame
    Barbara Heimannsberg Christopher J. Schmidt

Community and Confluence: Undoing the Clinch of Oppression
    Philip Lichtenberg

Encountering Bigotry: Befriending Projecting Persons in Every Day Life
    Philip Lichtenberg

Becoming a Stepfamily
    Patricia Papernow

On Intimate Ground: A Gestalt Approach to Working With Couples
    Gordon Wheeler Stephanie Backman, editors

Body Process: Working With the Body in Psychotherapy
    James I. Kepner

Here, Now, Next: Paul Goodman and the Origins of Gestalt Therapy
    Taylor Stoehr

Crazy Hope Finite Experience
    Paul Goodman, edited by Taylor Stoehr

In Search of Good Form: Gestalt Therapy With Couples and Families
    Joseph C. Zinker

The Voice of Shame: Silence and Connection in Psychotherapy
    Robert G. Lee & Gordon Wheeler, editors

Healing Tasks: Psychotherapy With Adult Survivors of Childhood Abuse
    James I. Kepner

Adolescence: Psychotherapy and the Emergent Self
    Mark McConville

Getting Beyond Sobriety: Clinical Approaches to Long-Term Recovery
    Michael Craig Clemmens

Back to the Beanstalk: Enchantment and Reality for Couples
    Judith R. Brown

The Dreamer and the Dream: Essays and Reflections on Gestalt Therapy
    Rainette Eden Fants, edited by Arthur Roberts

A Well-Lived Life: Essays in Gestalt Therapy
  Sylvia Fleming Crocker

From the Radical Center: The Heart of Gestalt Therapy
  Irving and Miriam Polster

The Gendered Field: Gestalt Perspectives and Readings
  Deborah Ullman & Gordon Wheeler, editors

Beyond Individualism: Toward a New Understanding of Self, Relationship, and Experience
  Gordon Wheeler

Sketches: An Anthology of Essays, Art, and Poetry
  Joseph C. Zinker

The Heart of Development: Gestalt Approaches to Working with Children, Adolescents, and Their Worlds (2 Volumes)
  Mark McConville Gordon Wheeler, editors

Body of Awareness: A Somatic Developmental Approach to Psychotherapy
  Ruella Frank

The Unfolding Self: Essays of Jean-Marie Robine
  Jean-Marie Robine; edited and translated by Gordon Wheeler

Encountering Bigotry: Befriending Projecting Persons in Everyday Life
  Philip Lichtenberg, Janneke van Beusekom Dorothy Gibbons

Reading Paul Goodman
  Gordon Wheeler, editor

The Values of Connection: A Relational Approach to Ethics
  Robert G. Lee, editor

WindowFrames: Learning the Art of Gestalt Play Therapy the Oaklander Way
  Peter Mortola

Gestalt Therapy: Living Creatively Today
  Gonzague Masquelier

The Secret Language of Intimacy: Releasing the Hidden Power in Couple Relationships
  Robert G. Lee

CoCreating the Field: Intention and Practice in the Age of Complexity
  Deborah Ullman & Gordon Wheeler, editors

Aggression, Time, and Understanding: Contributions to the Evolution of Gestalt Therapy
  Frank-M. Staemmler

Gestalt International Study Center

Transforming the way we live and work in the world

GISC is a diverse worldwide learning community based on trust, optimism and generosity. We study and teach skills that energize human interaction and lead to action, change and growth, and we create powerful learning experiences for individuals and organizations.

- **Leadership Development**
    - Leadership in the 21st Century
    - Leading Nonprofit Organizations
    - Graduate Leadership Forum
- **Professional Skill Development**
    - Cape Cod Training Program
    - Introduction to the Cape Cod Model
    - Executive Personality Dynamics for Coaches
    - Applying the Cape Cod Model to Coaching
    - Applying the Cape Cod Model in Organizations
    - Finding Your Developmental Edge
    - Women in the Working World
    - Advanced Supervision
- **Personal Development**
    - The Next Phase: A Program for Transition & Renewal
    - Optimism & Awareness Essential Skills for Living
    - Couples Workshop
    - Building Blocks of Creativity
    - Nature & Transitions
- *Gestalt Review*

Launched in 1977, Gestalt Review focuses on the Gestalt approach at all systems levels, ranging from the individual, through couples, families and groups, to organizations, educational settings and the community at large. To read sample articles, or to subscribe, visit:

www.gestaltreview.com

For more information about any of GISC's offerings or to read our newsletter, visit:

www.gisc.com